Instituting Thought

Instituting Thought

Three Paradigms of Political Ontology

Roberto Esposito

Translated by Mark William Epstein

polity

Originally published in Italian as *Pensiero Istituente. Tre paradigmi di ontologia politica*

The translation of this work has been funded by SEPS
Segretariato Europeo per le Pubblicazioni Scientifiche

Via Val d'Aposa 7 – 40123 Bologna – Italy
seps@seps.it – www.seps.it

Polity Press
65 Bridge Street
Cambridge CB2 1UR, UK

Polity Press
101 Station Landing
Suite 300
Medford, MA 02155, USA

ISBN-13: 978-1-5095-4642-8 – hardback
ISBN-13: 978-1-5095-4643-5 – paperback

A catalogue record for this book is available from the British Library.

Library of Congress Cataloging-in-Publication Data
Names: Esposito, Roberto, 1950- author. | Epstein, Mark William, translator.
Title: Instituting thought : three paradigms of political ontology / Roberto Esposito ; translated by Mark William Epstein.
Other titles: Pensiero istituente. English
Description: Medford : Polity Press, 2021. | Includes bibliographical references and index. | Summary: "A leading Italian philosopher develops an original perspective on the crisis of contemporary politics"-- Provided by publisher.
Identifiers: LCCN 2020057166 (print) | LCCN 2020057167 (ebook) | ISBN 9781509546428 (hardback) | ISBN 9781509546435 (paperback) | ISBN 9781509546442 (epub) | ISBN 9781509548040 (pdf)
Subjects: LCSH: Political science--Philosophy. | Ontology.
Classification: LCC JA71 .E68213 2021 (print) | LCC JA71 (ebook) | DDC 320.01--dc23
LC record available at https://lccn.loc.gov/2020057166
LC ebook record available at https://lccn.loc.gov/2020057167

Typeset in 10.5 on 12 pt Sabon
by Fakenham Prepress Solutions, Fakenham, Norfolk NR21 8NL
Printed and bound in Great Britain by TJ Books Ltd, Padstow, Cornwall

For further information on Polity, visit our website:
politybooks.com

Contents

Introduction

1. The title and subtitle of this book are related in a doubly asymmetrical manner. First because the title – *Instituting Thought* – only refers to the third of three paradigms mentioned in the subtitle; but also because, instead of examining it from without, I place myself and proceed from within, attempting both its definition and its radicalization. Setting up in an already established construction site, modifying its outlines to the point of reconfiguring them into a new shape is, moreover, a consequential way of proceeding for a programmatically instituting thought. As in the case of the first two ontologico-political paradigms, I also interpret the third through the work of a twentieth-century author: the French philosopher Claude Lefort. Thanks to the still somewhat limited circulation of his thought – at least as compared to Heidegger and Deleuze, the referents of the other two paradigmatic axes – one can still question it in ways that are less conditioned by other interpretations, thus foregrounding, whether explicitly or implicitly, that which refers to the lexicon of institutions or, perhaps better, of instituting. This subject matter, organized into an ample series of textual and conceptual cross-references, becomes both the gravitational center and the theoretical purview of the entire book.

The pronounced heterogeneity of the three paradigms is highlighted by the shared weave that they partake in, which is defined by the category of political ontology in its specific postmetaphysical acceptation. To fully capture its meaning and scope, one needs to start by acknowledging the peculiarity of the politico-ontological approach, as compared to all other kinds of theory, sociology or even political philosophy. Unlike these, which are circumscribed within a specific regional ambit, political ontology does not relate to the area of being that concerns politics, but rather to the essential relationship that conjoins being and politics. And this is the case for both sides of the relationship – the necessarily political configuration of political praxis as well as the ultimately political character of every event. As concerns the first side, it is obvious that any political action implies a conception of space, time, and human beings – and therefore of being. One can certainly state that the different rankings of political philosophies, ancient and modern, are predicated on the more or less intense awareness that their authors had of this implication. The extraordinary philosophical prominence of the political works of Plato, Aristotle, Hobbes, Rousseau, and Hegel is due to their being not only theories but precisely political ontologies. This is true also of the great political thinkers of the twentieth century, from Weber to Schmitt, Arendt, and Foucault – who are all authors of political ontologies in the fullest sense of the term, rather than of philosophies. Moreover, every philosophical definition of being entails presuppositions and effects of a political nature – even those that deny that this is the case, since this very negation is based in principle on an opposition between the political and the impolitical. To claim that something, an action or a discourse, *is not* political already situates it within an opposition of a political nature. That which presents itself as apolitical or antipolitical does so as a consequence of removing its instituting moment, which, as such, is always political. Additionally, any modality of being – beginning with its own "power to be" – expresses all the political tension of the relationships it originates from and tends to alter.

Of course, the relationship between being and politics – which is constitutive of political ontology – has been understood in very different ways in the course of time. For a long period, indeed for the entire course of the history of metaphysics, it was interpreted as a basic foundation of a substantive kind, one that was destined to guarantee the correctness of political action. In other words, one imagined that politics could, or should, be guided by specific principles, grounded in the sphere of being and expressive of it. This kind of presumption characterized a significant part of the philosophical tradition, both of Platonic and of Aristotelian origin – but also the one that derives from Christian roots. Obviously it is not possible to establish any continuity between ancient and modern politics, given their crystal-clear lexical dissimilarities. When compared to ancient politics, which was still bound to metaphysical presuppositions, whether theological or natural, modern politics begins with and is constituted precisely starting with their revocation. Modernity, in the most pointed sense of the term, implies the negation of that which precedes it, of every transcendent presupposition. The abandonment of the state of nature as a preliminary condition for the state of politics, as theorized by Hobbes, bestows on the category of negation a central role in the modern configuration of power: only by negating that which precedes it can the political order establish its place. But, even though it characterizes the foundation in negative terms, modern political philosophy remains tied to the logic of foundation, brought to its culmination by Hegel precisely through the dialectical use of negation. Only with the crisis of Hegelianism does this *dispositif* begin to show the first signs of degradation, which Nietzsche will push to a point of no return. After Nietzsche, all attempts at restoration notwithstanding, the hypothesis of grounding politics in the sphere of a substantive being seems to be definitively exhausted, a process tied to the ongoing deconstruction of the notion of substance itself.

This, however, does not mean that political ontology itself disappears. Instead one could say that it is precisely the consummation of the metaphysical foundation that entails the need for a different establishment of the political. Only now it is inscribed in the fissure into which the foundation has precipitated – in other words, in its *not* being a foundation any longer. From this point on, any political conception presupposes a negative horizon: not only a negative foundation, one already theorized by modern political philosophy, but a *non*-foundation, a lack of foundation. Starting from this point, the relationship between being and politics no longer refers to presence but to absence, to a void, a gap. This explains why the principal political ontologies of the twentieth century are all inscribed in the groove of difference: from the point of view of ontology, politics is defined by the relationship between being and difference. This is what opposes them to the ancient and medieval ontologies of identity, pushing the ontologies of difference toward contemporaneity. In this sense, to borrow Foucault's celebrated expression, they are all "ontologies of actuality."

But they do exhibit a decisive variation, precisely as regards the role of difference, which changes as a function of the theoretical frameworks of which it is a part. Inside the paradigmatic triangle formed by being, politics, and difference, the three terms constantly change position and meaning, combining with one another in unprecedented ways. It is these shifts that define the diversity of the three paradigms we examine here. Politics can exhibit a trait that reproduces ontological difference within itself, as Heidegger maintains. Or it can instead constitute the intrinsically differential characteristic of a being extended over a single plane of immanence, as in Deleuze's perspective. Finally, in yet another semantic register, interpreted by Lefort – but one that we can also define as neo-Machiavellian or conflictualist – social being is instituted by a symbolic difference that possesses the characteristics of politics. These are precisely the figures delineated by the three most important ontologico-political paradigms of contemporary philosophy: the post-Heideggerian, the Deleuzian, and the instituting paradigm, which is still in the process of being elaborated. These three paradigms don't succeed one another chronologically but exist contemporaneously, interweaving in complex ways, which sometimes juxtapose them and sometimes exhibit one as the reverse of the other. But they do give rise to a diversity of effects on the philosophical debate, effects that the following pages emphasize, motivated by an intent that is itself ultimately political. My thesis is that, while the first two paradigms – the post-Heideggerian and the Deleuzian, which follow different and sometimes opposed modalities – are inscribed in the current crisis of the political and thus contribute to its exacerbation, only the third, the instituting, is able to reverse this drift with a new, affirmative project. What divides them is the role that the negative plays for each one with respect to the constitutive relationship between ontology and politics. In Heidegger the negative is present with such intensity that it opens up a gap between the two, while in the Deleuzian paradigm, conversely, it is erased, owing to their complete overlap. What characterizes the instituting paradigm, on the other hand, is a productive relationship with negation that allows one to articulate being and politics in a reciprocally affirmative relation.

2. Tracing the first ontologico-political paradigm – which is oriented toward the deactivation of action, and therefore also definable as a "destituting" paradigm – back to Heidegger is neither a foregone conclusion nor one devoid of problems. This is not only because he never claimed to be a political thinker, not even in the dark period of his rectorate, but also because all contemporary philosophers who, in various ways, could be ascribed to the destituting paradigm are situated in a political orbit that is radically counterposed to Heidegger's. And yet, this very clear distance in political orientation notwithstanding, all of them, from Schürmann through Nancy to

Agamben, consider him an essential theoretical point of reference. In this respect the same paradoxical relationship that had tied Heidegger to his great Jewish disciples – Marcuse, Arendt, Löwith – repeats itself. In this case, too, naturally, each of the philosophers I mentioned follows his or her own original path, in which references to Heidegger alternate with just as frequent ones to Bataille, Benjamin, and Foucault. And yet the traces left by Heidegger in their thought remain indelible. How come? What paradigmatic thread ties intellectuals of the extreme left to a thinker whose political orientation was always toward the right? In order to answer this question – which has made people use the phrase "left Heideggerianism" – one needs to look at Heidegger not from the perspective of his inauspicious political commitment in the 1930s – a perspective that is all too much in evidence today – but rather from that of the impolitical turn that succeeded it, and in ever more pronounced forms, from the postwar period to the 1960s.

The following pages provide a fairly detailed account of Heidegger's itinerary, reconstructing the transitions and the discontinuities of a grand thought that ever more clearly modifies its conception of politics. These are pages that never elide the profound connection to the theoretical center of gravity of his work as a whole, represented by the "negative" *dispositif* of ontological difference. From this angle, one can even trace an obviously imperfect parallel between ontological difference and the political–impolitical bipolarity. In both cases the relationship is characterized, and constituted, by a negation. Just as *alētheia* is recognizable only in the negative modality of "non-concealment," analogously politics originates negatively from an impolitical presupposition that both founds it and defies it. Having originated from something non-political – the impolitical site of the *polis* – politics is not able to correspond to it with a sufficient degree of radicalism. The complex equilibrium that still allowed Heidegger in the 1930s to imagine the instituting of the political, even if by thinkers and poets, breaks at some point, projecting the two poles, the political and the impolitical, in ever more divergent directions. When this happens, the impolitical – understood, up to a certain moment, as the negative foundation of politics – becomes its absolute negation. This is the case when politics – any type of politics, including that to which, in the early 1930s, Heidegger had entrusted the task of saving the West from the anti-metaphysical grip that was strangling it – appears to him to be incorporated and perverted by technological *Machenschaft* [machination], a legacy contemporary to the Romanization of the Greek language. That is when, having lost its contacts with an ever more degraded politics, the impolitical expands to the point of occupying the entire ontological horizon, clearly separating itself from the destiny of humankind. From this point on, the only way for humans to respond to that which calls them is to deactivate their action, ready to listen to a poeticizing or meditative thought.

All of Heidegger's work, starting in the early 1940s, revolves around this destituting paradigm. That which was conceived as the negative presupposition of all political institutions and of instituting itself now becomes its very clear rejection. Politics, which at this point has been entirely absorbed by technology, should no longer be instituted, but destituted. Any kind of "doing" should be undone. Only the radical tonality, the decisive lexicon related to taking a decision, is what remains of the political – a decision that now coincides with a non-decision, one that corresponds to the oxymoron of the will to not will. But, once all political possibilities have been voided, even the impolitical, deprived of its original foundational power, ends up annihilating itself. If the impolitical is thought of as the source of the political, when the latter implodes into technology, the impolitical ends up sliding into nothingness aswell. Once the political has been annihilated, the impolitical, deprived of a point of contrast, sinks with it. Insofar as human beings are concerned, since they are ontologically prevented from transforming reality, they can only wait for the fulfillment of destiny. What is striking in Heidegger's language is the activist tone taken by that which one can subject oneself to only in a passive manner: the non-postponable nature of the ultimate option that continues to suggest the category of potentiality – but only so long as it remains unrealized, sheltered from an activity that, in realizing it, would empty it. It is this impolitical intensity of the deactivation of all politics that post-Heideggerian thinkers absorb from Heidegger, transposing it, in similarly radical fashion, into a horizon that is as theoretically revolutionary as it is practically inert.

One needs to add that the Heideggerian roots of this destituting line are not the only ones. At its origin, not always fully consciously, lies a paradigm that in its day was defined as impolitical, inscribed on the reverse of the official side of twentieth-century philosophy. I am thinking of authors who were not professional philosophers, such as Karl Barth, Simone Weil, Georges Bataille, Hermann Broch, Elias Canetti. They are the first to coin the, elevated and tragic, language of dis-activation: from "decreation," to "passive action," to "non-agent," "not translated into act," "decreation," "blocked at the stage of pure potentiality." The entire lexicon of the destituting paradigm was born between the 1920s and 1930s and was then resemanticized at the end of the century. At its center we find a negative presupposition – expressed by the prefix in im-political – which excludes any affirmative judgment. In this world one finds nothing but conflicts of power and interest, separated by an invisible line from what is not and will never be able to be. The impolitical is not something situated beyond it, that does not exist as such, but that invisible line itself. It accomplishes nothing but express the impossibility of representing goodness, justice, and value politically. But the impolitical, in turn, cannot escape the contradiction of being able to define itself only on the basis of the political, from which it distances itself. It is this insurmountable antinomy that places it on the same slim ridge that both conjoins and disjoins gnosticism and mysticism, pushing one into the reverse of the other. That which ultimately remains, notwithstanding everything that distinguishes individual interpreters from one another, is the shared depoliticizing outcome that the entire paradigm of deactivation produces. Removed from any perspective oriented toward action, protected from the temptations of work, bent on the anarchical removal of principles, it dissolves the possibility of the political in the as yet unrevealed enigma of a potentiality devoid of act.

3. The ontologico-political paradigm whose influence is most strongly felt in Deleuze's works is antipodal to the post-Heideggerian paradigm. Deleuze himself, while recognizing Heidegger's philosophical stature, views his own oeuvre as a sort of confutation of the latter's. While they both share a number of themes, what sharply separates them is the plane, which Deleuze himself defines as one "of immanence," that is in principle destined to abolish all kinds of ontological difference. Since being is univocal, in other words constituted in the unique form of difference, instead of being separated from an ontic dimension, difference coincides with the becoming of being itself. Without dwelling on the transitions that lead Deleuze to elaborate this plane of immanence, we can state that its effect is the exclusion of the notion of the impolitical itself, a notion that, on the other hand, Heidegger's political reflections do revolve around. Once the negative presupposition of the political has been suppressed, the latter expands to the point of filling the entire movement of reality. This is what Deleuze argues, at least starting from 1968; and this period is identified, not only by him, as the period in which the realization of the political and the politicization of the real resolve into each other without residue. From this perspective the French

philosopher's work – especially the *Anti-Oedipus* and *A Thousand Plateaus* – can be seen as the most intense political ontology of the twentieth century, in other words a work in which the two terms, ontology and politics, experience the highest degree of superposition, one that frontally collides with the irremediable fracture Heidegger opened between them.

This does not mean, however, that the matter is closed. It is in fact precisely this superposition that prevents Deleuze from elaborating an effective political thought, almost as if the three areas of being, politics, and thought could not find any possible articulation within his philosophy. This also helps explain the sharp distinction between a first, more technically philosophical part, essentially devoid of political references, and a later one, which exhibits a strong political orientation but is perhaps not as philosophically rigorous. The impression one receives is that, the more politics is superposed on being, becoming the constitutive cipher of its becoming, the less it is being thought of in its specificity. Once it has been extended to the entire ontogenetic process and is its immediate expression, politics ends up losing its own contours, and in the end confuses them with those of being, in which it inheres. If being is political as such, according to Deleuze's own explicit declaration, how can a specifically political activity be distinguished within it? What differentiates it from that which it is not? Or from another kind of politics, oriented in the opposite direction? I believe that the reason for this impasse – which has not prevented a motley galaxy of political thinkers, in addition to neo-naturists, post-humanists, and hyper-immanentists, from drawing inspiration from the Deleuzian paradigm for their theses – should be sought in Deleuze's loss of contact with the category of negation. It is true that his emancipation from the negative – which does constitute the principal explicit objective of his ontology – never happens all at once or completely. One can instead say that his work is indeed troubled by it in all its parts, without ever managing to completely discard it. So he passes, sometimes on the same page, from the mutual implication of difference and negation to the opposition between them, from a conception of difference as a figure that affirms the negative to another, which instead excludes it, and he never opts definitely for one of the two. This is the reason for a tragic vein that runs through an oeuvre that is all too often interpreted in an insufficiently problematic fashion. The fact remains that the greater the influence of Bergson, this staunch proponent of the misleading and therefore non-existent nature of the negative, the more Deleuze abandons the category of the negative. This development, in turn, has entropic effects on the determination of the political, since one cannot ask oneself what politics is, even a certain kind of politics, without simultaneously knowing what it is *not*. This is the way in which a position that is programmatically hyperpolitical – in the sense that it interprets any event in political terms – is reversed, if not into a depoliticizing outcome, at least into a failed determination of the political: of its subjects and objects, of its ends and means, of its organizational forms and strategies. And this is not due to a default, as in the case of Heidegger, but to an excess of politics – which, being defined as identical to everything that exists, risks becoming something that is not at all defined.

If the Heideggerian paradigm can be called destituting, the Deleuzian, even taking its most influential political translations into account, can be called constituting. Obviously, not in a technical – that is, juridico-political, sense; but certainly in an ontological sense, as an eternally creative form, and also, precisely for this reason, one that is decreative of the reality just created. Just as the primacy of constitutive power – one proposed, within the same ontological perspective, by Antonio Negri – overwhelms constituted power, so the infinitely productive power of being resolves each "state" into its own becoming, dissolving it as such. This is the effect of the substitution of the category of production, transposed to an ontological level, for that of praxis, a category still too charged with the negative to be able to merge with the plane of immanence. In the course of an extensive interpretation of *creatio ex nihilo* – taken beyond the moment of Genesis and rendered co-eternal with the world – productive creation exposes the created to an unceasingly renewed creation, which is made possible only via the abolition of what precedes. In the Deleuzian paradigm, even thought is qualified by the continuous creation of new concepts rather than by a differential resumption of that which has already been thought. This is the same relationship that exists between the virtual and the actual: the latter is no more than the momentary and deceptive fixation of a process that flows ceaselessly from one virtual to the next. Understood in this manner, the constitutive act, which "dissolves" being into an eternal becoming, is at the same time destitutive of that which it creates, and therefore ultimately also destitutive of itself – just as desire, which moves the entire Deleuzian political ontology, is always at the same time a desire for life from the universal point of view and a desire for death from the individual point of view: a desire for escape and abolition, for emancipation and self-repression. This is true of any desire, which is limitless and therefore also inclusive of its opposite.

This is what explains the insuperability of capitalism, as elaborated upon by the philosopher. Within Deleuze's ontological *dispositif* there are two ways in which capitalism cannot be denied: on the one hand, because negation does not exist, only affirmative difference does; on the other, because no other social formation can unleash the flows of desire and nomadic movement to the degree capitalism can. It is true that capitalism simultaneously harnesses them with bonds, blockages, and striations that must be vanquished by means of what Deleuze refers to as "counter-effectuations." But this occurs from within capitalist effectuation itself – since there is nothing external to it. It is an effectuation that needs to be fully completed, freed from its contradictions and indulged in, in an ever-accelerating fashion. In this sense *acceleration*, or intensification, appears to be Deleuze's only political category: one oriented not to changing the present state of affairs, but rather to pushing it toward implosion. What needs to be accelerated or intensified is always the reality that is unfolding, never a different one, which is declared impossible. As in the case of Nietzsche, the only way of facing nihilism is to drive it to its extreme outcomes, making what had been passive up to that point active. This is how Deleuze believes that capitalism – with all the slivers of fascism that characterize it – should be led to self-destruction: by infinitely accelerating its movement, in a coincidence of creation and destruction, constitution and destitution. Driving affirmation to its acme also means affirming that which is counterposed to it, thus leading to the collapse of both forces. As Hegel had explained, absolute affirmation coincides with absolute negation. At the apex of its development, the constituting paradigm tends to join the destituting paradigm from the opposite side, in a shared rejection of instituting thought.

4. What distinguishes instituting thought from the destituting paradigm and its messianic matrix, as well as from the constituting one and its eschatological inspiration, is its taking leave of the lexicon of political theology while it remains aware of the incompleteness of modern secularization; this awareness is especially strong in Lefort. The instituting paradigm is protected from the return of the theological because it is extraneous to the presupposition of the One that, albeit in different forms, remains at the heart of both Heideggerian and Deleuzian ontologies. Social being is neither univocal nor plurivocal, but conflictual in the instituting paradigm, and this is why it can be defined as neo-Machiavellian. What characterizes the social – all interhuman relationships – is neither the absoluteness of the One nor

the infinite proliferation of the manifold, but the tension between the Two. Even when it proclaims its compactness or seems to fracture into infinite differences, society is always characterized by a fundamental antagonism, one that ultimately all the others can be related back to. The role of the political, both central and ineradicable, is to stage this division, raising it from the empirical plane of the clash of powers and interests to the symbolical one of the government of society. The institutional bent that gathers the social around the division that runs through it is symbolic – in its distinction from both the real and the imaginary. *Sumbolon*, according to its own etymon, evokes an order that is not alternative to the conflict but is produced by it and productive of it, in a form destined to constantly change on the basis of the power relationships that are established each time between the parties to the conflict. This does not mean that instituting praxis, from its Machiavellian matrix through all its subsequent incarnations, is neutral. It certainly takes sides, it is partisan – oriented toward an expansion of freedoms and a narrowing of inequalities. It is difficult to imagine something that represents the instituting paradigm better than the Roman institution of tribune of the people [*tribunus plebis*], mentioned by Machiavelli in his *Discourses*. Born of the conflict with the nobility and itself a generator of new social clashes, this is perhaps the clearest example of an instituting power that does not destroy a given institutional equilibrium, but innovates it in an affirmative sense. From this point of view Machiavelli's thought is at the heart of the instituting paradigm. The political is that which unites society via its divisions, rendering a fracture that had not reached awareness and was therefore potentially destructive up to that point symbolically manageable. Within the instituting paradigm, difference remains what it is, without splitting into the ontological fracture between the political and the impolitical, as in Heidegger, or being flattened out into the Deleuzian coincidence of ontology and politics. If the political is made into the institution of the social, it is thereby contained in the social, but not identified with it. One is holding fast to the symbolic limit, thus preventing the social from coinciding with itself and subsiding into absolute immanence.

Obviously such a dynamic, which inscribes transcendence into immanence, so to speak, presupposes a radical revision of the category of institution, by comparison with the canonical ways in which it has been treated in the domains of political science, sociology, and the law. The passage from the noun ("institution") to the verb, "to institute," already points to a deep transformation with respect to all the katechontic, eschatological, and messianic *dispositifs* of political theology, which are all explicitly hostile to any encounter with history. Rather than referring to a consolidated order of rules and laws, instituting refers to a task that coincides with that of politics and is destined to continually change the normative framework in which it operates – and to do so without either deactivating it in a salvific mode or dissolving it in the name of a creativity so accelerated that it destroys what was just created. An instituting logic exhibits a profound relationship with the historicity of existence, one that is far removed both from the deactivation of destituting power and from the acceleration of constituting power. The instituting movement is always a *creatio ex aliquo* – neither a **decreatio* nor a *creatio ex nihilo*; it keeps together origin and duration, innovation and conservation, functionalizing the one toward the further empowerment of the other. As Lefort's teacher Merleau-Ponty argued, the institution, however original, always arises in the context of a preexisting situation; it always makes use of fabrics that were woven previously, in the fields of the arts, the sciences, thought, and, naturally, politics. It does not entrust itself either to the Heideggerian temporality of the event or to the Deleuzian one of repetition – exceeding both the severe majesty of being and the inarticulate flow of becoming. To institute in the grooves of what was already instituted creates stability and stabilizes creation – and does so without revolutionary proclamations, messianic prophecies, or anarchistic intentions, since there does not exist and there has never existed a society able to forgo power. Instituting praxis deconstructs any substantiality of power, doubts any claims to belonging, reveals its empty center, which can be occupied each time only by the forces that prevail in that moment, before they are substituted by others, which are just as replaceable. Within the instituting paradigm, political subjects do not precede the conflict in any substantive fashion but are shaped and transformed by it. The category of subjectivation, which coincides with the always collective movement of instituting, takes the place of the category of subject.

An important contribution in this direction was provided by the legal institutionalism of the first decades of the last century, represented by figures such as Maurice Hauriou, and especially Santi Romano. At the center of their work, whose foundational value was also recognized by Carl Schmitt, are the challenges they pose not only to the obligatory relationship between institution and legal person – via the reference, brought into play by Hauriou, to an institution-thing that recalls the category of the "impersonal" – but also to the identification of institution and state, an identification Romano declared was "in crisis" already in the first years of the twentieth century.

Their work exhibits elements of a rupture with the legal lexicon that has not yet been sufficiently exploited in its ontologico-political and even philosophical presuppositions. This is about the paradigmatic contrast between institution and law, which was then taken up and even developed with originality by the young Deleuze. The state not only is not the sole – or the main – form of institutional arrangement, but it always coexists with other institutions subordinated or superordinated to it, which are autonomous and compete with it because they are situated outside the sovereign regime, if not actually opposed to it. But in Romano's elaboration these can be considered institutions to all effects and purposes, so long as they meet the condition of being internally organized; and this applies even to those that the state declares illegitimate on the grounds that they are hostile to it, as in the case of revolutionary associations. This does not necessarily mean that they have reasons that are ethically inferior to its own – in fact they are often superior. It is difficult not to grasp, or to underestimate, the innovative power of the instituting paradigm with respect to the two currents of legal normativism and decisionism, with which it was necessarily in conflict. A radically different conception of the law separates them: the first two currents rely on a paradigm that is enclosed in the language, also sovereign, of the primacy of the written law and of the will of the legislator; institutionalism on the other hand relies on a paradigm that is open to the pressures of society and to the exigencies of history, it has to respond to the urgencies of necessity and to the needs of life. In this sense the law is the object of a struggle that centers on its own meaning even before centering on the issue of specific rights. To say that the law, instead of responding to institutions that are fixed in time, never ceases to institute means attributing a performative force to it that unleashes all its performative power. Precisely insofar as it is "unnatural" – entirely artificial – instituting law can intervene effectively in life: not in order to save it or re-create it anew, as the paradigms of political theology propose in a politically inactive manner, but in order to change it from within. This is a possible starting point from inside the crisis of contemporary political philosophy. Today the only paradigm of political ontology that is capable of politically rearticulating being and thought is the one that refers to instituting praxis.

*

The first person to talk about a postfoundational political ontology is Oliver Marchart: he does so in an important book, dedicated to the thought of

Nancy, Lefort, Badiou, and Laclau, which opportunely substitutes this term for the excessively generic and trite "poststructuralism." As he develops the tension between the polarities of politics and the political, *la politique* and *le politique*, *Politik* and *das Politische*, he sees the second term as possessing that energetic element that is destined to confer vitality to the first, which is still devoid of a foundation. The impolitical, conceived of as a supplement to the lack of legitimation in postclassical political ontologies, withdraws at the very moment at which it institutes the social. This withdrawal is not, however, equivalent to the negation of the foundation – which would restore the same metaphysical mechanism that had been deconstructed, only in the negative – but instead intends to assume it in a weak version, which oscillates between presence and absence without ever coinciding with either one or the other. According to Marchart, one should beware of confusing postfoundationalism with anti-foundationalism or, even worse, with the postmodern thesis that "anything goes," "since a post-foundational approach does not attempt to erase completely such figures of the ground, but to weaken their ontological status."[1] Having reemerged as "the political" – in a sense that does not coincide with that used by Carl Schmitt – this artificial foundation has the function of preventing "politics" from closing in on itself, flattened out into mere administration. In this fashion something similar to what Heidegger defines as "ontological difference" would be inscribed at the heart of political ontology. Resting on an absent base, a new artificial foundation would work affirmatively, precisely because of its own negativity.

This perspective is not fully convincing, not only because it makes reference to a weak ontology,[2] but also because it takes a very heterogeneous group of philosophers back to the same paradigm. While Marchart does reconstruct their different itineraries, pointing out semantic and conceptual dissimilarities, he does so within a single horizon. A problem of this kind – also present in Carsten Strathausen's book on neo-ontology,[3] where he assembles a series of thinkers who share an overcoming of Marxian and post-Marxian dialectics but do not really have much in common – is instead absent in Lars Tønder and Lasse Thomassen's research on political ontology. They divide the thinkers included in *Radical Democracy* into the opposed categories of lack and abundance: "two different versions of radical democracy follow from this: one that emphasizes the hegemonic nature of politics, and another that cultivates a strategy of pluralization."[4] The former, generally thinkers with a Lacanian background, like Laclau for instance, think of the political starting from a constitutive lack, and institutionalize it as an absent foundation. Not only democracy, but also the hegemonic alternatives that succeed one another within it are always internally destabilized by a lack of substance that renders them structurally incomplete and impermanent. On the other hand, the ontologies of abundance, in which one can easily recognize Deleuze's profile and that of nomadic thinkers, create ever new networks of materiality, flow, and energy. The sign of some sort of lack transpires in their case too, but it is always filled by new differences, which succeed one another in a potentially infinite becoming. In this game of mutually reflecting mirrors, there seem to be two political theologies that face each other, counterposed and complementary, one negative, the other positive. For one – one could say – there is nothing within being, for the other, nothing external to being.

1

Destituting Power

1. One cannot state that the relationship between Martin Heidegger's thought and politics has been fully explored – regardless of the growing interest directed at the issue, which has led to its becoming a focal point of interest in contemporary philosophical debates. Even more than the objective complexity of the issue, the fashion in which it has been undertaken, which was mostly prejudiced, has prevented this exploration from occurring more fully. Facing off and confronting each other frontally are two widely divergent lines of interpretation, which provide opposing evaluations of the philosopher's well-known compromises with Nazism. Where some interpreters have seen them as a point of coalescence that leads to a precipitate of his thought, and therefore the key to interpreting all of Heidegger's thinking, others have attempted to isolate them, reducing them to a mere biographical episode, of little relevance with respect to his work as whole. The presupposition – but ultimately also the consequence – of both perspectives has been the selection, within the vast Heideggerian corpus, of those texts that best seemed to bolster their respective interpretive strategies. Where those who argue for the centrality of the Nazi option privilege his writings from the 1930s where it is more explicit, their adversaries focus their attention on those that follow or even on those that precede them chronologically, starting with *Sein und Zeit*, and put aside those texts that are more directly implicated with the regime. Subsequently, especially with the recent publication of the *Black Notebooks*, the gray area within Heidegger's work has appeared to grow ever larger, taking on

various shadings of antisemitism. At this point, in the course of an unusual crescendo of disagreements and polemics, the hermeneutical confrontation shifted to the incriminated texts, which were examined not only from an ideological and political point of view but also from a philosophical one.

What remains at stake, regardless, is the configuration of the relationship between politics and thought. In what sense can Heidegger's thought, given all the changes it underwent in the course of time, be considered "political"? And to what extent do his political stances, taken during the Nazi years, retain some philosophical importance when considering his thought in its entirety? The answer to this dual question has up to this point oscillated between two extreme polarities, whereby in one case one tends to politicize all of Heidegger's philosophy, while in the other one tends to affirm its substantially impolitical nature. Each perspective, however, has had to confront irrefutable matters of fact. If the hyperpolitical interpretation – which depicts the philosopher as a crypto-Nazi – does not manage to explain the extraordinary theoretical depth of some of the most fundamental works of twentieth-century philosophy, the impolitical one is led to ignore the just as indubitable influence of Heidegger on ample areas of contemporary political philosophy. I am not only referring to Hannah Arendt and Herbert Marcuse, avowed political thinkers and Heidegger's students,[1] I am also referring to a number of philosophers with strong political inclinations such as Nancy, Sloterdijk, Agamben, who have all been intensely influenced by the Heideggerian paradigm. In truth an observation of this kind could be extended to the entire area of continental thought. While one must certainly make all the necessary distinctions, the Heideggerian tone of philosophers such as Derrida, Schürmann, and Vattimo, themselves important interpreters of Heidegger, is not in doubt. But which thinkers of the second half of the twentieth century, with the exception of the analytical school, can be considered completely extraneous to the Heideggerian lexicon? The fact that a majority are located on the political left – to the extent that some have talked of a *gauche heideggerienne*[2] – only increases the problematic nature of the issue.[3] If Heidegger's political engagement – whatever its nature and duration – was situated on the German right, why did it arouse such an enduring interest among what, starting with Sartre, can be defined as the European philosophical left? Why did engaged thinkers on the left, communists if not also anarchists, not only never cut the thread that tied them to Heidegger's philosophy, but instead appropriated some of its constitutive categories and reworked them as their own?

To provide an answer that is not limited to empirical circumstances of a biographical or editorial nature – after the war, these had a far from negligible impact on the circulation of his thought – one has to take into account the interpretive contrast between a political and an impolitical reading and attempt to rethink it in a theoretically more articulated form. What appears in the Heideggerian literature as an interpretive dichotomy – between political and impolitical – should be recognized as a *dispositif* that is internal to his thought. The hypothesis I advance here is that Heidegger's philosophy, and not only that which addresses the political, is constituted in and by its relationship with this *dispositif*. In other words, it is constituted along the mobile line where the two vectors of the political and the impolitical reciprocally imply each other and continuously translate into each other, albeit without cancelling their difference and in fact reinforcing it. The specificity of the Heideggerian conception of the political resides precisely in its antinomical relationship with the impolitical dimension. Far from delineating an area external to the political horizon, this relationship represents both its necessary presupposition and its internal challenge. The issue should be viewed from both sides: if the political is always generated from an impolitical ground, the latter in turn takes on a political significance, entering into tension with the former. One should actually talk about a single unit of meaning rather than two opposite elements, a unit that can be viewed from different angles. This is the reason for the divergent perspectives it gave rise to in the critical literature, exhibiting either political or impolitical characteristics. Even if one divides this unit into distinct paths, one should not lose sight of the contradictory node that is formed by their intertwining, because it is the only one capable of providing the overall cypher of Heideggerian thought.[4]

The fact that the two layers of Heidegger's discourse, while inseparable, are never unproblematically superimposed on each other but, on the contrary, become increasingly conflictual along the arc of his entire oeuvre represents a hermeneutical difficulty for those who approach his thought. What is at stake is precisely the figure of their difference, in a manner that in some ways recalls the ontological difference between Being and beings: although it reveals itself through beings, Being cannot be limited to them. In their turn, beings can never exhaust the being that they "are," but rather tend to forget it. The political is also traversed, if not constituted, by a difference between what it is and what it is *not* and ultimately can never be. From this point of view, as is the case with all the other most important concepts of the philosopher, starting with *alētheia*, the positive can never be defined except by starting with the negative, in fact from the modality of the double negation, as the opposite of that which is not. This is also the case for the political – except for a brief period, which ran its course in the mid-1930s, when Heidegger attempts to express it directly – which only becomes meaningful by carving itself out from a non-political background that constitutes its condition, but never coincides with it. In the course of time, what changes is the relationship between these two registers of the negative: that which is, so to speak, constituting, on the one hand, and the destituting, which is destined to increasingly exclude the former, on the other. If the negative presupposition, that is to say, the impolitical, is that from which the political stems and takes shape, from a certain point onwards it becomes the explicit negation of the political. What was initially a tension internal to a single process diverges into a laceration between contrastive poles, destined to mutually annul each other.

From that point on the impolitical is on an ever more marked collision course with the political, which is homologized into a single nihilistic dimension, one that coincides with the generalized domination of technology. The impolitical therefore transitions from the role of a necessary background to that of functioning as a critical *dispositif* in its relationship with the political. What was a negative presupposition that enabled one to think of the political becomes its pure negation: no longer the "non-political" from which the political starts, but that which negates it in its very possibility. In this case, however, one should not understand "negation" to mean any active modality, an action against, but rather a "non-action" in the radical sense of an abandonment of the category of "action" itself. If all existing manifestations of politics are part of the same destructive technology – as Heidegger, starting from a certain phase, will argue with ever greater conviction – the "impossible" task of the impolitical becomes that of their deactivation. That such a task is consciously impossible is due not only to its inability to translate into action but also to the absence of any subjectivity capable of enacting it. It is precisely the paradigm of "putting to work," moreover – which Heidegger in the mid-1930s still thought of affirmatively – that subsequently becomes the target of his polemics. The impolitical – which by now is the focus of his attention, an attention critical of all actual politics – coincides with the placing into unworkability[5] of any political operation and with the destitution of any institution, even though no entity, individual or collective, can put it into practice, since it is the very notion of praxis, before anything else, that is deactivated. The impolitical, in other words, is not an active option for human beings, but the condition that necessarily makes any such option vain, annulling any decision other than to "let be" what is.

This is how the antinomy of Heidegger's reflections on the political come to light, expressed by the negative character of the impolitical – negative with regard to any kind of politics, resisted from the very roots of its technical–nihilistic drift, but also negative in relation to itself. How can the impolitical, in its withdrawal from workability, continue to exercise any critical function whatsoever? And, even prior to that issue, how can it assume any differential relief with respect to the political, if it constitutes its negative presupposition? Non-action cannot be thought of logically outside of the relationship with the action it negates, just as destitution does not make any sense without any institution to destitute. But if this is the case, if action and inaction are the inseparable surfaces of one sheet of paper, the impolitical loses all consistency and dissolves as such. So long as it inheres in the political, it is no more than its inner fold, as is the case with some Heideggerian texts of the 1930s. When instead, in subsequent works, it becomes the motor for the deactivation of a politics that at this point coincides with technology, it loses all possible connotations. Taken to its greatest intensity, negation ends up negating even itself, annulling itself as negation. In this sense one could conclude that, for Heidegger, politics in its ultimate version coincides with the movement of its self-destitution.

*

A quasi-transcendental presupposition of the entire western conception of the political is that it has a negative foundation. The political seems to be recognizable only starting from its external limits.[6] Analogously, in the world as experienced by the Greeks, the *polis*, to the extent that it is non-political, can be thought of only against the background of the *oikos*, *praxis* is defined in opposition to *theōria*, and *vita activa* in opposition to *vita contemplativa*. In the modern period the civil order is seen as rising from the abandonment of the natural one, while the public sphere, in its turn, is built as an alternative to the private. In any case, to define itself, the political needs a negative background from which to detach itself. Over time obviously the political and the non-political are interpreted in different ways, which modify both the relationship between the two terms and the value given to them individually in each particular instance. In the Greek world, while *polis* and *oikos* remain separate, they mutually imply each other in a recursive fashion: while from a genetic point of view the *polis* follows the formation of non-political communities, from a logical or metaphysical point of view it precedes them as their presupposed essence.[7] This means that the *oikos* is situated in a pre-political context rather than in an apolitical or non-political dimension, one that waits to be fulfilled by the advent of the *polis*, just as generic life waits to be brought to perfection by the "good life."

The situation of the relationship between the political and the non-political is different in the Christian world, where, at least in its Augustinian version, the "non" is more pronounced with respect to the political world. Rather than pre-political, *civitas dei*, the city of God, is radically apolitical and even post-political – in the sense that it is destined, at the end of time, to definitely take over from *civitas hominis*, the city of humans, which it is not placed next to horizontally, but to which it is counterposed vertically. In its turn, the human city can fulfill itself only by negating itself in the city of God. Although they commingle in the course of history, the two essentially incompatible cities are destined to be irreversibly divided on Judgment Day, when only one will remain. In the modern conception inaugurated by Hobbes, the presupposition of the political, in other words of the state of nature, tends to be seen in a light where its negative aspects are emphasized. This is not only an a-political condition or a simply non-political one, but a decidedly anti-political one, given that, in its irrecoverable lack of order, it contradicts the only possible political order, which is made possible solely by excluding the natural order. The subsequent distinction, typical of the bourgeois world, between public and private or, starting with Hegel, between state and civil society nuances and reduces this separation but does not eliminate it, giving rise to an antinomical dialectics that in Marx is resolved in revolution. Before him, even with all the conceptual reversals, one could argue that the thought of the political remains suspended by the presence of a negative element, which is necessary to delineate its specificity. With the advent of Nietzsche, this horizon is transformed and ultimately breaks up. Not only do none of the previous dichotomies seem to remain standing, but it is the very machine of negative presupposition that runs aground, not because the negative presupposition fails but because it begins to penetrate the political itself, expanding and deforming its contours. If there is something that, for all their profound differences, unifies the perspectives of Schmitt's, Arendt's, and Foucault's political ontologies, it is precisely their perception of the implosion of the negative foundation and of the risk it entails for the existence of the political itself. The amalgam of the statist and the political in Schmitt, of the social and the political in Arendt, and of the political and the biological in Foucault seem to determine a turning point that cannot be grasped by means of classical categories, ancient and modern, that are involved in the very subsidence of their object. From another perspective, we are dealing with the same drift that Heidegger recognizes in the complete overlap of technology and politics that is destined to crush the latter in the cogwheels of the former. What these authors – with the exception of Foucault – share is the politically dissolving outcome to which the disappearance of the negative presupposition of the political leads. Without a contrastive backdrop, the political can no longer be thought, because it has lost its contours in an indistinction from society, nature, and technology that is irreversible at this point. The category of the "biopolitical," which grasps the commingling of politics and life genealogically, appears to be the only one capable of subtracting contemporary political thought from this negative logic – or, perhaps better, of subtracting the negative from the logic of negation, reconverting it into an affirmative perspective.

*

2. What distinguishes the rectorial address (*Rektoratsrede*) of 1933 – in which the surrender to Nazi ideology is exhibited in its most obvious form – is the absence of any impolitical reservation with regard to its explicit political goals. These goals fill the entire frame, eliminating any critical tension within it. Later Heidegger will argue that, in accepting the position of rector, his intention was to save the university's autonomy from national socialist "political science" – in other words from a coarse instrumentalization of learning for apologetic ends. And his talk in fact theorizes the topic of the autonomous mission of science in the presence of the joint body of faculty and students. Yet it is precisely this mission that conveys a tone that is inseparable from the political framework of which it is a part. The very purpose, announced at the outset, of "guiding the guides" of the German people – destined, in Heidegger's intentions, to move the center of gravity of *Führung* [guiding] from the field of power to that of knowledge – in fact simply translates the subordination of the latter to the exigencies of the former. In order for the German university to recognize its fundamental task, which gushed out from the foundation of its *Dasein*, it must will with a decisiveness that is at one with its political enactment. The result is an integral superposition of levels bound together by the primacy of the will of the German people and their state: "The will to the essence of the German university is the will to science as the will to the historical mission of the German people as a people that knows itself in its state."[8] Knowledge, people, and state are bound together in a single will that responds in a single voice to the call of the new Germany.

Certainly, in the tight mesh of a text that is so integrated in the dynamics of the ruling power a margin of difference remains: it is the different level at which the rector situates his own discourse with respect to the language, deemed to be significantly inferior, of a regime that was not adequate to the task of culturally forming the next generations. This is where one gets the sense, which one can derive from Heidegger's words, of an infinite intellectual superiority with regard to his political interlocutors – who were, moreover, scarcely disposed to tolerate it for any length of time. Heidegger used his premature resignation from the rectorate, which was due to the inevitable failure of such a pedagogical project, as a belated proof of his lack of guilt. As has often occurred in analogous situations, he subsequently argued that he acted in a responsible manner, to avoid a greater evil. Apart from the morally sticky nature of such an argument, it in no way modifies the heavily ideological scope of the *Rektoratsrede*, which is oriented toward the full integration of philosophy and politics. As has been noted,[9] it borrows from Plato's Syracusan project – which in its own time also resulted in failure – of providing politics with the legitimation of a knowledge oriented toward operational perspectives and adapting it to the new conjuncture. At its base one can recognize an energetic notion of *poiēsis*, in which Nietzschean accents and Jüngerian references to the "warrior worker" are melded. Recalling the myth of Prometheus as the first philosopher worker already tends to negate the idea of a *theōria* withdrawn into pure contemplation. According to Heidegger, the Greeks fought against it so as to express "the highest mode of ἐνέργεια, of man's 'being at work' [*am-Werk-sein*]."[10] If one considers that, in the writings that follow Nazism's defeat, the philosopher will proclaim, with ever increasing urgency, the need to deactivate all workability, the choice of this term seems all the more significant. If to this we add his emphasis on the "work" of thought, the reference to the operative power of theory seems to impart the foundational tone for the entire *Rede*. The triple service that is requested of students – work (*Arbeit*), defense (*Wehr*), and knowledge (*Wissen*) to the benefit of the German people – only strengthens the character of active militancy of the task to which they are destined: "This people shapes its fate by placing its history into the openness of the overwhelming power of all the world-shaping powers of human being (*Dasein*) and by ever renewing the battle for its spiritual world."[11]

It is true that these expressions preserve a significant distance from the much more elementary Nazi jargon. First there is the argument for the primacy of the spiritual element as against the strictly biological one – which, however, *does not* prevent Heidegger from specifying that the spiritual world "of a people is not the superstructure of a culture, no more than it is an armory stuffed with useful facts and values; it is the power that most deeply preserves the people's strengths, which are tied to earth and blood; and as such it is the power that mostly deeply moves and most profoundly shakes its being (*Dasein*)."[12] Second, there is the Heraclitean meaning of *polemos* [war] given to the term "struggle" (*Kampf*), to be related to an *eris* [quarrel], or *Streit*, which does not mean "war" but rather "contest" between adverse parties bound in a shared *Auseinandersetzung* [confrontation]. Even the "overwhelming power" that Heidegger talks about should be referred not to any historical subject, but to a destiny marked by the "provocation" of technology. And even the self-affirmation to which the German people is called could appear to follow from the absence of a foundation for Dasein that had been theorized in previous texts such as *The Essence of Ground*, *The Essence of Truth*, and *Plato's Doctrine of Truth*. One could add that the historicization of *Mitsein* in the "community of the people" had already been anticipated in paragraph 74 of *Sein und Zeit*, thus proving an element of continuity with the original inspiration of his work that not even the wretched turning point of 1933 can definitely break.

But it is another element that confers a slender margin of autonomy to the *Rektoratsrede* with respect to its immediate political circumstance. This is the reference to Greek origins and the discontinuity they bring about within the racial continuity that the Nazis asserted about their presumptive Germanic ancestors. Heidegger's insistence on the difference between the genealogical concept of *Geschichte* and the chronological one of *Historie* is well known. In the allocution he delivered in November 1933 during the student matriculation ceremony, he reminds the Germans of what it means to be a "historical people." This does not coincide with the simple fact of "having" a history, which is true of any community. What he intends to convey is rather "*to know, as a people*, that history is not the past, let alone the present; it is an acting and an undertaking that grasps the present in its entirety and holds on to it with a view to the future *that presses upon us*. The future of a people does not in any way consist of *that which is not yet*. It is precisely because it is a coming."[13]

Hence the polemics against those forms of knowledge that limit themselves to glancing back only a couple of decades, thus preventing themselves from acquiring a deeper dimension of historicity. They flatten the present onto itself, preventing its accession to the future by means of that step backwards that only a referral to origins allows. Heidegger asserts the primacy of philosophy over all the sciences against this form of reduction of essential historicity to simple historical succession, since it is the only one capable of conversing with Greek beginnings. This pushes knowledge far away from the direction taken first by Christian and then by modern culture, according to which what comes first flows linearly into what comes after. Against the erasure of origins proclaimed by modernity, it is necessary to know that "[t]he beginning still *is*. It does not lie *behind us*, as something that was long ago, but stands *before* us."[14]

And yet, all these considerations notwithstanding, a real caesura is not introduced into that amalgam of philosophy and politics produced by the *Rektoratsrede*, even when viewed from this angle. It is true that the projection of Greek origins onto the present opens up a perspective that differs from simple historical succession. But the difference that had thereby been outlined is immediately neutralized by the insertion of a new German beginning in the wake of the Greek one. If in the 1940s and 1950s this joint presence will seem to be precluded by the irreproducibility of the first beginning, at this juncture it is precisely what the *Rektoratsrede* does claim for the future of the *Tausendjähriges Reich*: "The beginning has invaded our future. There it awaits us, a distant command bidding us catch up with its greatness. ... But if we submit to the distant command of the beginning, science must become the fundamental happening of our spiritual being [Dasein] as part of a people."[15]

In this unbroken continuity, which conjoins the new Germany with ancient Greece, any difference of levels is destined to be lost. Hinging on the forced convergence between Greekness and Nazism, the political dimension ends up absorbing the knowledge that should direct it. Sweeping away the distinctions that still characterized the texts that straddle the 1920s and 1930s, the *Rektoratsrede* incinerates any impolitical reservation toward an integration of politics and thought that does not contemplate any remainder.

3. This paroxysmal politicization of thought, which sees its culmination during the year of the rectorate, does not last long. Already in the course of the 1934–1935 winter semester, devoted to Hölderlin's hymns "Germania" and "The Rhine," something changes in Heidegger's conceptual language,[16] also as a result of his resignation from the rectorate. He naturally continues to declare himself a Nazi, but in at least one passage in the first course one can find some fairly explicit distancing. Speaking of "lived experiences," Heidegger reminds us that they can be interpreted, with Spengler, as an expression of the soul of culture or, with Rosenberg, as an expression of the soul of race, and in several other ways as well. All these, the philosopher continues, may in fact be accurate, but that does not mean true. Never as in this case does what is correct prove to be essentially false, especially when such modes of thinking claim

to be scientific and philosophical. At this point Heidegger quotes the Nazi writer Edwin G. Kolbenheyer as an example: according to him, poetry "is a necessary biological function of the people." Heidegger immediately follows this with an extremely ironic observation: "one does not need to be endowed with great intellect to note that this is also true for digestion, which is also a necessary biological function of the people, especially of a healthy one." It is true that Heidegger is just as critical of Spengler's thesis. But it is also obvious that the sarcasm reserved for the racial biologism of Rosenberg and Kolbenheyer is specially emphasized, rounded off by a final consideration to the effect that "[a]ll of this is so wretchedly banal that we speak of it only reluctantly."[17]

The distance from the previous year's *Rektoratsrede* cannot be reduced to this qualification. Without withdrawing his support for the regime, Heidegger is even more convinced of its cultural inadequacy, which is expressed in its bluntly direct conception of the relation between theory and politics. To tighten the knot between them to the extent of eliding any intermediate articulation, as he had done in *Rektoratsrede*, seems to him a mistake he should not repeat. This is the historical and biographical framework for his lessons on Hölderlin, considered by Heidegger to be not only the greatest German poet but also a thinker at the level of Schelling and Hegel. It is precisely this passage through *Dichtung* [poetry] that, for Heidegger, is a sign of a marked difference with regard to the position he had taken the previous year. The bond between politics and thought, between thinkers and statespersons remains firm: both are creators that detach themselves from the mass, reaching the peaks of thought and action. It is, however, no longer a direct link, because it requires the mediation of poetry, which, placed between them, produces their first disarticulation. Political action, to reveal itself, needs to pass through poetry.

This is no trivial change, when compared to the synonymy of philosophy and politics that Heidegger had argued for the previous year. Politics and philosophy still cross paths, certainly, but only if the latter converses with the writing of poets. According to the famous verse in *Andenken* [memory] according to which "[w]hat remains, however, the poets provide," the practice of instituting, which also characterizes political action in a fundamental fashion, originates with the poets. Just as poetry establishes the truth through the word, politics institutes the state by means of its actions. In both cases we are dealing with a foundation; and in both cases "foundation" should be understood in its most intense acceptation, as "enactment of the truth." But the category of "workability" that continues to characterize the Heideggerian lexicon during this phase now refers, even before thought, to art. The politician is a kind of creator who resembles an artist, from whom he derives this specific, form-giving attitude. Their homology passes through common linguistic usage, which is necessary both for poetry and for the life of a historical people. The poet has the civic function of gathering the word of the gods so that it may be "built into the foundational walls of the language of a people by the poet."[18]

In order for *Dichtung* to be able to inform politics, breaking its immediate relationship with thought, two conditions need to be met, which Heidegger assumes as presuppositions of his own perspective: on the one hand, the separation between aesthetics and art, which is removed from the category of the beautiful and assigned to the institution of being; on the other, the withdrawal of the meditation on the political into its essential dimension. And what does this withdrawal into the essential nucleus mean, in terms of thought about politics, if not to once again propose the question of origins, to which poetry also refers as its enigmatic source? In each of these cases, presence needs to be deferred, creating a bridge between the now and the originary. This is what Hölderlin has taught us: once the ancient gods vanished, it is precisely the vital relationship with their origin that human beings are at risk of losing. The philosopher is now reasoning in a negative register. Unlike in the *Rektoratsrede*, where the reference to a Greek beginning was directly functional to a political purpose, it now traces a groove within the political that excludes its immediate effectuation. Hölderlin's poetry reveals a conceptual landscape marked by an irredeemable void. It is certainly no accident that Heidegger reminds us that "the time of the creators and peoples is cleaved by an abyss; it is not the common road on which everyone can race away and race past everyone else."[19] Therefore the political, like the poetical, not only lacks itself, but is defined precisely by this lack. This is the case because both resort to that language that is revealed as "the Most Dangerous of Goods"[20] – since it entails the threat to being from the side of non-being. Whether this takes place in 1801, in Hölderlin's time, or in 1934, during Hitler's rule, nothing changes.

But this *does not* exhaust the shift in emphasis by comparison to the *Rektoratsrede*. Naturally the conceptual lexicon – that of the "being put to work" and of the "foundation" – remains the same; so does the reference to a *technē* still understood in a mythopoeic sense – in the triple dimension of *Dichtung*, *Sprache*, and

Sage – poetry, language, and myth. But what fissures is the closed nature of the *Rektoratsrede*, which is now replaced by a centrifugal tendency toward the outside, which ruptures its internal compactness via a series of differential caesuras. Seen from this perspective, the Heideggerian interpretation of "The Rhine" turns out to be even more consequential than that of *Germania*. The reason is not that faith in the refoundation of the German people through the *Dichtung* of its greatest poet has diminished, but that this project *does not* take the form of a glorious ascent. To rise again, it must first experience descent into the abyss, as *Germania* reminded us. Only the passage through the abyss creates an opening for one's land and allows one to attain the fatherland. But how does one recognize one's land and take ownership of the fatherland? It is to these questions that Hölderlin's poem provides the most problematic answer, destined to fissure the apodictic certainties of the *Rektoratsrede*: the fatherland can be reached only by means of an estranging encounter with strangers. This is what Hölderlin had written his friend Böhlendorff on December 4, 1801.[21] The matter at hand at the time was the same relationship between the Germans and the Greeks that the *Rektoratsrede* had alluded to, but with a decisive difference: unlike on that occasion, when Heidegger imagined that he could graft the new German beginning onto and in continuity with the Greek one, the latter now appears unattainable. As Hölderlin teaches us, the relationship between Germans and Greeks can no longer be direct. It does not express the figure of either analogy or opposition, but that of the chiasmus, because each of the two peoples can relate to itself only via the teachings provided by the other – in other words by renouncing what was initially its own. While the principle of the Greeks is Dionysian fire, that of the Germans is Apollonian order. For each people to be able to realize its own, it must appropriate the principle of the other, transforming that which is naturally given into a task that is difficult to accomplish. This is the reason why the Greeks – to whom Heidegger continues to refer as an essential archetype – now appear inimitable to him: not because they are too distant from us but, on the contrary, because, just like us, they also were not able to grow on the foundation of their original nucleus. Paradoxically, the one thing that they have and that we can imitate is lack, their constitutive alterity. The conquest of one's own (*das Eigene*) therefore presupposes the riskier transition through the alien (*das Fremde*), just as the political can find itself only by presupposing something that, from within, distances it from itself – its impolitical reverse.

4. The three 1936 conferences collected under the title *Der Ursprung des Kunstwerks* mark a new transition within Heidegger's reflections on the political. This is obviously not the conferences' main object – which is instead the work of art, questioned as to its essential meaning. But they are indeed tied to the political by more than one thread, primarily via the category of "work," which I have already recalled in the preceding pages. Philippe Lacoue-Labarthe in particular has identified both the very paradigm of Nazi politics and, albeit via a series of distinctions, that of the Heideggerian concept of the political in this category of "work."[22] On the basis of this reading, Heidegger would seem to have tapped into the Jena Romantic model – that of Hölderlin, the Schlegel brothers, Schiller, Schelling, and the young Hegel, following a thread that leads to Wagner and Nietzsche – and into the idea of *Gesamtkunstwerk* [total work of art], interpreted in an intensely political manner. Like the work of art, the state should also be considered the product of a forming activity oriented toward *Bildung* [construction], understood simultaneously as formation, fiction, and figuration of a mythopoeic kind. After the failure of his plans for the rectorate, Heidegger shifted his political reflection from the horizon of philosophy to that of art, situating it at the crossroads of *Dichtung*, *Sprache*, and *Sage*. As occurred in the case of Homer for the Greeks and Hölderlin for the Germans, only myth allows a people to access its own language and to situate itself at the center of its own history. Hence a sort of "national aestheticism," different from but parallel to national socialism, on whose basis the people, gathered in the state, gives itself its own representation.

In *The Origin of the Work of Art*, moreover, it is Heidegger himself who includes the action that orients a state toward the institution of truth, religious sacrifice, and the questioning of thought among the figures of "putting to work." But the relationship between politics and the work of art can also be part of a more intrinsic relationship, which is related not only to the artistic tone of politics but also, at least in a certain sense, to the political semantics of the work of art. I am obviously not referring to a form of politicization of art, an idea that is very far removed from Heidegger's intentions, but rather to the conflict that traverses the form of the work itself, whose characteristics orient it in a political direction. To better understand what is meant, one needs to briefly retrace the steps in the arguments that articulate the text. Having started with a question about the essence – and therefore the origin – of art, Heidegger discards all the conventional answers provided by the discipline of aesthetics, which is subordinated to the metaphysical tradition. The work is not made of a material substrate to which one then adds an aesthetic value. To penetrate the enigma of art, one should not go from the thing – marble for sculpture, canvas for painting, and language for poetry – to the work, but rather from the work to the thing. The material entity as such is silent – that is, before the work establishes its truth, opening it to the dimension of being. Art, in this sense, is constituted by the "setting itself to work of truth" (*das Sich-ins-Werk-setzen der Wahrheit*). This, however, is just a first answer to the initial question about the relationship between art and truth; that question is followed by a second one, which pertains to both terms: "What is truth itself, that it sometimes comes to pass as art? What is this setting-itself-to-work?"[23]

That which opens in this fashion is the historicization of truth in the work – its relationship with what Heidegger starts to refer to as "event" (*Ereignis*) in the contemporary pages of *Beiträge*. In order to clarify what he is referring to, he observes: "It is the temple-work that first fits together and at the same time gathers around itself the unity of those paths and relations in which birth and death, disaster and blessing, victory and disgrace, endurance and decline acquire the shape of destiny for the human being." He then adds, with a clear reference to the political: "The all-governing expanse of this open relational context is the world of this historical people. Only from and in this expanse does the nation first return to itself for the fulfillment of its vocation."[24] At this point Heidegger introduces the decisive argument for the institution of the political precisely on the basis of the structure of the temple. It rests on its rock foundation, from which it rises on high, as if coming out of what the Greeks called *phusis*. This foundation from which human inhabiting emerges is defined by Heidegger as "Earth" – by which he does not mean either a stratified mass or the planet, but precisely the "where" thanks to which what rises is at the same time hidden and protected.

The dynamics that art "puts to work" is thus already defined in its two constitutive elements: "The temple-work, standing there, opens up a world and at the same time sets this world back again on earth, which itself only thus emerges as native ground [*heimatliche Grund*]."[25] At this point Heidegger proceeds to qualify the two terms, distinguishing them from meanings attributed to them by others. To accomplish this, he proceeds, as usual, by following a negative path, and begins to clear the field of all non-pertinent references. The world – which was already at the center of *Sein und Zeit*, only characterized in a slightly different fashion – is not the mere ensemble of all things; but it is not a simple representation added to their sum either. It is not an object – in fact it is what cannot be objectified. "Those decisions of our history that relate to our very being"[26] are internal to it, whether they are then realized or abandoned. With the opening of a world – of course, for the living human who makes it such – everything acquires the rhythm of rest and movement, the measure of its extension, and the possibility of its recollection. It is for this reason that the work's role is to expose the world, keeping its opening uncovered.

But, Heidegger adds, the exposure of a world is only one of two vectors joined together in the work: the other one concerns the Earth. This, as was stated, is that from which the world emerges. Its emergence is, by way of contrast, made possible by the work's withdrawal into its own material substrate: into the heaviness of rock, the flexibility of wood, the hardness of metal – but also into the light of color, the tonality of sound, the power of the word. It is this withdrawal into an inviolable impenetrability that allows the opening of the world. Exposing a world and placing the Earth here are therefore the two traits through which the work expresses the historicizing of truth. But what is their relationship? This is the question that leads back to the issue of the political and, more precisely, to the two polarities – political and impolitical – into which it splits. If the world is thought of as the locus of political institution, the Earth, in its withdrawal into itself, recalls the hollowed profile of the impolitical. As with the Earth with respect to the world, the impolitical is the politically unrepresentable foundation from which the possibility of something like the political emerges.

What brings the relation between political and impolitical into a close parallelism with that between world and Earth is the specificity of their relationship, simultaneously inevitable and oppositional, inseparable and contrastive. Heidegger begins by saying that Earth and world, connected in the work, are not related to each other in the figure of rest, unless it is a rest that presupposes and includes movement; actually only that which moves can also rest. But how does it move? With what type of motion? We are dealing with an inexhaustible struggle. And in fact, resting on the Earth, the world aspires to dominate it, while in its turn the Earth, since it wards and seals, tends to absorb the world. A struggle, Heidegger immediately clarifies, does not mean a brawl or a simple contest. It is not characterized by perturbation or destruction. Not only because one pole cannot do without the other, since it derives from it in the negative, but, to a greater degree, because it proceeds via the strengthening of its opposite – exactly as occurs in Hölderlin between own and extraneous: hence the indissolubility of the contenders, but also the continuous recurrence of a *polemos* that cannot cease without, in the process, vanquishing the fighters and what they stand for. The instituting role of the work is to sustain the struggle's tension and, with it, that of the forces that express it. If we relate this dialectic back to the relation between political and impolitical, we once again find the same superposition of opposites – the one determined, but also countered, by the coexistence of the other. This dramatic interplay is based on the antinomy of a negative that impacts that which it serves to found, destituting it. This is the same perspective that, working against its modern interpretation in terms of correctness or correspondence, sees truth as nothing more than "*non*-concealment." Heidegger insists on the dual status of this "non" – not only external, but also internal and foundational with respect to that which it negates: "Truth is un-truth [*Unwahrheit*], insofar as there belongs to it the reservoir of the not-yet-uncovered, the un-covered in the sense of concealment. In unconcealedness, as truth, there occurs also the other 'un-' of a double restraint or refusal. Truth occurs as such in the opposition of clearing and double concealing."[27] Concealment is not only the opposite of illumination but also its dark apex. If it does not appear, this is not due to a lack, but to an excess, of light – because, to allow for a more intense illumination, it conceals itself, annulling itself. Analogously – or so one could argue – the impolitical, to subtract itself from any political dimension, also ends up dissolving itself.

*

The category of the "impolitical" is also tied to the negative, up to and including its very designation. The insoluble antinomies that articulate its conception in all its possible twentieth-century formulations also derive from this aspect.[28] Once the essential difference between this notion and all apolitical or, worse, anti-political conceptions has been established, the problem of its definition remains open. While it cannot be assimilated to the categories of the political, from which it distances itself, the impolitical adheres inextricably to them like a shadow. One must therefore reiterate that the impolitical is not, nor could it be, the negation of the political, but is rather its negative. It cannot be its negation, because otherwise, by opposing the political, it would fall back into its language, via the inevitably political semantics of conflict. But, more importantly, it cannot because it does not outline a reality beyond the only existing one – that of the political, of which it constitutes only the external border or, more precisely, the impossibility: that which the political truly cannot be. Whatever name one wants to assign to this "non" – goodness, justice, value – its political unrepresentability, the closure of any dialectical transition between two irreconcilable polarities, remains. If there is one thing that the thinkers of the impolitical exclude, that is the dialectical convertibility of power into goodness. But, let me repeat, this insuperable difference does not open a space of workability that differs from that governed by power. As Canetti observes, history is completely occupied by it:

> [It] places itself on the side of that which occurred and detaches it from what didn't occur, while building solid connections. Among all the possibilities it bases itself on the only one that survived. This is how history acts, as if it were on the side of the *strongest* event, in other words the one that really occurred: it could not have remained un-occurred, it had to occur.[29]

By placing itself on the side of the "non-occurred," the impolitical renounces historical existence. It is other than history, in the sense that it does not belong to it. And yet the difference that is delineated in this manner cannot be measured, except from the side of history itself – the only effectual dimension of action. It is for this reason, to escape it, that the impolitical *does not* propose a different action, but the destitution of action. In this sense one can say that it inaugurates the paradigm of destituting thought.

This does not resolve the problem of its determination, however. Placed in an extra-historical space, and therefore non-existent as such, the impolitical runs the risk of being reduced to a mere negative presupposition of the political; however, by thus limiting itself to negating that from which it derives meaning, it remains devoid of an autonomous connotation. Hence the antinomic knot that none of the impoliticals manages to solve. If the impolitical cannot avail itself of any definition, how is it distinguished from the political? When answering this question, a decisive one for the qualification of the concept, impolitical thinkers oscillate between the two options, both contradictory, of gnostic dualism and of coincidence with the political. All the stakes depend on the interpretation of the negative. What should be understood here by "negative"? As stated previously, it is not the negation of something by something else. It is rather the point of contrast on whose basis the political shows itself in its bare effectuality, the invisible margin that differentiates it from that which it is not and will never be able to be. But where is that margin drawn – inside or outside the political? Does it circumscribe the political from without or does it split it from within? If it circumscribes it, with respect to what horizon does it do it, given that no other exists? If it splits it instead, *is* the dualism *not* reconstituted within its borders? To avoid this outcome, the impolitical recognizes that there is no reality outside of the conflict of power. But in this fashion it does no more than repeat that which political realism has always affirmed, only in the negative, and ends up erasing its own peculiarity. It can escape this outcome only by alluding to an alterity that it knows is unattainable. Its tragic condition lies entirely in the insolubility of this tension – in knowingly tending toward the unattainable. The person who expresses this antinomy with the greatest intensity without attempting to neutralize it is Simone Weil, when she writes: "There is no other force on this earth except force. That could serve as an axiom"; but she then immediately adds: "As for the force which is not of this earth, contact with it cannot be bought at any lesser price than passing through a kind of death."[30] The awareness of the necessity, and at the same time impossibility, of this passing through is impolitical.

Like Heidegger, Weil also looks for the leap toward this impossible not through action, but through its deactivation. An action that is halted at the stage of pure potentiality is deactivated, it is denied the possibility of becoming act – or at least an act that is not its own withdrawal. This is the motif, which was present already in her earliest writings, of "passive power" or "non-acting agency," on the basis of which "to act is never difficult: we always act too much and we ceaselessly consume ourselves in disorganized acts. To make six shirts with anemones and remain quiet: this is the only way we can acquire power."[31] To act passively, by *not acting*, "the only strength and the only virtue is to abstain from acting,"[32] she writes, in this case also separating the potentiality from the act. Like Heidegger, Weil also belongs within the destituting paradigm, which she expresses by means of the Kabbalistic concept of de-creation – a creation that proceeds by self-annulment. But she does so with a decisive difference by comparison to Heidegger. While for him deactivation means the abandonment of action, Weil places herself within its space, which thus leads to its reconversion. What is no longer there is not action itself, but the interest on the part of whoever enacts it, the goal-orientedness that triggers it: "To act not for an object, but *because* of a necessity. I can't do otherwise. It is not an action, but a kind of passivity. Non-acting action."[33] Non-acting, but still action – removed as much from actions oriented toward a goal as from inaction, because "Your right is to action alone;/Never to its fruits at any time – Arjuna recommends in the *Bhagavad Gita* – Never should the fruits of action be your motive;/ Never let there be attachment to inaction in you."[34] So, in the same years in which Heidegger theorizes the "letting be," Weil leaves for the Spanish Civil War and asks to be sent to the front against the Nazis.

*

5. The comment, contained in the *Introduction to Metaphysics*, to the first chorus in Sophocles' *Antigone* reproduces, in an even more antinomic fashion, the same conflictual dynamic as that between the political and the impolitical. In this case it is neither Hölderlin's *Dichtung* nor the origins of the work of art that are being investigated, but the contrastive conjunction of Being and beings. Yet what confers a more intrinsically political tone to these pages is the place where this confrontation occurs – which is the limitless one of violence and,

finally, of the *polis* itself, in which this violence is unleashed. The line along which, in *The Origin of the Work of Art*, world and Earth were counterposed now cuts across a single territory, dividing it into two divergent fronts. Heidegger's point of departure is the Parmenidean saying on the coexistence of being and thought, which in its turn is analyzed starting from the Greek conception of human beings. This is where the celebrated definition of humans as the most disquieting (*das Unheimlichste*) within disquiet itself comes from. The Greek term used by Sophocles is *deinon*, understood as the "terrible," humans being its most cutting edge – *to deinotaton*. The semantic duplicity of *deinon* is delineated within this superlative, which introduces some separation between the condition of humans and what looms over them. It is as if it pushed a part of itself into an extreme area, in which violence is at risk of splitting apart into two counterposed entities, each one saying the same thing, only differently. Within the generalized domain of violence, in fact, it is possible to recognize two impulses, simultaneously superposed and juxtaposed, which face off in a perpetual struggle. A first meaning of *deinon* is "the terrible in the sense of the overwhelming sway [*überwältigendes Walten*],"[35] inclusive of all other entities. A meaning centered not simply on how it imposes itself, but on its constitutive character. From another point of view, which intersects the first while also contrasting it, *deinon* is "the violent in the sense of one who needs to use violence – and does not just have violence at his disposal but is violence-doing,"[36] in an active fashion.

This second modality of *deinon* – not external, but included in the first – belongs to humans who are oriented toward violence to the point of being defined by it in their essential traits, much more than they are by reason or language. This means that violence is not a qualification that is added subsequently to the being of humans or, even less, that it is dependent on their will, but is the only possibility assigned to them within the horizon of the predominant in which they are inscribed. Human violence is an integral part of the violence that encompasses it, the violence that absorbs it into a more inclusive circle, even though it distinguishes itself from the latter by a particular trait. To talk of "distinction," however, is not sufficient, since human violence is not limited to differing from, but is actually directed against, the other, presupposed violence that includes it. This clash occurs because humans tend to shatter all limits, including those of the horizon in which they are inserted, which is itself violent. For this reason they do violence to violence, simultaneously obeying and transgressing it: obeying it because they act violently, transgressing it because, in doing so, they force the limits of the "first" violence, attempting to impose themselves on its imposition.

The entire antinomy of the human condition is revealed here: although it is part of the disquieting in the primordial sense, Dasein tends to exit it, opening a breach in its borders and projecting itself outside it. This is, however, revealed to be an illusory move, because an outside does not exist, since the prevailing violence occupies the entire field of the existent. In fact it is precisely the absence of an exteriority – or, better, its coincidence with interiority – that is violent to the utmost degree. From this point of view the human situation is without escape. It continuously faces its own impossibility of overcoming the non-overcomeable. Its attempt – or, more precisely, its temptation – to violate the violence that surrounds and penetrates it is destined to failure. Whatever their efforts, the violators can never subjugate the predominant, since ultimately this very intent comes from it – from the same coercion they are trying to escape from, accomplishing no more than a strengthening of the predominant itself. To exceed – in other words to exit from something that has no outside – is impossible. But resignation to immobility is not possible either, because the movement to exteriorization is also imposed by our invincible disquiet. From this point of view the two sides of the *deinon* cannot be disjoined, not only because they are internal to one another but because both are aimed at the disclosure of that which is, which ultimately all violence refers back to as its essential destination. Violence is essentially of an unveiling nature – it provokes to appearance. This is why the opening of a breach is indispensable both to the violating *deinon*, which is led to force the horizon in which it is enclosed, and to the predominant *deinon*, which needs to disclose itself via human violence. But, in both these urgencies, the violator remains exposed to the excessive power of the predominant. This explains the violator's resistance to it – nevertheless, a move that turns out to be useless because the force it is resisting coincides with its own destiny. The only occurrence that can break this circle is death – which, however, quintessentially represents that from which there is no escape, the emblem of the without escape.[37]

The same occurs in the ambivalent relationship – both a contrast and a homology – between *technē* [art, skill] and *dikē* [justice]. It corresponds to that between the two modes of *deinon*, since *dikē* – to be understood not as "justice" but as imposition – also includes *technē* within itself. The latter, in its dual aspect of producibility and unveiling, resists the former, while constituting a modality internal to it. Even though it rises up against it, *technē* is part of *dikē*, which in its turn is expressive of the opening of *phusis*. The specificity of the political, to which the last verses of the chorus return, frames this opposition of forces, which are simultaneously divergent and coincident. Heidegger's attention focuses on the relation between the expression *pantoporos aporos* [all-inventive with no way in] and the one that immediately follows, *hupsipolis apolis* [proud citizen without a city]: if, with the first expression, the chorus refers to the different paths that open up for that which is, with the second it names the place or site at which they intersect – where Dasein historically subsists. The *polis* is the context in which history occurs, to which belong essentially – in other words, in what they are – kings, temples, gods, poets, thinkers, armies, ships. Heidegger's intention is to affirm that the *polis*, translated improperly with "city" or, even worse, with "state," has very little to do with what we generally understand as "politics." This is perhaps the first time that the rift that splits the political, separating it into two diverging semantic ganglions, one simultaneously foundational and deconstructive of the other, is made explicit in the Heideggerian corpus. *Polis* is not a political regime, as a philosophical tradition that culminated with Hegel always imagined, but rather that from which the political originates: not so much as its epiphenomenon, however, but rather in a form that maintains all its difference from it. This separation within its very own roots refers back to what was just said about the binary nature of violence. The *polis* constitutes the most appropriate place for the wrangling of violence with itself, because it delineates the margin that both divides and conjoins inside and outside. Those who inhabit it are defined by the mobile relationship they entertain with the border they themselves instituted through the act of foundation. It is the limit they establish, so as to then go beyond it, before tracing it anew. Only in this manner can they maintain the role of creators to which Heidegger ties the function of the political:

> *Are* [Heidegger is referring to those he previously named as beings in the *polis*] – but this says: use violence as violence-doers and become those who rise high in historical Being as creators, as doers. Rising high in the site of history, they also become *apolis*, without city and site, lonesome, un-canny, with no way out amidst beings as a whole, and at the same time without ordinance and limit, without structure and fittingness, because they *as* creators must first ground all this in each case.[38]

As in the interplay between these two forms of violence, Heidegger, in this phase, refers political action back to the inexhaustible struggle against an enemy that cannot be defeated in the long term. The impolitical – in other words the *non*-political essence of the *polis* – rather than just being one of the "contenders," expresses the meaning of this inevitability, but also of the inexhaustibility of a struggle that this obstacle makes even more inevitable.

6. The *Introduction to Metaphysics* contains another opening onto the political that leads one back closer to Heidegger's position on Europe's crisis and Germany's role. This position emerges from the same question from which the text originates – "How does it stand with being?" – which follows the other one: "Why, in general, are there beings at all instead of nothing?"[39] According to the author, if we responded to such questions in the traditional terms of ontology, in other words within the lexical confines of a philosophical discipline, we would remain in the space of their unthought [*il loro impensato*]. But the same would occur if we adopted the language of a science, such as the historical, which is incapable, as a science, of instituting an essential relationship with history. This situation is especially serious if one considers that the interrogation of being is a properly historical question – in the historiological sense that it refers back to a necessary relationship with the origin – because, if the loss of the relation with being is an originary event, we must return to the origin to attempt to reactivate this relation in the form of a new beginning. Here "new" means one that differs from the first, which has definitely been lost at this point, "with all the strangeness, darkness, insecurity that a genuine inception brings with it."[40]

The irrecoverableness of the "first beginning" requires a decision that concerns historical existence in its entirety, and therefore also one's own times. This is where the political reference to the contemporary situation is introduced; Heidegger inserts it into the text not as a contingent element, but as its central core. It is closely connected, as outcome and possible reaction, with that forgetfulness of being that gave rise to the metaphysical question of the *Introduction*. Transposed from a traditionally ontological context to a more intensely historical one, this question is translated into another, which directly interrogates the part of the world we inhabit: "Is 'Being' a mere word and its meaning a vapor, or is it the spiritual fate of the West?"[41] It is precisely this fate that is put at risk by the forgetfulness into which not only being, but its very forgetting have fallen, owing to the advent of technology. This is the irresistible power that condemns Europe – to which Heidegger circumscribes the West – to blindness and possible self-destruction. The inherence of such a political horizon in the philosophical content of the *Introduction* is testified by the anti-metaphysical characterization used for the powers that have Europe by the throat – in other words America and Russia. The philosopher opposes "the metaphysical people" par excellence – the German people, naturally – to these two powers, but only if the German people are capable of reestablishing a living relationship with the question of being:

> All this implies that this people, as a historical people, must transpose itself – and with it the history of the West – from the center of their future happening into the originary realm of the powers of Being. Precisely if the great decision regarding Europe is not to go down the path of annihilation – precisely then can this decision come about only through the development of new, historically *spiritual* forces from the center.[42]

This is a motif that is destined to recur in all Heidegger's philosophico-political texts up to the conclusion of the war and even beyond, albeit with a series of variations pertaining to Germany's position. It joins what the philosopher defines as "the darkening of the world, the flight of the gods, the destruction of the earth, the reduction of human beings to a mass, the hatred and mistrust of everything creative and free"[43] into one single negative, or rather catastrophic judgment. These are all figures of speech expressive of the "darkening of the world" and the "*disempowering of the spirit*" that loom over the fate of the planet.[44] The outcome they point to is not only the reduction of everything to one dimension, "resembling a blind mirror that no longer mirrors, that casts nothing back," but a lack of understanding whose consequences are even worse, and Heidegger does not hesitate to define it as "demonic [in the sense of destructively evil]."[45] The issue is an immense shadow that at this point envelops the entire surface of the earth, Germany being the sole exception. It is Germany – given its eccentric position with respect to the global drift – that calls into question the role of the political in its contrastive relationship with the forces of technological depoliticization. Heidegger views this as only a partial and precarious exception, which is already threatened with disintegration from without and, above all, from within. Europe's situation appears all the more fatal to him the greater the extent to which its spiritual collapse originates from its very foundation. It is true that the more immediate risk is represented by the anti-spiritual forces that compress it in a pincer movement, but this would not have been possible had Europe's subsidence not been due to an endogenous matrix. It is a question of a spiritual sickness that does not spare Germany itself and that indeed arose even there, via the phenomenon that is designated as the dissolution of German idealism, even though it did no more than sustain an ongoing degradation that occurred in that period. The current drift started from that point in time and went through the degrading phases of the transformation of the spirit (*Geist*) into intelligence (*Intelligenz*), then into simple reasoning (*Verständigkeit*), and finally into instrumental productivity and the parades of the world of advertisement.

But – and here is where Heidegger operates the reversal of perspectives – if all this found its origin in Europe and, more precisely, in its German heart, it is from there that first a resistance and then a redemption can start: because it is only in this "land of the center" that, surrounded by silence, the voice of the political can still be raised in the form of a "decisive historical question of the earth."[46] Only such a literally metapolitical decision, in other words political *because* metapolitical, can reproduce the "decisive opening" (*Entschlossenheit*) that had already been invoked in the *Rektoratsrede*. These expressions alone are sufficient to prove the intensely political tone of Heidegger's entire discourse. But – to return to our initial problem – political in what sense? What does "political" mean for Heidegger? And to what extent is this term compatible with the metaphysical rank he assigns to Germany in the struggle against the anti-metaphysical powers that surround it? What "political" means for Heidegger – in the historiological sense in which he uses the term – is not assimilable to Nazi politics, from which it diverges radically by virtue of its spiritual tone. Even when he recalls a phrase from the *Rektoratsrede* of 1933, he refers it back to an idea of the power of the spirit that can only with difficulty be made compatible with national socialist biological politics:

> Spirit is the empowering of the powers of beings as such and as a whole. Where spirit rules, beings as such always and in each case come more into being [*wird ... seiender*]. Asking about beings as such and as a whole, asking the question of Being, is then one of the essential fundamental conditions for awakening the spirit, and thus for an originary world of historical Dasein, and thus for subduing the danger of the darkening world, and thus for taking over the historical mission of our people, the people of the center of the West.[47]

The manner in which the "historical mission" of the German people would be carried out, in the space of just a few years, is well known. This is not the point on which one should insist, however. It is the short circuit, which already starts to emerge here, between political and impolitical, that is really relevant to a definition of the Heideggerian political paradigm. At this moment – two years after Hitler's advent to power and four years before the outbreak of war – in Heidegger's eyes it is only Germany, in Europe and the world, that embodies the principle of the political against the depoliticizing powers, which are at this point enslaved by the domination of technology and besiege Germany itself. But the political, on which Germany has a monopoly, is itself characterized in impolitical terms, precisely because these are viewed from a spiritual perspective. The force that – in a deeply rooted connection with the recalling of being – it must oppose to the forces of nothingness is that of the spirit, and it is political only as such. It will be sufficient to await Germany's defeat, itself interpreted in metaphysical terms, for that politics to reveal its irreducibly impolitical nature. Then, when that occurs, not only will it no longer be able to be "put to work," but it will recognize its task as the systematic deactivation of any work.

7. The years 1937–1938 represent a break in the Heideggerian reflection on the political in which the novelties of the following period are already anticipated. In the *Beiträge zur Philosophie* written during this period, the topic of the *polis*, which is so present in the *Introduction to Metaphysics*, seems to sink into a meditation that leaves no explicit traces on the surface. This does not mean that the issue of which it is a bearer diminishes, but rather that it is situated in a semantic horizon in which the relationship between the political and the impolitical shifts in favor of the latter. As always in Heidegger's works, the shift in perspective does not lead to an abandonment of the previous lexicon, which mostly remains the same. All the motifs, and even the terms present in the *Rektoratsrede* and in other contemporary texts – from "people" to "decision" and on to "foundation" and "creation" – return in the *Beiträge*, but on a tone that ends up giving them a different meaning, suitable to the new theoretical background of which they are a part. At a biographical level, Heidegger has not ceased to hope that the national socialist revolution, at the height of its success, will embody the epochal turn he had wished for. This, however, does not prevent the philosopher from intensifying his critique of the way it is interpreted by its contemptible actors. A good case in point concerns the central concept of *Volk*: he not only fully recognizes its semantic ambiguity, but refers it back precisely to the ethnic–racial interpretation that

leads to an "*Idolizing*, raising to the level of the *unconditioned*, the *conditions* of historical beyng."[48] At the height of the *Beiträge* period, the people cannot be either the subject or the object of philosophy, in the author's view – a view that follows that Platonizing mode of thought he had not abstained from in the *Rektoratsrede*. But the mythopoetic model employed there is now rethought according to a modality that reverses the relationship between politics and thought. By comparison to what he had theorized in 1933, in fact, it is no longer philosophical knowledge that needs to conform itself to the destinal exigencies of a historical people – in this case, the German people – but it is the latter that must respond to philosophy's most radical question:

> A people first becomes a people when its most unique members appear and when they begin to experience a presentiment. In that way a people first becomes free for its law (to be achieved through struggle) as the last necessity of its highest moment. The philosophy of a people is that which makes people, people of a philosophy, grounds them historically in their Da-sein, and destines them to stewardship of the truth of being.[49]

The reference to "most unique members" marks a further distance from the preceding approach, severing any direct link between the *Volk* and its guide. It is true that previously, especially in the conferences on Hölderlin, Heidegger had spoken of "founders" or "creators" of peoples, assimilating them to artists in their poietic activities. Now, however, it is the characterization of *poiēsis* itself, together with that of *technē*, that undergoes some discernible conceptual movement. The heroic and Promethean connotation of the *Rektoratsrede* is no longer present, and one finds instead much more problematizing characterizations, in which critical and negative accents prevail. The confrontation from the *Introduction*, between the predominant and Dasein, which took place within violence, is attenuated in favor of a meditative tendency that pushes human action toward the background, not only because it has no possibility of countering the violence that assails it but because any working will is ultimately counterproductive with respect to the intention that moves it, because it is captured by the nihilism that it intends to counteract.

At the center of this theoretical transition one finds the translation of the Sophoclean term *mēchanoen* [crafty, ingenious] with the expression *Machenschaft* (machination), which is charged with negative connotations. This is a key concept in Heidegger's overall reflection,[50] and the entire transformation of his outlook, especially as regards the issue of the political – and therefore also of the impolitical – seems to revolve around it. The more political action is related to *Machenschaft*, progressively incorporating its traits the more the role of the impolitical, which constitutes its external limit, comes to the fore. In Heidegger's text, this shift is slow, far from linear, and in fact contradicted by a series of references that seem to go in the opposite direction. But, overall, it unequivocally marks Heidegger's path, starting from the "political" connotation that he assigns to *Machenschaft*. Without ever losing contact with the prevailing semantics of technology – in all the determinations that it will assume over the course of Heidegger's oeuvre, up to the late appearance of *Gestell* [framework] – machination is immediately provided with the hyperpolitical attributes of *Macht* [power] and of *Gewalt* [violence]. Certainly, at least during this period, the two lexical fields of technology and politics don't fully coincide, but articulate each other reciprocally in the shared prevalence of a negative lexicon: just as technology exhibits political characteristics – in the sense of conflict and violence – so politics begins to increasingly assume technology characteristics, which pervert its originary affirmative meaning, as Heidegger writes in his *Ponderings*: "*The new politics is an intrinsic essential consequence of technology*."[51]

What is the element that binds technology and politics together in a single negative node, in the figure of the *Machenschaft*? The answer is contained in the root of the term itself. It is a question of *machen* – in the sense of making, operating, effectuating – which destines a being to its "makeability" (*Machbarkeit*), thus distancing it from the Greek horizon of the *phusis*. Here the element Heidegger insists on is the mechanism of mutual implication between such a metaphysics of "doing" and the interpretation of the entity underlying it, as is made clear in a decisive passage of the *Contributions to Philosophy*:

> Instead, the name machination [*Machenschaft*] should immediately refer to *making* [Machen] (*poiēsis, technē*), which we assuredly know as a human activity. This latter, however, is itself possible precisely only on the grounds of an interpretation of beings in which their makeability comes to the fore, so much so that constancy and presence become the specific determinations of beingness. The fact that *something makes itself by itself* and consequently is makeable in a corresponding operation: the *making itself by itself* is the interpretation of *phusis* carried out in terms of *technē* and its outlook

> on things, in such a way that now already the emphasis falls on the makeable and the self-making (compare the relation between *idea* and *technē*), which is called, in brief, machination.[52]

In order to capture the movement of Heidegger's thought, one needs to keep his genealogical reconstruction of western metaphysics in mind, starting with the closure of the "first beginning," which can especially be referred back to Aristotle's philosophy. Already in the relationship that Aristotle establishes between *dunamis* and *energeia* the becoming of reality is conceived of as a continuous "being put to work" – in so far as it is both work and action. The medieval concept of *actus* constitutes a further step in the same direction and finds its culmination in the Christian idea of creation, which transforms the entity into *ens creatum*. But, in order to arrive at the modern idea of machination, one needs to pass through the activist orientation Leibniz impressed on modern metaphysics, in a direction that would lead to Nietzsche's "will to power" and Jünger's "total mobilization." On this basis, all entities become real to the extent to which they are "realizable," in other words inscribed within a general process of production and effectuation. Regardless of the fact that one of the basic features of machination is its own concealment – in conformity with a form of deceit we shall soon find also in the political – here the traits of the convergence between technology and the political, which lead simultaneously toward the politicization of technology and toward the technologization of politics, are already delineated. The technical artifact is one with political doing, in a metaphysical horizon "ordered" – in the dual sense of the term: organized and imposed – by machination, which has taken the place of the *deinotaton*, of the predominant violence that cannot be opposed by any *deinos* because it is inextricably part of it: "Machination as the sovereignty of making and of the realm of what is made. Yet that is not to be thought of in the sense of human activity and busyness and their management; on the contrary, such activity, in its unconditionality and exclusivity, is possible only on the basis of machination."[53]

If Heidegger ties politics to that technological machination in which the most violent trait of modern metaphysics is inscribed, it is obvious that at its external margins another space is freed up, one to which it is possible to assign the name of impolitical. Although the concept does not yet appear in the Heideggerian lexicon, it can be derived by contrast with the negative characterization attributed to the political. In at least one case, however, it already begins to emerge with clarity: it is the case of the motif of decision. In no other situation does the transition from the political to the impolitical appear in a fashion that is as clear and where the inactive characterization of the category is so emphasized. In paragraph 43 of the first part of the *Beiträge*, a paragraph appropriately entitled "Beyng and Decision," Heidegger intersects the two terms, making decision a trait of Being instead of a human faculty. It is certainly difficult, begins the philosopher, to approach the phenomenon of decision without connecting it to the idea of a choice with respect to an either/or, and therefore to the freedom of human action in a moral–anthropological sense. This is precisely what needs to be avoided, however, if one wants to regard it from the perspective of the event, to which Heidegger's entire text is devoted:

> What is here called de-cision then proceeds to the innermost center of the essence of beyng itself and thus has nothing in common with what we understand as making a choice or the like. Instead de-cision [*Ent-scheidung*] refers to the sundering itself, which separates [*scheidet*] and in separating lets come into play for the first time the ap-propriation of precisely this sundered *open realm* as the clearing for the self-concealing and still undecided, for both the belonging to beyng of the human being as the one who grounds the truth of beyng and the assignment of beyng to the time of the last god.[54]

This means that there is no decision from us that corresponds to the decision of Being, but there is instead an irreducible indecision, which does: that between decision and non-decision. The only decision – not one to be taken, but one to make room for – is "whether beyng conclusively withdraws itself, *or* whether this withdrawal, as refusal, becomes the first truth and the other beginning of history."[55] This is equivalent to stating that, far from conjugating decision and the political, we need to separate them radically and suspend any decision from the enigmatic space of the undecidable. If the political enters into the era of machination through work, in order to escape its grasp we can do no more than withdraw from collective work into the sphere of solitude, to which point the few "nexts" in the sphere of a non-acting action, of a de-creating creation that consigns all human works to unworkability.

*

The person who argued for the non-political – in fact rather ontological or, in a peculiar sense, ethical – character of Heidegger's category of "decision" was Jean-Luc Nancy, in a text entitled *The Decision of Existence*: "The thought of decision can have nothing to do with any 'decisionism' that might descend from on high to cut through to specific possibilities and objectives of existence. On the contrary, 'decision' is, for this thought, the undecidable 'object' par excellence."[56] But what is an undecidable decision, and what is its relationship with a thought, of which it would be, even if in quotation marks, the "object"? Nancy's answer is that, for Heidegger, the decision is not discharged onto the world but is the Dasein's modality of conduct in its existential inherence in it. To decide, in this sense, does not mean to take a position on something instead of something else but, on the contrary, to adopt the undecidable character of the existence and to expose oneself to the event: "We think, we write, we read philosophy the way *they* think, write and read. But what we cannot decide in this way is *the originary undecidability of Being-thrown-to-the-world* (to the "*they*"), in which, by which, and as which the Being of existence takes place."[57] This means that it is not the subject – a term Heidegger always avoids – that decides something; on the contrary, it is the decision to institute the subject in a form that no longer has anything subjective about it because it expresses the exposure of existence to its own constitutive opening. The semantic sequence *Erschlossenheit* [development], *Entschlossenheit* [determination], and *Entscheidung* [decision] articulates the rhythm of this opening – "deciding" but also "decided" – in an insoluble intertwining of mastery and passivity. It is, then, decision itself that is decided or rescinded: a decision that coincides with a Dasein that allows the possibility of its existence to be.

While this folding of decision onto itself excludes its political interpretation, placing it on a rigorously impolitical level, it does not preclude an ethical interpretation, so long as one takes ethics in an ontological sense, as Nancy does when speaking of an "originary ethics" or a "fundamental ethics." The ontological difference, in this acceptation, is not the difference between Being and being(s), but the manner in which a Dasein is called to an active relation with its own being. Dasein's reality is no more than *praxis*, doing: but "doing" understood not as a "producing" but rather as an "acting," or a "conducting oneself," one that does not differ from the act of thinking. Nancy feels the urge to divert the reader from an erroneous – because abstractly speculative – interpretation of the Heideggerian text, specifically with respect to this synonymy of acting and thinking. While admitting that it occasionally can give rise to misunderstandings, he underscores what is in a certain sense the "practical" character of thought itself as that which makes sense within acting: "Thought as such, therefore, requires action in the most active sense of the term. That which characterizes the 'active' character of action is not agitation – but meaning (or truth)."[58] That thought requires that action should not be understood as something that guides conduct from the outside with a view to a practical result, but rather as the active character of thought itself.

But how can one qualify an action that does not produce results, according to the ontological modality of Heidegger's originary ethics? It is defined above all by a negative trait that Nancy derives not only from Heidegger but also from Bataille, in a form that intersects the two authors without however superposing them. It is the kind of action that does not produce works, in other words it is unworkable (inoperative), *désouvré*, as community itself is defined in Nancy's fundamental essay: fundamental not only within Nancy's philosophical itinerary but for the entire destitutive paradigm that it in fact inaugurates. Nancy is the first to tie the political to the absence of works, recognizing in it the modality of a community that wants to escape both the abandonment to which the end of communism seems to consign it and any reclamation of a metaphysical nature: "'Political' would mean a community ordering itself to the unworking of its communication, or destined to this unworking."[59] The only way to escape the lack of community resulting from all individualisms, as well as the Marxist presupposition of human beings as producers of their own shared essence, is the refusal of a community that makes a work of itself.[60] This is possible not by negating the loss of community that articulates the entire modern experience, and perhaps even the ancient, but by recognizing this loss as the hollow center of community itself. Nancy arrives at this outcome, a decisive one for destituting thought, by invoking the Heideggerian recalling of the non-appropriability of one's own death, intersected with the Bataillian experience of the partition of beings. Consequently Nancy is led to derive the impossibility of a political orientation of community – with the exception of one in which the assumption of such impossibility as its own form is inscribed and acknowledged, where "[i]n a certain sense community acknowledges and inscribes – this is its peculiar gesture – the impossibility of community."[61] If the community coincides with its own impossibility, this must mean that the only non-metaphysical political relationship must be one that excludes the relationship itself, as the destituting thinkers will argue. As Nancy himself had already written, "[t]his suspension is what makes 'being-with': a relation without a relation, or rather, being exposed simultaneously to relationship and to absence of relationship."[62]

8. Between the end of the 1930s and the beginning of the 1940s, withdrawal from work becomes the privileged modality through which Heidegger thinks of the political. Once the entire political horizon is occupied by technology or sucked up into its *dispositifs*, the thought of the political contracts into the space of the impolitical. One will have to wait for the collapse of Nazi Germany and the alternative to depoliticization it had initially represented for the philosopher: only subsequently will this option become irreversible in Heidegger's reflections. While the motif of unworkability is destined to stabilize itself only at the end of the war, it does not represent an absolute novelty within Heidegger's works. In the writings on Hölderlin – where the activist semantics of "putting to

work" prevails – it is absent, or in the shadows: it announces itself for the first time in the 1920s, in his lecture courses on primitive Christianity and particularly on the Letters of St. Paul the Apostle. The Freiburg courses on the phenomenology of religious life, oriented toward the discovery of an experience that is free from the influence of Greek metaphysics, as the proto-Christian experience is, open up a workshop in Heidegger's thought that will never completely close. Moving against the objectivizing method of philosophical historiography, which reduces the Christian conception to a segment of the metaphysical tradition, Heidegger looks for something irreducible within it, to be understood in its absolute particularity. The first step in his approach is to eliminate any philosophical or dogmatic presupposition that would prevent an understanding of the concrete form of life. St. Paul's thought cannot be isolated from lived life – in Heideggerian terms, its "context of realization" – but constitutes the resulting outcome. This explains why the philosopher believes that it is the most significant antecedent of his "hermeneutics of effectiveness."

At its center we find a conception of temporality that is radically alien to the modern: it is produced by the unique and unrepeatable event of the advent of Christ. For the community that believes in it, this irreversibly changes not only the perception of the past and the future, but also their mutual relationship, which is now contracted along the line of the present. As emerges particularly from the Letter to the Thessalonians, the waiting for *parousia* has nothing in common with the quiet expectancy of an event that is included within a chronological succession. It completely upsets such a succession, intersecting the three dimensions of past, present and future in a completely unprecedented manner. With Christ's death, our time comes to an end, giving rise to a new *aiōn*, and it is only here that beatitude can be found. This is the reason why St. Paul is in a hurry – he "runs," as conveyed by the verb *trechein* – he can no longer tarry, irresistibly attracted by something that he already glimpses ahead of him. Each gesture or thought is oriented toward the event that is *already* unfolding, with the joy and suffering that such imminence determines. The future is not positioned "after," but already brings about restlessness in the present, pushing it outside itself. It is for this reason that becoming does not differ from being: it is superposed on it in the form of the *having become*.

But what does this mean, what does this imply, this contraction of time into present experience? What must Christians "do" to respond to their calling (*klēsis*), by contrast with those who were not "called" (*klētoi*) and who have therefore remained rejected? Heidegger insists on the relationship between temporal and modal experiences – between the "when" and the "how" of behaving. What results brings us back to the horizon of decision. For those who want to live as Christians, this is absolutely necessary: not only subjectively, but on the objective plane as well, since even those who don't care do so on the basis of a negative decision. The real decision, one could say, is the one that splits itself above all, over deciding or not deciding in favor of Christ. But this means that decision has no other content but itself, that there is nothing to be "put to work," if not the experience of implementation itself. Christians, moreover, should not abandon their daily occupations by transferring to a further dimension, which *does not* exist as such. Heidegger is careful to emphasize that there is a reason why "the connections Paul [makes] should *not* be *ethically* understood":[63] they do not prescribe or prohibit anything – otherwise Nietzsche would be right in accusing Christianity of ressentiment. Paul's words, even though they cannot be translated into practical precepts, should not be understood negatively. Even when he seems to negate the possibility of a law, he does no more than "fulfill" it in the modality of love. Instead of limiting himself to negating it, he makes love the new law. This means that the law remains but is deprived of its normative content, separated from its impositional meaning. In this manner it continues to remain valid, but in a form that subtracts it from itself, emptying it of its operationality. In this way the law is simultaneously affirmed and negated by a faith that suspends it in its effects, without excluding it in its modes.

To grasp the significance of the Christian experience as elaborated by Paul in Heidegger's interpretation, one needs to grasp this movement, which on the one hand is as imperceptible as the blink of an eye, and yet also possesses radical transformative power. In it, work – either emptied of grace or filled with it – continues to act, but in the modality of a passive, non-acting action, devoid of any goal-orientedness. It is only from this angle that one can penetrate a constitutionally antinomic experience like the Christian one, on the basis of which the most radical change has the form of an apparent immobility: "something remains unchanged, and yet it is radically changed."[64] The behaviors of those who have decided for Christ are completely new, even though they remain perfectly identical to themselves, given that what changes is not the "what," but the "how." This is how the Pauline proposition that "[t]he Christians should *be* such that those who have a wife, should have her in such a way, *that* they do not have her, etc." should be understood.[65]

What counts is not what one does, but how one does it – namely by "undoing it." Each work needs to be worked *as if it were not* such, withdrawn into itself to the point of annulling itself in the very act of fulfilling itself. The is the decisive formula of the Pauline lexicon, which Heidegger assimilates into his own conceptual language:

> In this having-become, how should the Christian comport himself to the surrounding world and communal world (I Cor. 7:20; 1:26ff. ...: the reality of worldly life is targeted). The reality of life consists in the appropriative tendency of such significances. But these do not all become dominating tendencies in the realm of the facticity of Christian life. Rather, *en tēi klēsei menetō* [remain in the condition in which you were called]! At issue is only to find a new fundamental comportment to it. That must be shown now in the manner of its enactment-structure. The indeed existing [*daseienden*] significances of real life are lived *hōs mē*, as if not [*als ob nicht*].[66]

Heidegger realizes that to translate that *hōs mē* with "as if" (*als ob*) would be incorrect, because it would exclude the references to the ambient world, when instead *hōs* [as] refers in positive terms to a new meaning that supervenes, while *mē* [no, not] concerns the enactment of the Christian experience. Already previously he had observed that, in the so-called "apocalypse" of the second Letter to the Thessalonians (2 Ts., 2, 2–13), *ouk* (*edexanto*) [(they did) not (show)] "is neither a *non privativum* nor a *non negativum*, but rather has the sense of the 'enactmental not' [*das "vollzugsmässige Nicht"*]. The 'enactmental not' is not a refusal of enactment, nor a setting-oneself-outside of the enactment."[67] It remains within what it contests, it is an affirmative negation or a negative affirmation. To sum up the perspective that Heidegger inaugurated on the proto-Christian experience, one can conclude that it in no way excludes action – and in fact requires it against all inertia – so long as it assumes the form of deactivation, exactly as the work realizes itself in the form of unworkability.

*

It is certainly not an accident that the relationship between action and deactivation – the critique of work[68] – is at the center of Karl Barth's second comment to Paul's Letter to the Romans, written in the same years as Heidegger's courses in Freiburg. The explicit target of Barth's critique is precisely the fundamental law that makes work the ultimate goal of humans.

The absence of God as an absolute object within our horizon is born precisely from the irresistible tendency to put our work at the center of this horizon itself. This is an unemendable fact not only because it is inscribed in human nature, but because even its negation – in the various modalities of quietism, renunciation, asceticism – is in the purview of work, even if negative work. It is for this reason that Barth writes: "No work, be it most delicately spiritual, or be it even a work of self-negation, is worthy of serious attention."[69] It would be located in the reverse of the all too human ethics that is interposed, like a distorting screen, in our relation with the object. The only way to break the dominance of the subject that this ethics presupposes is to empty work of all its productive substance, thus withdrawing it from the ambition of fulfillment. Only a work that recognizes its finitude, imperfection, incompleteness in its entirety can open to an authentic relationship with the other.

This critique of ethics corresponds to another, which is just as sharp and targets both politics as the supreme work of human beings and its impolitical emptying. But not even in Barth – and in fact least of all in him – is the "impolitical" intended as the negation of the political: his entire life, from his youthful social democratic militancy through his anti-Nazi commitment to the critical position he took during the Cold War, is a testament to the very opposite. The impolitical relates instead to a distancing from a form of political theology that was far from being absent in Germany in that period and that was inclined to sacralize power. It is against it that Barth proclaims the "great negative possibility" (*die grosse negative Möglichkeit*) – negative because critical of a politicization of theology, or of a sacralization of politics – at whose center we find the idea of work. Against it, Barth explicitly invites to "non-action" (*Nicht-handeln*). One cannot respond to the coercion to work other than thus: "And how can this end be represented, if it be not by some strange 'not-doing' precisely at the point where men feel themselves most powerfully called to action?"[70] Barth is not inviting human beings to give up, to escape or withdraw from their tasks by using these expressions, but, as we already saw with Weil, to excavate within action itself, in such a manner as to free it from its immanent purpose, its productive finalism. In this sense he reminds us that the Pauline "[t]o *be in subjection* is, when it is rightly understood, an action void of purpose."[71]

But in what sense? What is an action without a purpose, for Barth? And can it still be called action? It has nothing to do with what Heidegger means by entrustment to a destiny, or even to a "god that can save us." In his words there is no abandoning the field of battle, no retreat, no refusal of responsibility. On the contrary, his words resonate with the sense of a more intense responsibility, which cannot be translated into the ethics of works because they are radically critical of its subjective presupposition. The use of the negative notwithstanding, in fact precisely as a consequence of using it as its foundation, the "negative possibility" remains internal to the action it negates, affirming it in a more originary sense. It is not the action itself that is negated, but rather the presumption of the subject that brings it into existence without recognizing its own limitedness with respect to the object from which it originates. It is for this reason that Barth can state that the "good action," as "negation of the subject," is "the 'not-doing' by which all action is related to its Primal Origin."[72] The inaction that he refers back to is not at all the negation of action or its opposite, but its originary source. This is why, although "[w]e can do right only in the 'not-doing' of our relationship to God,"[73] we are called to "action [that] is in fact pregnant with 'not-doing.'"[74] In this fashion Barth is certainly still expressing himself in the language of the impolitical, not by opposing the political but by joining the two in a form that makes one the presupposition of the other.

*

9. The text in which Heidegger explicitly formulates his conception of the impolitical is his course from the summer semester of 1942 devoted to Hölderlin's hymn *The Ister*. As is always the case in his oeuvre, he maintains strong ties with the themes and the inspirations of the preceding courses on Hölderlin and with the *Introduction to Metaphysics* itself. By comparison with them, however, this continuity is characterized by noticeably different emphases, pertaining above all to the issue of the political. The same relationship of continuity and distance can be followed in the *Beiträge* as well, where, as we have seen, the term *polis* is absent, whereas it reemerges vigorously in this course from 1942. To grasp the many folds of meaning the term has for the philosopher, one needs to situate it within the interpretation of the hymn, devoting special attention to *Antigone*'s chorus. According to Heidegger, a shared note resonates in both Hölderlin's notion of "being at home" and Sophocles' tragedy, as expressed in the decisive moment of the chorus. In both cases, the relationship with "one's own" passes through the alien, in a "disorientation" that proves to be "disquieting." These are precisely the two terms that he uses to translate the words *deinon* and *deinotaton*, which appear in the first stanza of the chorus, in a manner that is perhaps philologically questionable but theoretically dense. We already came across these terms in the *Introduction to Metaphysics* – set in an endless struggle between predominant violence and the other kind, which is opposed to it, namely human violence. The same dialectic now returns, but with a different accentuation, no longer of an activist–Promethean nature, but rather suspended from the finitude of Dasein. There is a reason why the appeal to political creators in the *Introduction* is now directed to poets, after a transition, which was already underway, from a *Denken* [thought] that was oriented toward the political to a *Dichtung* that is constitutively impolitical.

The other element that distinguishes the Heideggerian interpretation concerns the relation between political and impolitical. The year is 1942, when German victory – almost certain in 1940 and probable in 1941 – begins to appear problematic, if not even improbable. Heidegger, however, continues to dialogue with Nazism, although he is increasingly annoyed by its most shameless apologists: "In the majority 'research results' [his irony is directed against the vulgar propaganda of the *Deutsche Wissenschaft*], the Greeks appear as the pure National Socialists. This overenthusiasm on the part of academics seems not even to notice that with such 'results' it does National Socialism and its historical uniqueness no service at all, not that it needs this anyhow."[75]

This is a jab balanced by a much harsher attack, against that "Americanism [which] has resolved to annihilate Europe, that is the homeland [*Heimat*], and that means: the commencement of the Western world."[76] That is, not to speak of Bolshevism, which represents a further degeneration of the latter. With respect to this geopolitical framework, the reference to Hölderlin – like the one made, during these same years, to Nietzsche – constitutes the philosophico-poetic alternative to a nihilist drift that at this point no political regime is able to confront without being engulfed by it, something that, under his very eyes, is affecting the Nazi regime as well.

What does this mean for the political? Instead of being thought of in itself, or even via the analogy with the work of art, the political needs to be tested by its opposite, according to that coexistence of contraries that runs through all the great words of the West. Heidegger lingers on two expressions, both of which we already encountered, and both of which are present in the chorus of *Antigone*. The first one is the play on antonyms *pantoporos aporos*. In it the estrangement of human beings is understood not as the situation of adventurers who have lost their way, but as the constitutive condition of those who, although they essentially belong home, cannot gain access to their essence. Although she or he arrives "everywhere," being *pantoporos*, "all-resourceful," the human being risks ending up in nothingness, by reason of being oriented toward an entity that is forgetful of being. In this fashion, although on the path toward home, a human is estranged – without a place, *aporos*, "with no way out." The same antinomy is present in the other hendiadys uttered by the chorus: *hupsipolis apolis*, which is concentrated around the term *polis*. The relationship between political and impolitical is preserved in it, and Heidegger's attention begins to focus on it and its surroundings. If one grants that, for the Greeks, everything is determined politically, the traditional interpretation becomes wrapped in a sort of hermeneutical vicious circle. If it is true that we can determine what is political from the *polis* – just as we infer what is logical from *logos* [reason] or what is ethical from *ēthos* [character] – the opposite cannot be true. If it were, we would explain the condition by means of the conditioned, losing the meaning of both. To avoid this interpretive misunderstanding, we need to reach the conclusion that, while that which is political is founded by the *polis*, the latter cannot be determined politically. It is therefore necessarily impolitical: "The *polis*, and precisely it, is therefore not a 'political' concept. This is indeed how things stand, provided that we wish to remain serious in our reflections and follow a clean train of thought."[77] This is stated even more clearly in the *Überlegungen*: "Politics [*Politik*] no longer has anything to do with the *polis* [*polis*, "city-state"] or with morals and least of all with 'becoming a people.' … 'Politics' is the genuine executor of the machination of beings."[78]

What was the *polis* for the Greeks, then? Probably, the late theories of Plato and Aristotle notwithstanding, not even the first Greeks knew exactly, given that what *does not* have a foundation, as is the case with the *polis*, preserves a threshold of necessary inaccessibility. This is the reason why, if we want to return to its original meaning, we must tear the veil that tradition has covered it with. In any case we should proceed by avoiding the misleading analogies between the *polis* and the city or the state – or, even more, their conceptual intersection in the "city-state." We must instead recognize the *polos* [axis, pivot] in it, in other words the "pole," the seat, the vortex around which everything turns. The two modalities of stability and change implicit in the word *pelein* [come to be] are superposed in it – in other words we are dealing with an intrinsically restless *status*, one that exhibits a considerably different semantic intensity by comparison with the modern "state" and that includes the polarity of own and alien within itself. It is in the oscillation between these opposites that the impolitical – to be understood as the "non" of the political, its constitutive absence, which contrasts sharply with the modern idea of the absolute primacy of the political – shines through. The fact that the *polis* is the "site" does not imply that the political predominates and that the *polis* should be understood politically. It means that what is essential in historical human beings should instead be traced back to their sojourn in the midst of being(s). It is from this site that everything else originates – religion, the law, politics, thought, art. This is what raises the *polis* to something worthy of being thought of as a crossroads in which all relationships with beings – and therefore also with the truth about being that this reveals, both disclosing and concealing it – are determined.

That the "truth," as *alētheia*, means the "not-hidden" is closely related to the "negative" semantics of the impolitical – which in this sense differs both from the "pre-political," with which Heidegger confuses it in some passages, and from the a-political, which ends up losing all constitutive relationships with the political. Aristotle's own definition of the human being as a *zōon politikon* [animal of the *polis*], but also one *logon echon* [that has reason], attests to the fact that "they [human beings] are not political without further ado."[79] In these same pages Heidegger lingers on the negative semantics, which does not pertain only to the formation of the impolitical but to the entire philosophical horizon. If Plato, even though he differentiated the negative from an empty nothing, did not fully penetrate its nature, Schelling's, Hegel's, and Nietzsche's philosophies did not result in better outcomes. Each one of their "affirmative overcomings" of the negative ended up relinquishing it to negativity, since the use of the term "negative" already forces the discourse into the circle of negation. For Heidegger, however, negation does not come close to exhausting the meaning of "non-." If, rather than as simple negativity, we understand it as the concealed face of Being, then the impolitical can also rediscover the bond that ties it, via its reverse, to the political. And it is precisely because it is non-political that the *polis* is the unfounded foundation of the political. From this moment the political will always be seen – and critically deconstructed – from the perspective of the impolitical. That the impolitical itself is a semantically negative term expresses the contradiction that Heidegger's theoretical *dispositif* begins to run up against, without being able to solve it: that of wanting to affirm, against the negativity of the political, a perspective that is itself articulated in negative terms.

10. The place in which Heidegger's interpretation of the political finds its most developed definition is the 1942–1943 winter course dedicated to Parmenides. It once again proposes the same definition of the *polis* provided in the lessons on the *Ister*: it is the central core around which everything in Greek culture that relates to being revolves, and is thus very far from constituting the genetic nucleus of what will become the modern state. When one compares this definition to that given in the previous course, one finds an added emphasis on its conflictual nature; if the *polis* is in a constitutive relationship with *alētheia*, it will reproduce the latter's clash between veiling and

unveiling, or between essence and non-essence: "then in the *polis* as the essential abode of man there has [*sic*] to hold sway all the most extreme counter-essences, and therein all excesses [*Un-wesen*], to the unconcealed and to beings, i.e. counter-beings [*das Unseiende*] in the multiplicity of their counter-essence [*Gegenwesen*]."[80] It is precisely in this contrastive tension that Burckhardt recognizes the element of horror and misfortune that characterizes the *polis*, which prefigures what Schlosser and later Ritter will call "the demonic face of power." In this regard Heidegger notes that Nietzsche owned the notes to Burckhardt's lessons, guarding them like a precious treasure, with a view to his future formulation of the will to power.

It is precisely this reference, however, that allows Heidegger to insert the observation – a decisive one for the overall architecture of his reasoning – that Nietzsche thought of the *polis*, and all of Greek culture, from a Roman point of view, one partially derived from that very Renaissance culture Burckhardt had transmitted to him. Already with these two, in fact, concepts of a Roman or Romanic mold – such as "state," "religion" or "civilization" – infiltrate the representation of the Greek world, gravely prejudging its comprehension. For Heidegger, this is a fundamental transition, because it is destined to shape in an almost definitive form the entire western conception of the political. His thesis, an intriguing one, is that Romanity – understood in a lexical and categorial sense – does not limit itself to polluting the Greek-derived conceptual aspects of language, but also irreversibly connotes all modernity. The fact that we view Greek culture with Roman eyes is not only an error of historiographical perspective, but something that impacts and disfigures our relationship with the entire ancient world, and therefore our definition of the modern.

At the source of this misunderstanding, whose consequences reach down to us, one finds that the idea of "truth" has changed: one can recognize this change starting from the metamorphosis of its opposite – falsity. This misunderstanding determines an initial problem of a semantic nature, and ultimately therefore a metaphysical one. While the contrary of the term *alēthes* – "true" – would be **lēthes*, the Greeks refer to what is "false" with the word *pseudos* [lie]. Unlike the postulated **lēthes*, this does not refer immediately to "veiledness" but rather indicates covering, concealment, dissimulation, understood in an objective sense – as when, for example, something that is interposed obstructs the view of what is behind. Now this objective view, independently of the subjective intent to deceive, continues to situate the meaning of *pseudos* in an area contiguous to the horizon of *alētheia*. The turning point, the Roman orientation, arises instead from the translation of *pseudos* with *falsum*. The term *falsch*, which derives from it, is not of German origin and was only subsequently imported into the Germanic area, as attested to by the Grimm brothers, along the etymological line that originates with the radical *fall*, to which the Greek *sfallō* [I overthrow] can be traced back. But even in the case of *sfallō* – which refers to a misleading dissimulation, something that is destined to "cause faltering," "falling" (*zu-Fall-bringen*), or "to fell" (*fällen*) – it is a meaning that is still compatible with the area of concealment and veiling.

What twists the meaning of "false" – to the point of losing any relationship with the semantics of *alētheia* – in the direction of deceit in the pursuit of domination is the Roman principle of *imperium*, understood as power oriented toward the submission of others: "*Imperium* is the territory [*Gebiet*] founded on commandments [*Gebot*], in which the others are obedient [*botmässig*]. *Imperium* is the command in the sense of commandment. Command, thus understood, is the basis of the essence of domination, not the consequence of it and certainly not just a way of exercising domination."[81]

The politicization of the paradigm undergoes another qualitative leap when the verb *befehlen* [to command] (from *Befehl* [command]) goes from the more neutral meaning of "sheltering," "guarding" to that, Frenchified and therefore Latinized, of *kommandieren*, which is assimilable to the Latin *imperare* [to order] or vulgar Latin **imparare* [to seize]. Even more relevant is its relationship with the concept of *ius* [right], which Heidegger, resorting to some significant etymological stretching, relates back to *iubeo* [to command], thus counterposing Roman *iustitia* to Greek *dikē*. While the latter remains within the horizon of *alētheia*, the former implies the submission of other peoples, realized by the Romans via peace treaties aimed at swindling or circumventing these subjected peoples as well as at outflanking them and giving them a run-around (*das Hintergehen* [the cheat]).[82] At the center of such a constellation of meaning – enlarged by Heidegger to include all modern conceptions of the political – one finds the Roman category of *actio* [action] as the essence of *imperium* [power]: "The essence of the *imperium* resides in the *actus* of constant 'action [*Aktion*].' The imperial *actio* of the constant surmounting of others includes the sense that the others, should they rise to the same or even a neighboring level of command, will be brought down – in Latin *fallere* (participle: *falsum*)."[83]

In this manner Heidegger reconnects to the point of departure of his analysis, articulating the political plane to the metaphysical one. The transition from the meaning of *pseudos* to that of *falsum* marks the history of the West in a form that internalizes the imperial Roman trait to the point of being hegemonized by it. With the advent of Christianity, it splits on the one hand into the state and on the other into ecclesiastical *imperium*, giving rise to a theologico-political *dispositif*; but from the metaphysical point of view it remains within the bounds of the mutation of the concept of "truth." Its slippage from *alētheia* as unveiledness to *veritas* [truth] as *rectitudo* [correctness] and *adaequatio* [adequateness, correspondence] forms a trajectory parallel to the one that goes from the (impolitical) idea of the *polis* to the (political) one of the modern state, all the way up to its current technical conversion, which transforms the state into a cog in the *Gestell*:

> The Greek *alētheuein*, to disclose the unconcealed, which in Aristotle still permeates the essence of *technē*, is transformed into the calculating self-adjustment of *ratio*. This determines for the future, as a consequence of a new transformation of the essence of truth, the technological character of modern, i.e., machine, technology. And that has its origin in the originating realm out of which the imperial emerges.[84]

With this latest transition, the entire western political lexicon reenters the orbit of "machination" ("invented" by the Romans), from which it borrows the capacity to conceal within the procedures of its opposite. From that point on, the sphere of the political, dragged in a technico-operational direction by its Romanization, drastically separates itself from the essence of the *polis*, understood as a site starting from which humans address the Being of what is. What had been, up to the course on Parmenides, a still mobile limit between political and impolitical now becomes an irredeemable distance, marked by the collapse of ontological difference into the ontic sphere. The impolitical – the *polis* – which is the unfounded presupposition of the political, diverges from it, projecting a negative shadow onto it. The manner of proceeding via negation – an assumption that Heidegger made from the very beginning when defining truth as *a-lētheia* – now pervades every node of the analysis, and finally occupies the entire field. "We want the 'positive.' Why then all this brain-racking over the negative?"[85] – Heidegger suddenly asks. And then he immediately answers as follows: "The essence of negativity is nothing negative, but neither is it only something 'positive.'"[86] While he does address it, Heidegger renounces any affirmative theorization of the political. Founded by something *non*-political – such as the *polis* – the political in its turn is thus pushed into the sphere of the negative, without anything positive being able to reactivate it. What remains possible, and necessary, for meditative thought is rather the antinomic task of deactivating it.

*

A striking homology exists between Heidegger's critique of *romanitas* and another critique, formulated in the same period, by Weil in her 1939 essay *Reflections on the Origins of Hitlerism*, in a situation that was the complete opposite when seen in human, political, and cultural terms. This surprising symmetry is, naturally, part of an anti-Roman propensity of the modern philosophical tradition that is most sharply represented by Hegel. When, in a celebrated passage, he writes that "the world is sunk in melancholy: its heart is broken,"[87] he steps over a threshold from which it is difficult to retreat, even if then Hegel himself will dialecticize his position, pointing to Rome as the *humus* [soil] in which Christian civilization developed.[88] In the twentieth century one can say that only Carl Schmitt, an adoptive "Roman," and Hannah Arendt will pronounce in favor of Roman political and juridical culture, albeit for different reasons. Heidegger and Weil position themselves resolutely on the other side of the twentieth-century philosophical landscape on the issue, formulating a negative evaluation with no mitigating circumstances. If for Heidegger, as we have seen, Latin culture irreversibly infects the Greek conceptual lexicon, Weil is, if possible, even more severe. Rome corrupted the spirit of all western civilization to the point of constituting the most relevant antecedent of the Nazi phenomenon. Her judgment is obviously not situated at a historical level. Her critique is instead genealogical, or rather paradigmatic, in the sense that it institutes ties between origin and actuality that are not of a chronological, but of an anachronistic or meta-historical nature, as she searches in the one for the keys to entry the other. Rather than wanting to establish a continuity, Weil intends, on the contrary, to insert the clearest possible discontinuity within the racial mythology that situates the roots of the Third Reich in the history of ancient Germans.

In her eyes, the name of this discontinuity is Rome. The Nazis are as distant from the ancient Germans as they are, paradigmatically, close to the Romans, whose terrible virtues – tenacity, determination, organization – but above all whose horrible vices they develop. Ruthless cruelty, cold perfidy, sense of superiority, the art of deception, spiritual baseness are the characteristics that, through the millennia, the Nazis inherit from Rome, becoming their most despicable and efficient imitators. What they learnt from them is "the cold, calculated cruelty, which constitutes a method, a cruelty that no instability of mood, no consideration of prudence, respect, or pity can temper, that one cannot hope to escape from either with courage, dignity, and energy or with submission, pleading, and tears"; "a similar cruelty is an incomparable instrument of domination."[89] What leads one to compare Weil's judgment with Heidegger's is not only the intensity, although certainly not a very equable one, of their critiques – both even refuse to acknowledge the standing of Roman juridical culture, which is represented as a refined instrument of domination; what makes them symmetrical is also the centrality of the category of *imperium*, understood not simply as political regime but as a deep trait of the Roman character, expressed in a mixture of force and deceit. Even more importantly than being a political form, the empire is the irresistible power which devastated the human soul – of both vanquished and vanquishers, who have slid to the lowest point of the spiritual scale – for centuries: "In Rome everyone bowed not to the emperor as a human being, but to the empire. ... The absolute authority of the state could not be questioned, because it did not rest on a convention, on a conception of faithfulness, but on the power that force possesses to freeze the souls of human beings."[90] It almost seems as if one could recognize the entire semantic spectrum of *falsum*, which Heidegger had opposed to the Greek *pseudos*, in Weil's reconstruction of the long series of betrayals, humiliations, and torments that Rome inflicted upon enemies and allies by using that very law that made them famous the world over, but a spectrum seen from another perspective, and one that relies on imposing historical documentation. It is the same mixture of deceit and violence employed by Hitler to force adversaries into war: "With regard to international contracts, the Romans never felt obligated to observe a treaty when violating it or circumventing it was to their advantage. When one attributes a juridical spirit to them, one becomes prey to equivocation; the compilation of vast collections of laws has no relationship whatsoever with the sanctity of contracts."[91] It is, however, above all the disproportion between Roman baseness and the worthiness of the Greek spirit that reproduces, almost word for word, Heidegger's merciless analysis: "If one compares them to the Greeks, their inferiority is overwhelming. Wherever forms of spiritual creation were concerned that could not be put into service for the cause of national grandeur, one could state they were non-existent."[92] If Rome ties Heidegger's and Weil's analyses together with an invisible thread, Greece separates them, especially as regards Christianity. While the Greece Heidegger is looking at is used to recover something that Christianity has destroyed, thus preparing the modern turning point in metaphysics, in Weil's case it is precisely the relation to Christianity that gives Greece the splendor that still enlightens us.

*

11. With the end of the war and the ruinous defeat of Nazi Germany, Heidegger takes his impolitical option to a point of no return. Twelve years after the *Rektoratsrede*, the impression one gets is that he not only changed, but actually reversed his prior

perspective, while never completely severing all relationships with it. Heidegger's philosophical lexicon is so distinct that it reproduces itself apparently unchanged, the most marked categorial discontinuities notwithstanding. Yet some of its technical terms still undergo such significant semantic modifications that they assume completely different connotations. For instance the references, which up to this point had been customary, to the "homeland" or the "national" lose ground within a conceptual horizon that is dominated by the reference to "machination," with the loss of distinctions this entails on the global geopolitical scene. Central to Heidegger's discourse is what today we would call "globalization" – which he understands in its most negative configuration. The peculiarity of the Nazi revolution, which was still celebrated in the *Introduction to Metaphysics*, has now been erased by a defeat interpreted in metaphysical terms as the final victory of nihilism. What is dissolved is not only the specificity of the German people – to whom, as late as the mid-1930s, the philosopher had entrusted the task of forming an antemural defense with respect to the planetary diffusion of the *Gestell* – but the very possibility of a political action capable of resisting what had at this point acquired the characteristics of a devastation of the western spirit.

A topical trace of this turn can be found in "Evening Conversation: In a Prisoner of War Camp in Russia, between a Younger and an Older Man," which dates from May 1945. Already the place in which it occurs – a camp surrounded by barbed wire in the infinite expanse of Russia – suggests the two polarities around which Heidegger's new thought is gathered: the desert of devastation (*Verwüstung*) and the vastness (*Weite*) of the open. The Russian plain – in which, for the first time, the Wehrmacht was overwhelmed by a predominant force – represents the place without space in which the *polis* itself, understood in its archetypical sense, imploded. And yet it is precisely this place, devastated and devastating, that contains a possibility for liberation and restores breath to those who risk suffocation:

> YOUNGER MAN The expanse delivers our essence into the open and at the same time gathers it into the simple, as though the expanse's abiding were a pure arrival for which we are the inlet.
>
> OLDER MAN This expanse provides us with freedom. It frees us while we here – between the walls of these barracks, behind barbed wire – incessantly run up and wound ourselves on what is objective [*das Gegenständliche*].[93]

What liberates us from the dominion of the object is not the forest, which is opposed to the desert, but the vastness (expanse) itself, of which it is the visible manifestation: just as devastation is not the outcome of a war that destroyed Europe but its precondition, of which war is only the most blatant expression. Vastness and devastation are the contrasting extremes that clash from the outset in a struggle without quarter whose stake is the destiny of the West.[94]

But the decisive element, insofar as the characterization of the political is concerned, lies in the non-contrastive, in fact synonymous relationship of the two poles that face each other in the final clash between evil and its opposite. As had already occurred in the relationship between the bipolarities world and Earth, own and alien, what predominates and what violates, devastation and vastness are not two reciprocally transcending powers but arise antinomically, one from the bosom of the other. They battle each other in the same agon, whose object is the ontological relationship between Being and beings. As was the case in *Being and Time*, the authentic is not a dimension that differs from the inauthentic, but a modified way of comprehending it: so now vastness is no more than a modified modality of devastation. Vastness is simultaneously that which is opposed to devastation and that which makes room for it, just as the latter, in its turn, is the degenerate and perverted outcome of vastness itself. It is this mutual inherence of opposites which precludes any space for the political, which by now coincides with the metaphysical machine that dominates it. Not only can human beings not take a position against devastation from within it, but they don't even have the possibility of expressing an opinion regarding something they are taken by: "[if] the devastation consists in the abandonment of being, then after all it no longer allows for any beings, such that anything whatsoever that could be affected by it is lacking."[95] But if the only subject – to use a completely inadequate term – of that which occurs, and in fact of the event as such, is Being, one can understand how the possibility of the political is completely dissolved in the *dispositif* that has incorporated it. The rupture of the differential margin between ontological and ontic, with the flattening out of the former onto the latter, entails an irreversible metaphysical collapse. For this reason expressions like "progress," "development of all spheres of production," "equal work opportunities for everyone" are devoid of foundation and are in fact destined to strengthen the very process they would want to oppose, because they are internal to the category of "realization," from which devastation itself arose.

If this is indeed the case, if devastation is produced by the obsession with realization, then the only way of countering it is with an equal and contrary deactivation, one capable of destituting what human works have instituted. The impolitical is dedicated to this task; and, at this point, defeat having already occurred, it is the only political thought that is still practicable, in the form of its negative, however – precisely as im-political. We are facing the confrontation of two specular forms of negation. Just as, from the impolitical point of view, the political assumes the demonic aspect of machination, the latter, in its turn, removes any affirmative power from the impolitical. Not only can we not expect anything, in fact quite the opposite – since to wait would still belong to the subjective sphere of action – but we should not even attempt to stop the advancing desert. We can only wait for it, while it annihilates itself in the process of annihilating everything. "To wait" (*warten*) is essentially different from "to await (to expect)" (*erwarten*), precisely because, unlike it, it has no object. It implies releasement – which is what the Eckhartian term *Gelassenheit* refers to – in other words letting what is be. This means dismissing any form of opposition to a devastating process, one whose completion should actually be wished for: as in the case of nihilism, it is not in our hands. We can only accompany it, backing the implosion that it would involve. Only then, once the devastating will have entirely desertified the world and nothing will have been left to devastate, will a crack toward the vastness open. The only behavior allowed us, because it is not even a behavior, is that of the releasement to what is coming:

> OLDER MAN As this present-waiting-toward, we release ourselves to the coming, because our essence is already released to it.
>
> YOUNGER MAN And so in thus releasing ourselves, we first come into our own.[96]

With the end of the *polis*, and therefore of any possible politicization of the *Da* ["there"], the political completely transfers into the horizon of the negative. If power, in all its possible configurations, has been definitively consigned to technical machination, freedom can no longer be understood as a subjective option but as the allowing of everything, devastation included, to be.

12. Before arriving at *Gelassenheit*, as a form of impolitical withdrawal from works, it would be good to look at Heidegger's "Science and Reflection" lecture, which he held in Munich in August

1953.[97] In it the motif of deactivation from works intersects on the one hand with that of the critique of *romanitas* he had started in *Parmenides* and, on the other, with the opposition between reflective and calculating thought, which dates to the years of the *Beiträge*. At the center of his argument is the concept of science at its moment of greatest expansion, not only in the western world but on the entire globe. As was already the case with technology, however, it would be misleading to consider the deployment of science as exclusively a product of humanity, in other words as being subject to revocation solely on the basis of its will. There is something else in it that still awaits investigation precisely because, like the machination in which it inheres, it remains concealed. What is at issue? What is the essence of science, now that the sciences are taking hold within all the institutions of modern life? The answer can be condensed in the simple phrase that sees science as "the theory of the real." Naturally, Heidegger warns us, this is true of modern science, but not of ancient science, especially Greek science, which still constitutes the former's original presupposition.

Both of the terms previously mentioned, "theory" and "real," bear the traces of this ambivalent relationship with Greek culture and are at the origin of what we could call "workable thought": "The real [*das Wirkliche*] brings to fulfillment the realm of working [*des Wirkenden*], of that which works [*wirkt*]."[98] But what does "working" mean precisely? In a more general sense, it means "making." And what, in its turn, does "making" mean? "To make," in German *tun*, which derives from the Indo-European radical **dhe-*, can be traced back to the Greek noun *thesis*, which means "placement," "position." But – and this is the decisive difference by comparison to our lexicon – in Greek the meaning is not circumscribed to human activity, in other words to action and activity. The growth and the production of nature is also a form of "making," precisely in the Greek sense of *thesis*. It is only at a later stage that *thesis* and *phusis* will diverge, but within a shared semantic horizon. The meaning of pro-ducing something, bringing it to presence, resonates in both. That which those who work do – not necessarily human beings – is to make present: "The real [*Wirkliche*] is the working, the worked [*Wirkende*, *Gewirkte*]; that which brings hither and brings forth into presencing, and that which has been brought hither and brought forth. Reality [*Wirklichkeit*] means, then, when thought sufficiently broadly: that which, brought forth hither into presencing, lies before [*Vorliegen*]; it means the presencing, consummated in itself, of self-bringing-forth."[99]

The German term *wirken*, which translates as "to work," derives from the Indo-European root **werg-*, which gave rise to both the German *Werk* and the Greek *ergon* [work]. However, this is precisely were one finds a difference from the modern derivation of "making work"; and, once again, it comes from the distorting twist imprinted by Latin around Greek elements. The fundamental trait of *ergon* is not that of the Latin *efficere* [to produce] and *effectus* [effect], but the "rising of the non-concealment," just as for Aristotle the category of "cause" does not correspond to what the Romans define as *causa efficiens*, insofar as it produces an effect. *Ergon* – and *energeia* [activity] – refer to what is produced in the fullness of presence, not to the modern disposition to work. It is once again the Romans who translated *ergon* with *operatio* [activity] and *actus* [impulse], meaning something that produces a result or has a consequence. At this point the "real," identified as "consequent," appears "in the light of the causality of the *causa efficiens*."[100] The Christian God, following this pattern, is therefore also represented as *causa prima*. In our modern vocabulary, as a consequence of further semantic slippage, the fact becomes "factual," in other words "certain," "assured" – that which is "factually" the case, that which differs from an appearance or a simple opinion. Simultaneously the thing effected comes toward us in the guise of an "object" – in German, a *Gegen-stand* – that we have in front of us, something that pertains to the sphere of objectivity.

A parallel transformation is undergone by the word *theōria*: the object, in the aforementioned sense, is presented as the "representable": if one continues to follow Heidegger in these etymological reconstructions, one finds that at the origins of the Greek *theōrein* there lies a mysterious meaning, connected to the two roots *theaomai* [I gaze] and *oraō* [I see]. Both allude to appearance, as when something comes to light, hence *eidenai* [to know] and *eidos* [form] in Plato. The *bios theōrētikos* [contemplative life] also reaches these levels of elevation in rank – it was understood by the Greeks as the perfect form of existence – and is connected with the unveiling dimension of *alētheia*. *Theōria* is the look we give the truth while guarding it. We are confronted with a translation betrayal [*traduzione-tradimento*][101] that will lead to our contemporary meanings and, once again, is the work of Romans, who introduced the concept of *contemplatio* [contemplation] in its place; and this one, in addition to a meaning that pertains more to the religious sphere, soon slid into the workable one of "treatment," whence the German *betrachten*, understood as "to work one's way *toward* something, to pursue it, to entrap it in order to secure it."[102] As one can see, we are in the proximity of what

Heidegger, in the *Parmenides*, defines as the "imperial" Roman trait, giving the term a marked political emphasis. From this perspective, work, both in the sense of political action and in that of action of science, relates to the same horizon of meaning represented by the concept of "reality" as an effective determination.

It is precisely this kind of determination that is the typical procedure of modern science, which subdivides the real into a series of sectors over which the individual sciences exercise their control, each one within its own field of research, unified by the same modality of knowing, which is simultaneously a measuring, a capturing and a securing. The specialization of the various sciences is not, in this respect, as is sometimes claimed, a degeneration, but an inevitable consequence of the essence of modern science itself: a science that reaches its limit, however, represented by the impossibility of its getting to the bottom of that very nature whose understanding it aims for, of its being able to embrace it in all its breadth. At the very moment in which it subdivides nature into the various compartments of knowledge, transforming it into a field of disparate objects, it loses its dimension of wholeness, which remains ungraspable. Nature thus becomes the "non-bypassable" (*das Unumgängliche*) – something that modern science, sectorialized into its different lexicons, cannot even grasp as a problem. Science – and therefore the individual sciences to an even greater degree – are not able to represent their own essence to themselves: just as one cannot establish what mathematics is by means of a mathematical calculation, all other forms of knowledge are subject to the same problem. There is certainly a reason why all the sciences – not only the natural sciences, but also the human sciences – struggle with something they cannot come to grips with, but that their field of research presupposes: nature for physics, human beings for psychiatry, history for historiography, and language for philology. This structural opacity of science is countered by reflection, oriented precisely toward those questions focused on meaning that the former is not even able to pose. They constitute the motivation and the objective of *Besinnung* [reflection], which is driven to question the sojourn to which we are destined – naturally, only on the proviso that we go beyond faith in the power of reason, which is oriented toward securing and production, and enter that condition of *Gelassenheit* to which Heidegger now refers his own impolitical reflections.

*

If we wanted to translate *Gelassenheit* into political terms, the paradigm that comes closest, while still not corresponding perfectly, is that of "destituting power." Although it has a different origin, which in this case is connected especially to Benjamin, the two concepts end up intersecting in their joint refusal of the work. Like releasement, destituting power is defined, in its most influential contemporary theorizations, by its inoperativeness: "If our hypothesis on the structure of the *archē* is correct, if the fundamental ontological problem today is not work but inoperativeness, and if this latter can nevertheless be attested only with respect to a work, then access to a different figure of politics cannot take the form of a 'constituent power' but rather that of something we can provisionally call 'destituent potential.'"[103] In Agamben the critique of constituent power arises because of its inseparableness from constituted power, which it always presupposes. As much as it may contrast it, or even overthrow it, constituent power will sooner or later be captured by the constituted power to which it gave rise, thus reducing itself to a simple power of revision of the constitution being enacted.

The even more intrinsic need to deconstruct the dialectics between constituent and constituted power lies in the fact that they are revealed as the two poles, opposite and complementary, of the category of "sovereignty." In *Homo sacer* Agamben had already noted that they correspond to the relation that Aristotle institutes between potential and act, as the two aspects of a sovereign self-constitution of being. When Sièyes theorized that the constitution presupposes a constituting power, he did not budge an inch from the semantics of sovereignty: "Just as sovereign power presupposes itself as the state of nature, which is thus maintained in a relation of ban with the state of law, so the sovereign power divides itself into constituting power and constituted power and maintains itself in relation to both, positioning itself at their point of indistinction."[104] In this fashion the two problems, posed but not resolved by the idea of constituting power, are superposed, thus mutually reinforcing each other; just as it is not possible to separate constituting and constituted power, it is equally impossible to release both from sovereign power. All attempts to do this – at both the political and the philosophical level – can do nothing but fail, as is demonstrated by the history of all revolutions. Whatever the degree to which they may each time be declared "permanent" or "uninterrupted," they have all inevitably slipped into the fixity of a new constituted power. Even Carl Schmitt, who places constituting power ahead of any constitutional legislative procedure, is incapable of distinguishing it from sovereign power, since both coincide with the will of the people and the nation: by exceeding the normative plane, they inextricably reconnect on the plane of decision. The very book by Antonio Negri on constituent power,[105] although it insists on their categorial distance, remains entangled in the vocabulary of sovereignty. Even when thought of as an instituting praxis that is irreducible to the fixity of a constitution, it remains trapped in the logic, itself constituting, of sovereign power.

According to Agamben, the only way to escape this logic is by operating an ontological shift – one that goes even beyond Heidegger's "releasement," which is still involved in the lexicon of the "ban" – by attempting to think of a power that is no longer constituent but rather destituent. Just as Benjamin distinguished between a violence that destroys and then recreates the law and a divine violence that deposes it definitively, so destituent power must be freed from any *archē* and recognized in its purely anarchical character. The pivotal reference to the concept of inoperativeness reappears. Destituent power also renders human operations inoperative without annihilating them, limiting itself to liberating their unexpressed potentials, orienting them to a different use. The reference, which we already encountered when discussing Heidegger's courses on primitive Christianity, is to Paul's messianic *katargein*, understood precisely as the capacity of rendering all power inoperative. In this manner the law is deactivated without being abolished, but instead fulfilled. Only by cutting the metaphysical knot that ties potency and act will it be possible to burn one's bridges to the excluding lexicon of sovereign power. The outcome of this attitude is a deposition without abdication. "Living in the form of the 'as not' means rendering destitute all juridical and social ownership, without this deposition founding a new identity."[106]

What the political meaning of this operation is – the disjoining of all relations – remains, in truth, rather enigmatic, unless the space of a politics to come coincides with that of the impolitical, thus following in the footsteps of a move already practiced by the impolitical thinkers I referred to. The fundamental problem is that destituting power remains included in the negative reverse of constituting power, just as the impolitical continues to adhere to the political from which it distanced itself. Raffaele Laudani, in his book on destituting power, observes that "the 'ontological' characteristics that Agamben assigns to 'destituting power' today are the same that in *Homo sacer* he assigned to the constituent power 'freed' from its willy nilly identification with sovereign power."[107] Moreover, at the genealogical level, it is not difficult to observe that, as in the case of the power of activation, that of the deactivation of the law is also a prerogative – and in fact the maximum prerogative – of sovereign power, as Bodin writes in the founding text of the modern paradigm of sovereignty: "the prince … Included in the power of making and unmaking law is that of promulgating and amending it when it is obscure."[108] *Derogatio* or the derogation of the law – even of one that prohibits it – is the power that more than all others measures the sovereign's omnipotence.

*

13. The term and concept of *Gelassenheit*, which appeared for the first time, in a not yet elaborated form, in *On the Essence of Truth*, and later in *What Is Metaphysics?*, becomes the object of a lecture in 1955 of precisely this title. *Gelassenheit* is a *terminus technicus* in both Catholic and Protestant mystical traditions and is used especially

by Meister Eckhart in the sense of an abandonment (releasement) to God made possible through detachment from one's passions and desires. Transferred from the original theological context to the philosophical one, with different nuances of meaning in authors like Schelling, Schopenhauer, and Nietzsche, it tends to assume a quietistic connotation of indifference or apathy, which accentuates its passive aspects. Heidegger, as usual, gives the concept a semantic twist, making it a pivot of his postwar reflections.[109] Even though he *does not* return to its theological characterization, he resurrects its antinomical semantics and ties it to the motif of inoperative action, which had already emerged in the Freiburg courses on St. Paul. Far from being pure passivity or simple disinterest, *Gelassenheit* implies a struggle against the will, of which *lassen* [let] and *wollen* [want] constitute the irreconcilable opposites. "Letting be" is opposed to the will to realization and is oriented toward its annulment. But – and here is the antinomy Heidegger is perfectly aware of – is opposing the will, in favor of "let it be," not also a voluntary act? And how can one voluntarily annul the will? This is ultimately the same irresolvable issue posed by the relation between the political and the impolitical: when the impolitical – which Heidegger relates especially to the *polis* – opposes the political, negating it, it is captured by the latter's contrastive semantics. If instead it avoids expressing any content whatsoever, withdrawing into its own negative etymon, it is dissolved as such, reducing itself to the pure deactivation of political work(s).

This issue, recognized in its aporetic dimension, had already been thematized by Heidegger in a previous text, one obviously connected to *Gelassenheit* and entitled, in its Italian translation, "Per indicare il luogo dell'abbandono." It anticipates the elaboration that would occur in *Gelassenheit*, shifting its center of gravity from the ontic level to the ontological one. While in the 1955 essay the issue is, above all, human beings' attitude to the planetary deployment of technology – to be turned toward reflective thought and away from calculating thought – in the lecture it is the opposition of will and thought that becomes central. "[SCIENTIST] Thinking is something other than willing," one of the protagonists remarks. To which comes the reply: "[TEACHER] And that is why, in answer to your question as to what I really wanted from our meditation on the nature of thinking, I replied: non-willing."[110] But it is precisely this expression – "[I want the] non-willing" – that is aporetic: "[SCHOLAR] Non-willing, for one thing, means a willing in such a way as to involve negation, be it even in the sense of a negation which is directed at willing and renounces it. Non-willing means, therefore: willingly to renounce willing. And the term non-willing means, further, what remains absolutely outside any kind of will."[111]

Since this second, more radical form of non-willing cannot be realized by means of an act of will, one can only turn toward the first form, which holds willing and non-willing together, precisely in the form of "willing to not will." This implies a kind of oxymoron, similar to the decision not to decide. Which still constitutes a decision – and therefore in this sense an action – but such as to annul itself the very moment it is enunciated.[112]

We are dealing with the kind of decision that, already in *Being and Time*, Heidegger had defined using the term *Entschlossenheit*, with the difference that back then the subject of the decision was precisely Dasein, in other words human beings themselves, while now they are excluded from it. One could say that, if in 1927 that decision could still be related to an action – and one could therefore translate it into political terms, as the philosopher would indeed, ruinously, several years later – now it implies suspension of the act, in a radically impolitical form. Its subject – but this is a term Heidegger would never have used – is no longer Dasein, but that which mysteriously addresses him, calling him to itself. It is that which, in the lecture, Heidegger defines with the term "region" (*Gegend*) or, in the archaizing form he preferred "open expanse" (*Gegnet*), which, in its foundational meaning, can be referred back to the gathering openness of Being. Human beings have an inevitably passive role with respect to it, one into which ultimately releasement is also sucked up – "releasement" being how *Gelassenheit* is translated into English. The problem is that, if this is the actual state of affairs, if releasement not only goes toward Being but also comes from it, the meaning of the resolute invitation to practice it gets lost.

This is also because what is revoked is "practice" itself, which is inevitably tied on the one hand to the will that triggers it and on the other to the effects it induces, both of which – will and effects – have been declared external and extraneous to the semantics of *Gelassenheit*. Heidegger looks for a way out of the antinomy – which he himself produced, between a will that does not will and the not willing even this – via a "trace" of will that is immediately erased. But what should we take an "erased trace" of the human will to be – a presence or an absence? A presence that becomes an absence: this is precisely what occurs to the impolitical. On the one hand it is taken as a distancing, or an alterity, with respect to the political. On the other, it is deprived of all active elements and therefore annulled by its very inoperativeness: it is an action, but one of deactivation; a work, but an inoperative one; a doing that is an undoing or a doing by the other, the "region," or Being, whatever one wants to call it. The High German term *Bedingnis* refers to this latest antinomy, as defined by the three interlocutors: "[SCIENTIST] It determines the thing as thing. [SCHOLAR] Therefore it is best called the determining. [SCIENTIST] But determining is not making and effecting; nor is it rendering possible in the sense of the transcendental ... [TEACHER] ... but only the determining."[113] This means, Heidegger concludes, that, for now, this is something that escapes thought and that therefore we must still learn to think. But not even this depends on us, but rather only on what is autonomously revealed, always concealing itself, to thought, precisely as in the case of the impolitical, which has no meaning beyond the merely negative one that defines it in opposition to the political – which it negates in its turn. At the end of his trajectory, enclosed in a double negation, Heidegger's political thought seems to fold in onto itself, without managing to break through the wall that separates him from what he wants to reach.

*

Reiner Schürmann, in a book he devoted to the relation between doing and acting, definitely rules out that a political, or practical, philosophy can be inferred from Heidegger's thought. Rather than ending the discourse on the political in Heidegger, the book's aim is to restart it, but on the basis of different presuppositions: it is not possible to pass from being to acting for the simple reason that, when one approaches being as "coming into presence," one is already within the horizon of acting. Following the destruction of metaphysics engaged in by Heidegger, what is removed is not acting, but the possibility that acting continues to be legitimized by an external principle. At this point *praxis* can no longer be founded by *theōria*. This means that in the postmetaphysical age "[t]hen in its essence, action proves to be an-archic."[114] But how should the term "anarchy" be understood? And is it possible to think of it in a political vein?[115]

Let's start from the first point. Anarchy, in Schürmann's sense, has nothing to do with the historical forms it assumed in the political programs of Proudhon and Bakunin. On the contrary, these programs, by shifting the location of the *archē* from a subjective command by human beings to a rational criterion, remain fully within that metaphysics that the anarchic perspective intends to deactivate. If metaphysics designates the principle on whose basis action is required to possess an ultimate foundation for it to be able to reconnect words, things, and gestures, anarchic is instead that condition in which action remains devoid of principles. This is the turn to which Heidegger's thought leads: in the age of technology it is no longer possible to identify a first principle from which the world could become intelligible and governable by means of *scire per causas* [knowing through causes].

Now, if this is the anarchy that Heidegger's thought refers to, is it possible to give it a political configuration and, if so, how? Does an anarchic political form exist?[116] A question reemerges, one that so far has not received a convincing answer. According to Schürmann, to find that answer one would need to substitute ontological difference with symbolic difference, which is able to express the dual movement of being. Since the latter reveals itself only by veiling itself, it is not possible to derive from it any form of behavior that differs from the "let it be" to which we are destined in any case. All types of political legitimation, as they have so far been historically given, need therefore to be dismantled together with the epochal principles that founded them. But, once this has been accomplished, what can define an action devoid of foundations? Schürmann points to five characteristics: the abolition of any teleological order, the refusal to entertain the primacy of responsibility, the protest against a technically administered world, a certain disinterest for the future of humankind, and the coincidence of thought and action. What articulates these categories to one another is the reversal of Leibniz's principle that nothing is without a reason into Meister Eckhart's principle that life is without a because. An anarchic politics is one that, in the name of such criteria, exposes itself to the absolute absence of principles, making the history of metaphysics implode.

In the process of assuming a series of principles that certify the end of all principles, a paradox emerges that Schürmann has no intention of concealing: he in fact considers it typical of the transitional stage between the age of metaphysics and the one after it, which inevitably still makes use of its "principled" language. But the antinomy that is thus created also impacts the concept of the political, in addition to the concept of history – which can be "overcome" only historically, because only one of these two cases can be true: either the political cannot be distinguished at all from the coming into presence of being, realizing itself and dissolving itself via the deactivation of principles; or it points to a specific modality, which differs from all other types of action, such as those of artistic creation or of scientific invention. But, to do so, in order to differentiate itself from the punctuality of creation or the unforeseeability of invention, it must institute a connection between present and future. It is true that ultimately any action, suspended as it is from the contingency of its realization, is autonomous from the principle that places it into being. But this does not mean that it *is not* situated in a network of dependencies from other actions, just as individual praxis is always articulated in a collective context – unless the only consequence of action were that of having no consequences. If that were the case, by defining action as anarchic, one could say, with the same degree of truthfulness, that all actions are political, but also that none is. Pasolini, who was always skeptical of commonplaces, has one of the characters in *Salò* state clearly that only power is truly anarchical.

*

14. The entire movement of Heideggerian reflection on the political, which so far I examined in some of its distinct moments, was in some ways summed up by the philosopher in a famous interview that he gave to the weekly *Der Spiegel* and that was published posthumously, in May 1976. One of its obvious aims is self-rehabilitation with respect to his sudden commitment to Nazism, whose circumstances, compromises, and misunderstandings are reconstructed in detail. In its broader outlines the interview goes over some of the actual transitions in Heidegger's thought in the area of the dialectics of the political and the impolitical. The starting point, which is also where I began, is the *Rektoratsrede*, whose "positive" characteristics he now emphasizes, for instance his opposition to the much vaunted academic freedom, which he defines as a "negative one: freedom *from* taking the trouble to reflect and meditate as scientific studies demand."[117] But – the author continues – the self-affirmation of the university also intended to counter the Nazi drift of *politische Wissenschaft*. What Heidegger intended to support at that moment was a third position, which differed both from the depoliticization of the traditional academia and from its uncontrolled politicization in the manner desired by the regime. To be more precise, he claims to have advocated a form of mutual implication of philosophy and politics that, instead of functionalizing the former in the service of the latter, would have established the primacy of a philosophical knowledge capable of "guiding the guides" of the country. In this sense, the order of the three "services" – labor, defense, and knowledge – required of professors and students needed to be overturned, moving knowledge from the third to the first place.

What Heidegger forgets to mention is, naturally, the circumstance that, whatever his intentions, his philosophical talk, delivered in the very year of Hitler's ascent to power, would be instrumentalized by a regime that was totally uninterested in its content but was well aware of the political importance of the greatest contemporary philosopher joining their ranks. As we saw, after this first phase – affirmative, operative, activist – of Heidegger's thought on the political, a second one followed fairly rapidly in its steps, one that gradually amplified the use of negative tones. Doubly negative, as a matter of fact: both in the sense of pointing to elements of inadequacy and regression in

Nazi politics and in the sense of an impolitical attitude, therefore as such non-political. It is certainly no accident that the philosopher accepts and adopts the definition proposed by the interviewer: "Perhaps we might summarize: in 1933 you were, as an unpolitical man in the strict sense, not in the wider sense, caught up in the politics of this supposed new dawn ..."[118]

Heidegger relates this impolitical perspective back to his first courses on Hölderlin, in the mid-1930s, and to the prolonged engagement with Nietzsche, observing: "Anyone with ears to hear heard in those lectures [on Nietzsche] a confrontation with National Socialism."[119] It is in this intermediate period that an element of national aestheticism also emerges: the political, like the work of art, is considered a creation brought about by creators capable of providing their various peoples with models of self-representation that are adequate to their historical roles not only in the world but also in Being. The people Heidegger is actually looking toward, however, is the metaphysical people par excellence, the German. His *Introduction to Metaphysics* bestows a political characterization on this absolute philosophical peculiarity of the German people, one constituted by the destinal necessity of defending the European West from the combined attack of the anti-metaphysical powers of America and Russia. This people, in order to reappropriate its essence, must pass through estrangement – just as, according to Hölderlin, happens to any people, starting with the Greeks – and thus expresses that dialectic of implication and tension between opposites that also recurs in the conflictual relation between world and Earth on the one hand and predominant versus human violence on the other.

The relationship between political and impolitical must also be understood in this vein, simultaneously inclusive and oppositional. In a historical sense, until a certain point is reached, the political finds its foundation in an impolitical *polis* that institutes it, but without losing its difference from it. Deviations imposed by history notwithstanding, the political remains positively marked by the constitutive relation with the *polis* from which it emerges – until this connection is broken, thus separating and opposing political and impolitical. This occurs when the political – all the political, including the German, which emerged defeated from the war – takes on a technical connotation, becoming a simple link in the transmission internal to "machination," which increasingly orients the fate of the world. This development entails a significant theoretical reorientation as regards technology, which goes from the affirmative articulation of *poiēsis* to the category of *Gestell*, understood as the general *dispositif* that governs the very humans who are under the illusion of governing it. For the Heidegger of the 1940s this refers not only to Americanism and communism but also to Nazism. This explains the difficulty, manifested by Heidegger, of attributing a political system to the age of technology – including the democratic system. This difficulty is determined not by excessive distance, but by democracy's inherence in technical–scientific machination. In this situation, which Heidegger begins to define with the term "devastation," alluding to a desert that has grown and occupies every space, the only possible form of resistance can no longer come from the political, but exclusively from the impolitical. When referring to this turn, the philosopher mentions his lecture on "poetizing and thinking" that dates to the winter of 1944–1945. In this same vein, when reflecting on questions about the philosophical current that would be best suited to the times, he asks himself "whether timeliness is the measure of the 'inner truth' of human action, or rather, whether thinking and poetizing are not the activity which gives us the measure, despite the heretical meaning we have given the term."[120]

At this point, however, neither thinking nor poetizing conserve the political dimension that Heidegger had assigned to them in the mid-1930s, when he saw a connection between the impolitical *polis* and the forms of the political – or at least one of them. Now that the political is completely subjugated by the technological and has definitely shattered all connections with the *polis*, poetizing and thinking assume a strictly impolitical dimension – devoid of any effect with regard to a human reality, which is in its turn completely uprooted from its essential site. This is the sense in which what is perhaps the most celebrated passage of the interview must be understood: "Philosophy will not be able to effect an immediate transformation of the present condition of the world. This is not only true of philosophy, but of all merely human thought and endeavor. Only a god can save us."[121]

Heidegger's reply is actually decisive as regards the issue of the political: not so much for the indeterminate reference to a possible god as for the threshold he traces to his own previous thought about the political, which is at this point completely enclosed in the negativity of an impolitical dimension completely devoid of effects, because founded on the distancing from the category of "effectuality": a category to which he responds with the belief that the only attitude worthy of our life on the earth is that of the deactivation of all technico-political *dispositifs*. It is a deactivation, however, that is no longer dependent on humans, because it is internal to the flow of the event, which they can only ready themselves to welcome, annulling their will in the decision of not deciding anything. In this fashion, held tightly in the pincers of the negative – of technology, which has sucked it up, that of the impolitical, which counters it inoperatively – the political, as thought of by Heidegger, implodes without leaving any further traces.

2

Constituent Power

1. Rarely have such diverging opinions been recorded as those that concern Deleuze's political ontology. While some regard it as the most radical of contemporary political philosophies, others think it should not be deemed politically significant. While one side sees it as the most transparent expression of our times, to the other side, and for the very same reason, it appears devoid of any critical potential with respect to our times. The issue is on the one hand the relation between an intensely political biography and an oeuvre that is rigorously focused on its own internal development, and on the other the relationship between the first and the second part of his work, defined precisely by the encounter with the political, as the author himself reminds us: "I, for my own part, made a sort of move into politics around May 68, as I came into contact with specific problems, through Guattari, through Foucault, through Elie Sambar. *Anti-Oedipus* was from beginning to end a book about political philosophy."[1]

It is precisely on issues involving the articulation of these two terms – philosophy and politics – that interpretations tend to diverge, however. François Dosse, both in his recent *croisée* [intersecting] biography of Deleuze and Guattari and in an essay in the journal *Cités*, argues that the "political horizon in the broad sense of the term fertilized all of Deleuze's thought,"[2] and in the editorial of a collective volume devoted to *Deleuze politique* one reads that "politics is not at the heart of Deleuze's thought, as could be the case in Foucault, but it is not on its periphery either, instead it rather surfaces here and there in the form of the non-philosophical with which philosophy must necessarily come to terms."[3] In other words it is as if, in order to create a path into his work, politics ought to be situated in the philosophical voids that are revealed within it. In order for a political semantics to emerge in Deleuze's writing, one needs to wait for his philosophy to retreat, freeing up the field for a lexicon that, however, ultimately does not manage to integrate with it. When answering the question whether "something like a Deleuzian politics" exists, Alain Badiou provides an essentially negative answer. Although Deleuze talks a lot about politics, its relationship with his philosophy remains wanting. If prior to 1968 his work does not deal with politics, his subsequent work consists in an analysis of capitalism that is so internal to its object that it inhibits a point of view that is alternative to it. In both cases, what proves to be absent is a political philosophy in the specific sense of the term: "Deleuze believes that there is a politics of art, a politics of science and a politics of philosophy. But, if you allow me this expression, he does not believe there is a politics of politics."[4] Caught between the event of 1968, which exceeds the continuity of history, and a genealogical analysis of capitalism, politics, in Deleuze, misses the encounter with philosophy. Even Foucault, in the preface to Deleuze's most political book, prefers not to use the term and replaces it with the much less challenging "ethics." *Anti-Oedipus* – he writes – "is a book of ethics, the first book of ethics to be written in France in quite a long time ... [it] is an *Introduction to the Non-Fascist Life*."[5]

Slavoj Žižek goes even further in this direction: "It is crucial to note that *not a single one* of Deleuze's own texts (those which he wrote by himself) is in any way directly political; Deleuze 'in himself' is a highly elitist author, indifferent towards politics."[6] One should keep the observations in parentheses in mind, since they are paramount to Žižek's interpretation. It is true that the books born of the collaboration with Guattari, especially *Anti-Oedipus*, push Deleuze's thought toward political shores; but, in doing so, they weaken its philosophical nucleus, distorting it. This weakness, whose cause and outcome can be traced to the meeting with Guattari, would seem to arise from the philosopher's inability to come up with a convincing answer to the crisis of structuralism, from which his work originates: "Is *Anti-Oedipus*, arguably Deleuze's worst book[,] not the result of escaping the full confrontation of a deadlock *via* a simplified flat solution ...?"[7] Starting from this renunciation, and I am here still following Žižek's account, Deleuze's thought not only loses its philosophical center of gravity but ends up becoming the unwitting ideology of that capitalism it would want to oppose. Where do the desiring links and the nomadic flows that Deleuze and Guattari would want to deploy against it come from, if not from the capitalist *dispositif* itself?

Žižek, however, adds a further, even more paradoxical observation to this radical critique. If the politicization of the *Anti-Oedipus* and *A Thousand Plateaus* has a counterfactual outcome, it is precisely the least politically connoted parts of Deleuze's work that contain a possible political resonance, but one he is apparently unaware of. According to Žižek, in fact, in his writings one should apparently be able to recognize two mutually incompatible ontologies. The one dealt with in *Difference and Repetition* and *The Logic of Sense* expresses the gap between the generative process and its immaterial effects. The other, later one is instead characterized by the productive becoming of molecular multiplicities. What differentiates them is their relationship with the negative, which is still recognizable in the first ontology but is instead erased in the second, an ontology that is more influenced by the thought of Spinoza, and especially of Bergson. Following this interpretation, Deleuze seems to derive a purely affirmative view of being from them that, in filling the gap of the symbolic, ends up eliminating any distance between ontology and politics, flattening one onto the other:

> What Spinoza excludes with his rejection of negativity is the very symbolic order, since, as we have learned already from Saussure, the minimal definition of the symbolic order is that every identity is reducible to a bundle (*faisceau* – the same root as in fascism!) of differences: the identity of the signifier resides solely in its difference(s) from other signifier(s).[8]

Without necessarily following Žižek in his raids on the philosophical tradition, the point that should be held firm is the one that concerns the relation between the abandonment of the negative and political entropy. While Deleuze's first ontology, still traversed by a negative fold, did not confront the political directly, it did make its articulation possible, while the second, which entirely adheres to the plane of immanence, would seem to lose any relationship with it. The moment the philosopher declares that "Being itself is in this sense political,"[9] in other words directly productive of effects, the political loses its specific importance. The origin of this transition is the problem, never fully resolved by Deleuze, of the relationship between negation and affirmation. Until the latter withholds the negative inside itself in the form of difference, it is still possible to articulate a political question. When instead the tendency he inherited from Bergson, of reducing negation to a simple error of perspective within an entirely affirmative framework, prevails, the political, compressed into the self-generative process of being, loses the critical shore to push off from and is at risk of dissolving into the indeterminate. Hence the paradox recognized by interpreters of Deleuze: the political, precisely when it occupies the entire ontological landscape, loses specificity and ends up as pure becoming. It is therefore possible to read the most critical point of his relationship with the political precisely in his intentionally political works. Once everything – the constitution of being itself – is declared to be political, nothing continues to be so in a recognizable manner.

If we return to what was said in the first chapter, we cannot but remark how the problem of political ontology now presents itself as reversed. While in Heidegger's case a productive relationship between being and politics was impeded by the negative principle that both of them presupposed, in Deleuze's case the political seems to be inhibited by an excess of affirmation that shades its contours, making it indistinguishable from the ontological horizon in which it is inscribed. In this fashion the deactivation theorized by Heidegger is reversed into a constitutive moment that is equally devoid of a grip on reality, because completely immanent in its objective development. The incorporation of the political into the uninterrupted flow of becoming entails its dissolution as an antagonistic force. In *Out of This World: Deleuze and the Philosophy of Creation*,[10] Peter Hallward reinforces this interpretive hypothesis. The difficulty of identifying a properly political dimension in Deleuze's work derives from the fact that in his ontology it is being alone, translated into becoming, that is the creative source of all its manifestations. These are obviously not all alike, since the creative process reproduces a continuous differentiation. But this process never breaks through the circle of repetition in which difference is inscribed: each difference does no more than create new differences. This is true for all areas of experience. To live, to be, to think, to write, to act are all creative acts that continuously transform that which they create, undermining its stability. This drive, which is simultaneously constitutive and "dissolutionary," also characterizes politics, where each constituted form is only a moment of stasis that needs to be overcome as soon as possible by a new constituent power. To become the vehicle for new creation, the creature needs to free itself from its characterizing traits, becoming other than itself. The same duality of creation and creature, virtual and actual, constituting and constituted power is only an illusion of perspective. In reality there is nothing but creation, virtuality, constitution – a perennial differentiation of that which only erroneously appears as identical to itself. The actual is nothing but a momentary transition, due to practical exigencies, from one virtual to the next, as it was for Bergson, from whom Deleuze derives this assumption. The task of philosophy is to shed light on this dynamic, liberating it from its limits or erroneous perceptions. Individual organic life itself is no more than the momentary consolidation of an impersonal and inorganic flow of life, one of cosmic dimensions, to which the former must return. Within this entirely immanent ontological horizon – where affirmation affirms itself, creation creates itself and difference differentiates itself – the political has no space of its own, because it is included, yet also dissolved, in a being that is itself provided with an infinite power of innovation. In this framework, its only task is to remove the limits, the obstacles, the blocks to becoming, accelerating its productive flow. Acceleration is the only impulse that the political can impress on the unstoppable movement of a real intent on affirming itself infinitely.

*

Benjamin Noys, in an essay entitled *The Persistence of the Negative*[11] that goes against the mainstream, rereads all contemporary continental philosophy through the lens of the relation between affirmation and negation. The decline, if not the stoppage, of the political in our times is the outcome of this encounter – of an affirmative accelerationism that is incapable of translating itself into political practice. At its origin is the refusal of the negative, compressed in its dialectical configuration or assimilated to that nihilism, which is produced precisely by this affirmative drift. The defeat of the category of negation, in European philosophy, occurred between the 1970s and 1980s, when the dike that the Frankfurt School had built collapsed in the face of postmodern immanentism. This is when a neolibertarian current, in principle opposed to the capitalist front, ended up ultimately converging with it, losing the relationship with the political. In this manner, when it attempted to invoke either Nietzsche's "great politics" or Spinoza's "savage ontology," it proceeded along a path that was as radical as it was devoid of a political outlet. If one reads sequentially the works that have been influential in the construction of this *doxa*, for example Deleuze's *Anti-Oedipus*, Lyotard's *Libidinal Economy*, Baudrillard's *Symbolic Exchange and Death* (to which one could add Vattimo's *The End of Modernity*), it is easy to grasp the overall traits of a perspective that was both hyperpolitical and depoliticizing. It is true that at a certain point these thinkers did realize the risks that their thought was exposed to and partially modified its direction. But this was not sufficient to invert a process that, certainly not by way of linear transitions, has led to the current crisis of the European philosophical left.

The presupposition on which this conception is based, with all its internal differences, consists in the idea that all the forces that resist capital are internal to it – starting with the flows of desire that traverse it. These are not situated at the margins but in the deep nucleus of capitalism, to the extent that they constitute its characterizing trait. On the other hand, the thesis that capitalism freed humans from previous social bonds before creating new ones was already there in Marx. But, while he dialecticized it using the category of negation, postmodern thinkers refuse to use it, reversing the negative into an absolute affirmation. Since the forces of emancipation are entirely immanent in the movement of capital, all that needs to be done is free capital from its own limits; hence the slippage from affirmation to acceleration. Acceleration does not contest, but strengthens, the object it impacts. Seen from this point of view, the task of radical thought is not one of interrupting or contrasting capitalist flow but one of favoring it, indulging its destructuring logic. The problem, for postmodern thinkers, is that capital does not take its destructuring operations to their conclusion – it does not deterritorialize sufficiently, it slows the lines of escape down, it blocks desire, impeding enjoyment. It is for this reason that its movement should not be negated, but accelerated to the point of implosion. Since negation has vanished into absolute immanence, all that remains to be done is to bring affirmation to its culmination – affirming even that which one intends to oppose. In this sense, every "countereffectuation," as Deleuze defines it, is internal to the effectuation it seeks to contrast, and thus ultimately strengthens it. The political, itself immanent in becoming capital, can consist in nothing more than favoring an increase of the productive process, bringing it to its acme. The category of "production," generalized from the economic context to the ontological one, allows one to perfectly articulate affirmation and acceleration. Shifted onto the plane of a being that is always becoming, it translates without mediation the political into the ontological and vice-versa. Within this interpretive framework, the political – completely absorbed into its critical object – can have no other task than indulging its dissolutionary dynamics, determining its own as well as the object's dissolution. Noys's thesis is that one should instead once again relaunch a thought of negativity, without ontologizing it into pure negation: "Reifying negativity into *the* negative, which is treated as synonymous with what is outdated or purely destructive, these ideological mystifications serve their purpose in blocking any thinking of negativity as a practice."[12] What this practice is, defined by the author with the elusive term "agency," is, truthfully, not completely clarified in the development of the argument; but the problem he raises is far from irrelevant.

*

2. For a long time the philosophies of Heidegger and Deleuze have been considered so heterogeneous as to not even be comparable. And

if, as is understandable, Heidegger never quoted Deleuze, the latter has referred to Heidegger almost always in a critical manner, finally getting to the point of pronouncing an irrevocable judgment against him:

> It had to be a philosopher, as if shame had to enter into philosophy itself. He wanted to rejoin the Greeks through the Germans, at the worst moment in their history: is there anything worse, said Nietzsche, than to find oneself facing a German when one was expecting a Greek? How could Heidegger's concepts not be intrinsically sullied by an abject reterritorialization?[13]

As the latest research has proved, however,[14] things are not that simple. Not only do Heidegger and Deleuze share, albeit from different points of view, an ample series of topics – the event, the political character of art, the people to come, deterritorialization – but they situate them within a shared horizon, characterized by the eminent role both confer on philosophical work.[15] There is certainly a reason why, to the book that he wrote with Guattari and that marks his distance from Heidegger the most, Deleuze gives the title of a famous Heideggerian essay: *What Is Philosophy?* It is true that never as in this case has the answer given to this question been to this degree the opposite of that provided by his predecessor; but such an opposition, when it is sought out, reveals involvement, even if of a contrastive nature, rather than simple distance – so much so that it has been possible to argue that *Difference and Repetition*, Deleuze's most important book, is an implicit reply to *Being and Time*.[16] In this sense a sort of chiasmus seems to delineate itself, in which the confrontation with Heidegger appears as the negative modality of Deleuze's intense interest in him. Deleuze's declaration that he had never been either a communist or a Heideggerian is an added element that reveals the weight given to a philosophical option that is put at the same level as an important political choice. Deleuze must have perceived his relationship with Heidegger as a challenge he could not avoid. When he laments that French philosophy has long been blocked by the hegemony exercised within it by the thought of the German philosopher,[17] implicitly he is proposing to topple him from that role and take his place. Heidegger's baleful political vicissitudes, which had also gained increasing notoriety in France, must have played a significant role in the growing harshness of the criticism Deleuze directed at him. The impression is that he fully understood the philosophical and political scope of a confrontation with a worthy adversary destined to shape the orientation of future thought.

That mixture of convergence and dissonance that situates the two philosophies at the polar extremes of a common semantic axis would not be understandable otherwise. It is constituted by the shared ontological plane on which both authors place themselves. For each, being constitutes the natural space of thought. Even though Heidegger situates it on the oscillating margin between disclosure and concealment while Deleuze reverses it into the immanence of an infinite becoming, it is, however, the horizon in which everything else acquires meaning. It is for this reason that the reflection on the political acquires an ontological standing for both thinkers. Not only do both elaborate a political ontology, but they situate it in a shared postfoundational regimen – characterized not by identity but by difference. For both Heidegger and Deleuze, the political relates to being via difference. However, if one formulates their relation more precisely, what most unites the two thinkers – the triangulation between the political, being, and difference – is also what most divides them. Deleuze's philosophy excludes the ontological difference between being and beings – and therefore also any element external to the plane of immanence, along which all that exists flows.[18] The category of the impolitical itself, thought of by Heidegger as the negative presupposition of the political, undergoes a loss of meaning for the French philosopher as a consequence. For Deleuze the political is not split by difference, but instead coincides with the very differential constitution of being. It is, one could state, no more than the difference of being – that which frees its flow from the bonds that occlude it. Constituent power, which Deleuze opposes to any destituent move, belongs to being itself, to its inexhaustible capacity "to create, within a state of permanent creation, new things that escape all recognition and every establishment."[19] The difference between the two paradigms hinges on the fact that, while Heidegger thinks of difference starting from being, and therefore also in relation to identity, Deleuze questions being from the standpoint of difference – or, better and more simply, *as* difference. The originality of the Deleuzian perspective within contemporary thought lies in the collapse, which it presupposes, of all distinctions between being and difference: being is difference. In this sense Deleuze can maintain that "the conjunction 'and' dethrones the interiority of the verb 'is.'"[20] This means that it is identity that emerges from difference and not vice-versa. It is not the case that Being precedes difference, as Heidegger wants, or that Difference precedes being, as Deleuze supposes instead, since they are the same thing: difference is, just as being is *different*. What is removed, on the plane of immanence, is the concept of precedence itself. There is only the "place," the "positive": neither imposition nor deposition – only position. To state, as Heidegger does, that all beings share the same being while not coinciding with it signifies conditioning difference on a negative presupposition, which needs in its turn to be negated so as to free its affirmative content. But only an additional negation can emerge from a double negation. To start from the One and then differentiate it is quite different from making the real the place for the deployment of difference. Heidegger looks at the manifold from the point of view of what is; Deleuze thinks of being in its constitutive multiplicity. So, if for the former being is plurivocal in the sense that it is said in as many ways as there are beings, for the latter it is univocal because it unifies them in their shared difference: "In effect, the essential in univocity is not that Being is said in a single and same sense, but that it is said, in a single and same sense, *of* all its individuating differences or intrinsic modalities."[21]

The vertical historicity of Heidegger is answered by the simultaneous horizontality of Deleuze. What, for one, possesses temporal depth for the other moves along a spatial line of escape. Since, on the plane of immanence, there is no succession between a before and an after, but only transformation of each thing into the other, the cause is already entirely in the effect and the virtual is, in and of itself, real. In this sense the issue of origins, which is central for Heidegger, disappears from Deleuze's universe. In its place we find a constituent power, which coincides with the flow of a being that is forever productive of further differences. The classic problem of the beginning, which is very present in Heidegger, is substituted by that of linkage. As Jean-Luc Nancy observes,[22] if Heidegger asks himself why and when being was "folded," and how it can be "folded" again in a new beginning, Deleuze is already situated within the fold. This means that there is no negative – neither in the form of provenance *ex nihilo* [from nothing] nor in that of process *in nihilum* [into nothing]. Death itself, which Deleuze certainly does not ignore, is inscribed in a natural horizon that excludes any mournful or melancholic, and therefore negative,[23] tones. In one of the notes in *Difference and Repetition*, the author situates his discord with Heidegger precisely within the issue of negation. While he admits that "the Heideggerian *Not* refers not to the negative in Being but to Being as difference; it refers not to negation but to questioning," he asks himself whether "[i]t can nevertheless be asked whether Heidegger did not himself encourage the misunderstandings, by his conception of 'Nothing' as well as by his manner of 'striking through' Being instead of parenthesising the (non) of non-Being."[24]

This clarification is important. If it is true that Heidegger's "no" cannot be identified with the absolute negative, Deleuze in his turn does not negate negation – for in this manner he would redouble it – but includes it in an affirmative horizon that converts it into difference. What counts, rather than the exclusion of "non-," is the affirmative angle from which it is viewed. Even when he contests the negative, Deleuze does not disavow its reality but, by translating it into difference, places it in a positive horizon. Only a completely superficial interpretation of Deleuze can ignore the dramatic, even tragic tone that disquiets all his work, as an abyss in which one can always slide. The author himself seems to dissuade the reader from a harmonious reading of his texts, evoking the figure of the beautiful soul, to which he counterposes "a sense for cruelty or a taste for destruction,"[25] brought to their culmination by a Nietzsche who knew the negative power exercised by reactive forces over active ones very well. And yet, in Deleuze's text, awareness of the ineliminability of the negative is balanced, and sometimes contradicted, by an opposing tendency to abolish it. One could say that to a "Nietzsche side" – or even a "Spinoza side" – there corresponds a "Bergson side." As is well known, for Bergson negation did not exist in reality, but only in the diverted imagination of those who undergo a sort of perceptual distortion, mistaking an affirmation they cannot accept for something negative. While he does not completely support this extreme thesis, Deleuze skirts along it more than once, as when he writes: "The negative is an illusion because the form of negation appears with propositions which express the problem on which they depend only by distorting it and obscuring its real structure";[26] or: "The negative is the image of difference, but a flattened and inverted image, like the candle in the eye of the ox."[27] This oscillation, which runs through Deleuze's entire work, is present in different modalities in all his texts, even though the overall orientation of his philosophical path leans toward an increasingly clear prevalence of an affirmative lexicon. The fact that this is accompanied by a progressive shift toward the area of the political – a shift that reaches its apex in *Anti-Oedipus* and *A Thousand Plateaus* – raises the level of the contradiction to a form that places Deleuze's text into always greater tension with its very own presuppositions. We already know its fundamental antinomy. The politicization of discourse does not imply an intensification of political reflection. On the contrary, one could say that the more his language gets charged politically, the more it ends up losing antagonistic energy, transforming itself into a pure power of acceleration.

*

In the preceding pages I spoke of "constituent power." Is it legitimate to use this expression for Deleuze? Probably not, if we understand it in a technical sense – as a metajuridical source of constituted power. Since a true philosophy of law is lacking in Deleuze, the term might appear misleading. Once we consider the philosopher's insistence on a jurisprudence that is continuously creating new *nomoi* [laws],[28] however, the expression seems less inappropriate. If we then detach it from the specific meaning it assumes in constitutional theory, and understand it more generally, the compatibility seems even more evident. Hallward himself, whom we mentioned earlier, does not distinguish between creative and constituent power at the lexical level. Like the latter, the former not only precedes its object but ends up removing all stable consistency from it. In a conception of being that is uninterruptedly mobilized in becoming, what is created is subject to continual recreation, which impedes its consolidation within specific contours. Deleuze sees in that which is constituted nothing more than the matter for the formation of a new constituting process. The actual is the momentary threshold that we ourselves fix, on the basis of practical exigencies, within something that does not cease to be virtual. That the creature – the current result of an uninterrupted creative process – appears to be autonomous from it is an optical effect due to our not being able to grasp the infinite play of differences in its entirety. What appears, in and of itself, to be individuated, or individual, is nothing but the instantaneous product of a single differentiating process. At its origin there is the constituent power of a dynamic that simultaneously constructs and deconstructs all constituted powers. Ultimately nothing exists except this movement of destituting constitution or constituting destitution. Fully real, one could say, is only the virtual. The bipolarity between creation and creature, or constituent and constituted, is only apparent, as is that between virtual and actual.

From this point of view Bergson's influence appears to be stronger than Spinoza's, or such that it incorporates it within itself. The transient character of the actual, as compared to the virtual, is one of the theoretical centers of gravity of *Matter and Memory*. Not only is the actual such only within the representational grids of our perceptual *dispositif*, but it is continuously subjected to a disintegration that brings it back to the virtual state in view of a new and always different actualization. One can recognize the theologico-political principle of divine creation as the basis for such a conception – in a heretical version that does not circumscribe it to the event of Genesis but extends it through time ad infinitum. But, as I was saying, Deleuze's closest referent is Bergsonian *élan*. It is true that, in Deleuze's ontology, one can also recognize a reference to Spinoza's *natura naturans* [naturing nature], which *natura naturata* [natured nature] presupposes, but the idea of flow prevails over that of substance. Or, perhaps better, substance is always conceived of as a differentiating flow. The transition from one difference to the other is unmediated, as is the entire productive moment of reality. This is another point of contact with the radical theory of constituent power: just as the constituent is never mediated by the constituted, so the different is never mediated by the differed. This means that, taken in its absoluteness, constituent power destroys constituted power. In Deleuze, the principle of creation coincides with that of destruction. One does not create other than by destroying that which impedes creation and, ultimately, the created as well, all with a view to a different configuration. My impression is that this self-dissolving dynamics depends on the preemptive exclusion of the negative. As Hegel had observed, the extreme result of absolute affirmation does not differ from that of absolute negation. Within the purely affirmative horizon of the plane of immanence, the only possibility left for the constituted is that of its own dissolution. Just as the end result of each individual life is annulment into cosmic life, the end result of each datum is to be dissolved in its generative process. It is possible to talk of constituent power in Deleuze in this sense, provided that one specifies that it coincides with destituent power.

*

3. While, overall, Deleuze's philosophy is oriented affirmatively, one should not believe that he undervalues the problem of the negative. On the contrary, one could say that his entire oeuvre is obsessed with it – one the one hand engaged in erasing it, on the other always exposed to its return. No matter how much it is shoved to the margins of the frame, the negative always reemerges in a spectral form in the fissures that open up in it: some sliver of transcendence inevitably returns to stage an appearance within immanence.[29] There is no definitive choice between the two ontologies mentioned by Žižek – the one that gives space to the negative and the other that excludes it – but instead an uninterrupted battle. From his first writings on the institution through those on the crisis of structuralism, through the diaspora of sense and the impact on the Outside, up to the self-destructive dialectics between state and war machine, one could say that "Deleuze's thinking remains inextricably bound to, or entangled, with negativity."[30] One would almost think that the true war that he declares on the category of negation originates from the pressure that this category exercised on his work from the very beginning. Already in the youthful collection of essays on the relationship between

natural tendencies and institutional *dispositifs*, Deleuze counterposes the positivity of the institution to the negativity of the law:

> The institution is always given as an organized system of means. It is here, moreover, that we find the difference between institution and law: law is a limitation of actions, institution a positive model for action. Contrary to theories of law which place the positive outside the social (natural rights), and the social in the negative (contractual limitation), the theory of the institution places the negative outside the social (needs), so as to present society as essentially positive and inventive (original means of satisfaction).[31]

Unlike those who see in institutions – whether political, familial, sanitary, military, educational – a negative power to coerce vital forces, Deleuze recognizes an affirmative power in them, one destined to favor their development. If one thinks of the clearly anti-institutional direction of the entire philosophical left – from the post-Freudian school to the Frankfurt School, up to the positions of Foucault and Bourdieu – the thesis proposed by Deleuze appears to be fairly isolated in the cultural landscape of his time: not only does the institution not suffocate the free unfolding of the instincts but, given certain conditions, it actually leads to their expansion. Instead of having an inhibitory effect on natural tendencies, it opens up a space for their satisfaction that would otherwise be absent. What helps measure the positive valorization of the institution is its contrast with the negativity of the law. While the latter encloses human action within confines that are predetermined by obligations and sanctions, the former provides functional models of realization. This is why, if one translates this alternative into political language, Deleuze can maintain that, if "tyranny is a regime in which there are many laws and few institutions; democracy is a regime in which there are many institutions, and few laws."[32]

Where does he draw these conclusions from, when he is still at the beginning of his philosophical itinerary? To what conceptual horizon do they refer? To answer these questions, one needs to look at his text on Hume, which appeared in 1953 under the title *Empiricism and Subjectivity*. It deals with this topic from the viewpoint of the relationship between nature and culture. The institution is the site in which they transition from one to the other without contradicting their characteristics, and in fact elevating them to a higher level. At the root of this line of reasoning, which has Hume as its referent, there is a clear farewell gesture to modern political philosophy, which

Deleuze correctly traces back to Hobbes. What Hume advances against the latter is a critique of contractualism later on brought to fruition by utilitarians. The resulting thesis almost literally redeploys the opposition between negative and positive outlined in the introduction to *Instincts and Institutions*:

> The main idea is this: the essence of society is not the law but rather the institution. The law, in fact, is a limitation of enterprise and action, and it focuses only on a negative aspect of society. The fault of contractual theories is that they present us with a society whose essence is the law, that is, with a society which has no other objective than to guarantee certain preexisting natural rights and no other origin than the contract. Thus, anything positive is taken away from the social, and instead the social is saddled with negativity, limitation and alienation.[33]

For Hume it is a question of reversing this schema, so as to target the Hobbesian presupposition of the obligating character of the law at its root. While the law, suspended from the punctuality of the contract, poses limits to action, the institution provides it with an operative model, preparing a system of means necessary for its enactment. What Deleuze finds in Hume's philosophy is a radically new way of thinking the traditional relationship between law, politics, and society. Unlike in the modern juridical model, the first two terms presuppose the third, which simultaneously constitutes the terrain for them to take root and their propulsive drive: political decision and juridical norm don't precede, but instead follow historically instituted needs. The true legislator, therefore, is not s/he who legislates, much less s/he who commands, but s/he who institutes. Hence a transition that is destined to re-tie that knot between natural state and political state that Hobbes had drastically cut, placing them in radical opposition. What allows this turn is precisely the category of institution, which Hume defines as a "general rule": "Utility – that is, the relation between institution and need – is therefore a fertile principle: Hume's general rule is an institution."[34]

This description, however, does not portray the situation fully. The negative, which has been expunged from the sanction-oriented side of the law, returns to peek out of the affirmative space of the institution. The connection we just defined between institution and utility is neither an identification nor a superposition: while it is definitely articulated with nature, the artifice of the institution does not coincide with it. It is one thing to say that natural tendencies are satisfied through institutions, another to say that the institution originates from these tendencies. A diaphragm remains between one position and the other that, regardless of how thin it may be, continues to separate them. It is true that the satisfaction of these tendencies requires an intervention by the institution; sexuality is satisfied by marriage, just as greed is by property. Marriage and property, however, are positioned on the other side of the instincts to which they respond, and preserve a margin of transcendence with respect to them. The negative returns to make an appearance within the affirmative flow that seemed to dissolve it. The transition from nature to culture, implicit in the institution, is neither immediate nor linear, but requires an implicit diversion into the instrument with which it is enacted. While the outcome of the process is affirmative because it expands these tendencies, the means used to this end do not directly stem from them but from a subjective faculty that, while invoking Hume, Deleuze defines as "imagination":

> The institution, being the model of actions, is a designed system of possible satisfaction. The problem is that this does not license us to conclude that the institution is *explained* by the drive. The institution is a system of means, according to Hume, but these means are oblique and indirect; they do not satisfy the drive without also constraining it at the same time.[35]

The negative element that is implicit in the affirmative process of the institution does not escape Deleuze's attention: not only does it not coincide with the natural tendencies that it fosters, but it favors them by holding them back, channeling their energies into an artificial basin that, in shaping them, withholds their impulses. After all, if this were not the case, if the institution were born within the tendency, the transition from one to the others would always be identical, as is the case with animal instincts, which are always satisfied in the same manner. But this does not happen with human beings, who differ from one another on the basis of the kind of artifice that they enact on each occasion. While birds, wherever they are, always build their nest in the same fashion, human beings, in different times and locales, build their dwellings differently. Since institutions are historical and not natural, they are always different, because they vary on the basis of region, custom, but above all the imagination of those who invent them. This means that the institution is not a simple extension of these tendencies, but their imaginary representation in reflection: to become institutionalized, the tendencies must resort to the medium of the image. Further on, when naming this reflective mechanism, Deleuze will use the term "fold." In *Empiricism and Subjectivity*, he refers back to the non-immediate character of the process of institutionalization. The reflection of the tendencies – the fact that they need to be reflected on a sort of screen – expresses the necessarily negative modality by which the institution affirms itself. While necessary to its satisfaction, the institution is *not* instinct: to function, it requires a distance that, if it does not negate it directly, as does the law, at least detaches it from itself, duplicating it via the diaphragm of the imagination.

If we return to the introduction of *Instincts and Institutions*, we find the exact same detour. On the one hand Deleuze says: "Neither does the negative explain the positive."[36] On the other, rather than erase it, he situates it within an institutional affirmation, making it simultaneously into a functionality filter and a sounding board; in any case the negative does not appear to be eliminable from the affirmative procedure of the institution. One could express the situation as follows: the institution is the affirmation of a negative, while the law is the negation of a positive. What opposes them is not an absolute choice between affirmation and negation, but the manner in which they intersect and the visual angle from which this intersection is observed. While the law looks toward the positive – the natural datum, the tendency – from negation's point of view, the institution looks at the negative from the point of view of affirmation. Deleuze is far from removing this antinomic element, far from hiding the negative that separates instincts and institutions. Ultimately negation is their very separation – the fact that they do not coincide. The permanence of the negative within the horizon of its opposite is expressed by the presence of an unconscious instance in the construction of models that are appropriate to the satisfaction of the tendency. This presence arises from the gap between the sphere of the individual and that of the biological species from which the individual emerges. The more perfect the instinct, the more it relates to the species, as is the case with animals. The more it is perfectible, and therefore imperfect, the more it refers to the individual intelligence of a human being. But – and the question remains – how can an instinct, which is in any case rooted in the ancestral past of the species, take on the characteristics of intelligence? Deleuze replies that between species and individual there exists an intermediate level, which is that of society. This is an answer that provides an interpretive key also with regard to the nature of the institution, which is simultaneously conscious and unconscious, voluntary and involuntary, contingent and necessary. It is situated precisely at the point in which the repetition of circumstances gives rise to a system of recurrences that allows one to anticipate their succession. Whether one eats at midday or one sleeps at night, this choice ends up shifting the tendency onto a social level that translates disorderly animal urges into human exigencies of stability. In this sense one can argue that "[t]he Human is an animal decimating its species."[37] The affirmative negation with which Deleuze recognizes the dual profile of the institution seems to be outlined in this expression. Far from being fixed in an unambiguous meaning, it oscillates on a threshold in which human beings experiment with their differential relationship with the world they come from and to which maybe they secretly aspire:

> In the end, the problem of instinct and institution will be grasped most acutely not in animal "societies," but in relations of animal and humans, when the demands of men come to bear on the animal by integrating it into institutions (totemism and domestication), when the urgent needs of the animal encounter the human, either fleeing or attacking us, or patiently waiting for nourishment and protection.[38]

4. While the essay on Hume already situates in the institution the problematic point of intersection of nature and history, individual and society, it is in the book on Nietzsche, which appeared seven years later, that Deleuze brilliantly inaugurates his political ontology. The challenge represented by Heidegger reappears, and is deepened in another direction.[39] While for the German philosopher Nietzsche represents the ultimate consummation of metaphysics, for Deleuze Nietzsche is the one who opens a passage to its exterior. Nietzsche's will to power, understood by Heidegger as the extreme culmination of modern subjectivism, is considered by the French philosopher to be the savage foundation of a being that coincides with its own creative power. Even in this instance, his divergence from Heidegger is outlined from within a shared presupposition, defined by the ontological primacy of being over the subject. Thought's starting point does not lie in a consciousness critical of itself, as in Kant, or in a substance destined to become subject, as in Hegel, but in a being that precedes any other determination. This is a being that is, naturally, quite different from the one delineated by Heidegger, defined by a difference that separates it from beings. The being to which Deleuze refers is constituted by the immanent discord of a plurality of rival forces. It is precisely this play of antagonisms that

bestows that eminently political connotation on it, one that is silent in Heidegger's impolitical ontology. Already beginning with the first pages of Deleuze's text, it is fixed in the destituting relationship between being and force:

> We will never find the sense of something (of a human, a biological or even a physical phenomenon) if we do not know the force which appropriates the thing, which exploits it, which takes possession of it or is expressed in it. ... All force is appropriation, domination, exploitation of a quantity of reality. ... The history of a thing, in general, is the succession of forces which take possession of it.[40]

The terms used by Deleuze – appropriation, domination, struggle – confer an almost military, rather than political, imprint on his treatment. Nothing escapes the battle between opposing forces. Strictly speaking, one cannot even say that they clash over the conquest of an object, because even the object is a force that exerts itself on these clashing forces. It would be difficult to imagine a more intrinsically political ontology than Nietzsche's, which Deleuze pushes to such a degree of polemicalness as to be on the verge of a hermeneutical distortion. By contracting all of Nietzsche's philosophy, with all its range of tones, into the vortex of a conflict between adverse forces, he turns Nietzsche himself into a force that he hurls at his philosophical enemy, which from the outset he has identified as Hegelian dialectics. Following the well-known principle that one can derive each person's identity from the one whom that person opposes, it is precisely this enemy that identifies Nietzsche's thought, giving it meaning and internal compactness: "If we do not discover its target the whole of Nietzsche's philosophy remains abstract and barely comprehensible. ... Anti-Hegelianism runs through Nietzsche's work as its cutting edge. We can already feel it in the theory of forces."[41]

At the center of this no-holds-barred clash between philosophers and philosophies is the issue of the negative – which almost from the outset is provided with an ambivalent characterization. Deleuze considers the negative, rather than as a presupposition, as the product, the outcome of a struggle that, tearing it from its originary non-being, makes it real:

> The negative is not present in the essence as that from which force draws its activity: on the contrary it is a result of activity, of the existence of an active force and the affirmation of its difference. The

negative is a product of existence itself: the aggression necessarily linked to an active existence, the aggression of an affirmation.[42]

What is destined to remain a point of suspension or a line of oscillation in Deleuze's political ontology is laid out right here, through Nietzsche's perspective. On the one hand the negative is denied an autonomous status of existence: it is only the inevitable consequence of a contrary power that, since it tends to affirm itself without limits, gives the negative an importance it would otherwise not possess. On the other hand is an indispensable element of the framework, not only in determining the affirmative forces contrastively but also in triggering the essential dynamics of all types of forces. In Nietzsche's world, which Deleuze makes entirely his own, there is no possibility of a stable equilibrium – which, by discharging the forces' vital energies, would render them inert. No force exists that does not fight, to defend itself or to extend its domain. Even negative forces, those to which a primary existence is denied, are real forces, since they are fighting for their own existence, waiting for the moment to move on to the counterattack and submit the positive ones – even when they limit themselves to enduring the domination of the latter and to obeying them. An obedience of this kind is in fact charged with a resentment that is ready to reverse onto the enemy forces the pressure they momentarily endure: "Inferior forces do not, by obeying, cease to be forces distinct from those which command."[43] Certainly, they are forces of conservation or, even better, of reaction, precisely because they react to the action(s) of superior forces with a different kind of action. Their historical existence, even if "secondary," is demonstrated by the fact that, for an extremely long period of time, which still continues uninterrupted, they have prevailed over their adversaries. In fact, Deleuze adds, "[w]e can say that negation has dominated our thought, our ways of feeling and evaluating, up to the present day. In fact it is constitutive of man."[44]

But then, one could ask, does the negative exist or does it not exist? Is it the result of a perspectival hallucination or a reality that is so real that it is "constitutive of human beings"? One can say that Deleuze's entire philosophy flows along this antinomic ridge, bending sometimes toward one side, sometimes toward the other. As we have already seen, the first answer to this question is of a performative nature: it is the development of the active forces that confers the attributes of reality on entities that, on their own, would not possess them, since it is only the active forces that can produce all that exists, including the reactive forces (these are but an effect of the former). At this point, however, what had been an image acquires actual depth. Once they have been produced by the affirmative forces, the negative ones acquire a sort of second-degree power, which is destined to overwhelm their adversaries. A later answer offered by Deleuze, and one that is not alternative but complementary to the first, is that the error, shared by consciousness and science, is not that of inventing "negation" but of designating difference with this inadequate term, making of an affirmative negation, which is what difference is, an absolute negation, in other words a negative one. This occurs because consciousness is itself reactive with respect to the unconscious, and therefore incapable of grasping affirmation in its pure state. But, once more, how does that which is only consciousness manage to transfer itself into reality to the point of occupying it? And, above all, what is the reason why the reactive and negative forces prevail over the active and affirmative ones? Since they do not have any creative power – which lies entirely on the side of affirmation – they limit themselves to working on the affirmative forces, separating them from their root and twisting them against themselves. In this fashion a part of the active forces, dismembered and contaminated by the passive ones, is sucked into their horizon, to the point of being mixed up with them: this is how the reactive forces' strategy becomes victorious. Since they are not successful at adding themselves to one another – which would constitute a positive action – they proceed by subtraction, producing not a fullness but a void, which, at the culmination of the dynamic, assumes that profile of nothingness, whose philosophical name is "nihilism."

This being the situation – upon completion of a process that, at least since the advent of Christianity, has seen the progressive reinforcement of negative forces – what can be done? One path seems precluded: that of negating them frontally. First of all because, to negate a negation, outside a dialectical perspective, would mean to strengthen it by doubling it; but above all because this would presuppose that, behind these forces, there are subjects intent on using them for their ends – something that Deleuze's ontology refuses as a form of anthropological illusion. The only possibility – one grasped by Nietzsche in the transition from passive to active nihilism – is that of assuming the inevitability of the process of expansion of the forces of nihilism, and thereby accelerating their destructive dynamics to the point where destruction embroils them as well, vanquishing them. In this case these negative forces would end up objectively reverting their direction, thus proceeding inevitably on an affirmative path. This is precisely the discovery that Nietzsche hands us, through the figure of the eternal return, when he talks about the "joy of affirmation" and the "affirmation of the flow and annihilation":[45] "the *will to destroy* as an even deeper instinct than the instinct to self-destruction, a *will into nothingness*."[46] It is not therefore the choice, in and of itself counterproductive, of opposing the negative, but that of accelerating it, leading it to disown itself by becoming an affirmative power. The connection, a central one in Deleuze, between affirmation and acceleration – acceleration as a motor and outcome of affirmation – returns. As a result, the negative would not disappear but would be transformed, or transvalued, into affirmation – or so the argument goes; not into an affirmative negation – which is what negative forces do – but into a negative affirmation, productive of its opposite: "In the man who wants to perish, the man who wants to be overcome, negation changes sense, it becomes a power of affirming, a preliminary condition of the development of the affirmative, a premonitory sign and a zealous servant of affirmation as such."[47] But, in order for the process of conversion from the negative to the affirmative to be fully completed, it is necessary that the age of the last human be overcome in favor of that of the overman [*Übermensch*], prospectively outlined by Nietzsche and which we can barely glimpse: "In the man who wants to perish the negative announces the superhuman, but only affirmation produces what the negative announces. There is no other power but affirmation, no other quality, no other element: the whole of negation is converted in its substance, transmuted in its quality, *nothing remains of its own power or autonomy*."[48]

What is outlined in this manner is an ontology that is affirmative to such a degree that it identifies being and affirmation – not only in the sense of affirming being but also in the more extreme sense of claiming that being is in itself affirmation: "Being is not the object of affirmation, any more than it is an element which would present itself, which would give itself over to affirmation. Affirmation is not the power of being, on the contrary. Affirmation itself is being, being is solely affirmation in all its power."[49]

*

If the prevalent modality of Deleuze's political ontology is that of acceleration, one must recognize that Nietzsche is "his" philosopher – more so than Hume, Spinoza, Bergson, Leibniz. We already saw how it was through Nietzsche that Deleuze settled his score with Heidegger once and for all. As always in these cases, the greatest distance develops where the two authors ought to be, as a matter of principle, closest – in other words as regards the relation, constitutive for both of them, between being and time. The term that divides them is "becoming," which is a Nietzschean term. It is not the same thing to affirm that being is time and to say that it is becoming, as Deleuze does, thus joining Nietzsche once more: this is because, while in the first case the central figure, in its temporal configuration, remains being, in the second it is becoming. The emphasis is not on the being of becoming but on the becoming of being. The different role played by difference is what is inserted between the perspectives of the two philosophers. For Heidegger, it is situated between being and beings. In Deleuze, it is that which translates being into becoming. Acceleration, one could state, is the becoming nature of being.

The figure in which such "acceleration" of being in becoming is realized is that of the eternal return. In the preface to the American edition of *Nietzsche and Philosophy*, Deleuze supports the connection between eternal return and becoming, against an inadequate interpretation that compresses it into the identity of being: "only that which *becomes* in the fullest sense of the word can return, is fit to return. Only action and affirmation return: becoming has being and only becoming has being."[50] That which does not become simply is not, because "[t]hat which is opposed to becoming, the same or the identical, strictly speaking, *is* not."[51] In the conclusions of the Nietzsche conference held in Royaumont and devoted precisely to the concepts of will to power and eternal return, Deleuze refers to the latter as the becoming of being and by the term "intensification." It differs both from the quality of extension and from that of physicality, and the eternal return unfolds in "a domain of pure intensities."[52] Intensification is another name for acceleration – which is how Deleuze thinks of the politicalness of being. There is certainly a reason why intensification is what ties eternal return and will to power together in a single move. As against all its false politicist interpretations, the latter should also be understood as an intensive principle: "because the will to power does not mean wanting power; on the contrary, whatever one desires, it means raising this to the ultimate power, to the *nth* power. In a word, it means extracting *the superior form* of everything that is (the form of intensity)."[53] Acceleration, or intensification, is the form in which being and becoming become identified, making of the latter the only mode of being of the former. Being, insofar as it is becoming, is the point of implication of difference and repetition: differential repetition and eternally repeated difference. But it is also the only way of thinking about the political from the point of view of pure immanence. Unable to escape outside itself – since there is no outside or, on the contrary, there is only outside – being cannot express itself except by intensifying or accelerating itself into becoming. What is excluded from becoming is only negative being – the negative of being. In truth, even in this case, in order not to open a space for transcendence, the negative is not excluded, but transvalued in an affirmative sense. Not even nihilism, in the Nietzschean perspective that Deleuze makes his own, is negated – but transmuted: from negative, reactive, passive, into active. Active nihilism emerges not by opposition to, but via acceleration of, the preceding configurations, which are brought to the point of conversion into their opposite. Since it cannot be fought by an external force – which would insert a point of transcendence into the plane of immanence – nihilism can only self-destruct, by mutating, via progressive intensifications, into its opposite. In Deleuze's immanent universe affirmation and negation can never confront each other frontally – this would bestow full reality on the negative – but only twist one into the other: "Destruction becomes active to the extent that the negative is transmuted and converted into affirmative power."[54] Once it has imploded into its opposite, negation reveals itself as nothing more than a negated affirmation.

*

5. Before such an affirmative outcome can consolidate in Deleuze's work, it is necessary to identify not only the irregular transitions that precede it, but also the points of resistance that obtusely collide with it. One of the sharpest can be identified in the formidable watershed essay on Proust. Published immediately after the books on Nietzsche and Kant, *Proust and Signs* constitutes the hermeneutical fault line that disarticulates the philosopher's first works from what follows. It would be reckless to read the essay on Proust from the perspective of the works that followed, searching for conceptual junctions that will stabilize theoretically only later on. It goes without saying that some of these already do make an appearance, even if in a form that is more alluded to than fully developed. The relationship of thought with the forces of the "outside" for instance, already present in *Proust*, will return, reelaborated, in *Difference and Repetition* along a path that leads up to *What Is Philosophy?*. But it is precisely this topic that highlights an element, if not of transcendence, at least of exteriority, that only with difficulty could be related to what later on will be designated as the "plane of immanence." Instead the Proustian analysis in *Remembrance*, with its exhibition of signs, seems to prelude to what the author will later define as the "philosophy of expression." In Proust's universe, as reconstructed by its interpreter, there is no "Kantian" separation between high and low, aesthetics and analytics, sensibility and intellect. This is because any plane that would stand above the plurality of signs – to which the interpretation refers as to an origin to decipher or, even less plausibly, restore – is missing. From this point of view, Deleuze's distance from the Heideggerian paradigm is very clear and exhibits no hesitations. Being is completely expressed in the repetition of its differences, following a formulation that will come to full maturity in *Difference and Repetition*: "repetition constitutes the degrees of

an original difference, but diversity also constitutes the levels of a repetition no less fundamental."[55]

What specifically characterizes *Proust and Signs*, however, is the circumstance that the chiasmic play of difference and repetition does not assume the form of an erasure of the negative, as will occur elsewhere. On the contrary, the entire Proustian essay is entirely split by the line of negativity. This is so as regards both the attrition between signs and thought and the definition of their internal structure. What is even more relevant from my point of view is the metapolitical characterization that the structure of the negative assumes in both cases. It is, first of all, determined by the place in which all the semiological dynamics unfold – a force field that explicitly crosses over into violence. Signs, even before they indicate something, exercise a force – a force that compels one to interpret them as an injunction one cannot resist. This transition is a consequence of presupposing that, contrary to what the work's title leads one to foresee, the object of Proust's *Remembrance* is not "things past," but rather the truth that they vehicle. But even more important for my argument is the fact that this research is neither spontaneous nor natural, but imposed by something that obliges us to undertake it from the outside:

> *Who* is in search for the truth? And what does the man who says "I want the truth" mean? Proust does not believe that man, nor even a supposedly pure mind, has by nature a desire for truth, a will-to-truth. We search for truth only when we are determined to do so in terms of a concrete situation, when we undergo a kind of violence that impels us to search. ... There is always the violence of a sign that forces us into the search, that robs us of peace.[56]

Philosophy's fault – which keeps it on this side of thought, as Deleuze argues with an inflection that is still Heideggerian – is that of presuming, in human beings, some form of willingness to think, a natural desire for truth. This optimistic idea is born of an abstract intelligence, instead of "a violence or of an encounter that would guarantee their authenticity. ... truth is never the product of a prior disposition, but the result of a violence in thought."[57] To the idea of "method," which is typical of the philosophical tradition, Deleuze's Proust opposes a mixture of contingency and compulsion that inevitably refers to a negative semantics. Even the concept of things past, far from limiting itself to recalling a past with the help of memory, seems rather to allude to an irreparable loss that anticipates final annihilation with a dramatic intensity that is very different from the fully affirmative one of Bergson: "There are signs that force us to conceive lost time, that is, the passage of time, the annihilation of what was, the alteration of beings. ... Proust does not in the least conceive change as a Bergsonian duration, but as a defection, a race to the grave."[58]

This hollow structure, this structural lack, characterizes, in different ways, all the signs of *Remembrance*, following the three typologies into which Deleuze subdivides them – worldly, amorous, and sensuous signs: all signs of a lost time, and ultimately also lost themselves. This is the case with worldly signs – emptied of meaning as a matter of principle, because enclosed in a ritual circuit devoid of external referents. They have an excluding function. The ceremony that is celebrated by worldly signs is always a rite of exclusion, on whose basis one includes some only so as to be able to exclude others: "Thus the apprentice's task is to understand why someone is 'received' into a certain world, why someone ceases to be so."[59] If the negative traverses the worldly signs, it connotes the amorous ones with even greater intensity. They constitute the narrow door through which one enters the universe of love. To fall in love means to choose someone on the basis of the signals they transmit. To love means precisely to unravel the hidden signs that are wrapped up in the behaviors of the person one loves. But this is exactly where the trap of the negative snaps shut, since we cannot penetrate the world of a loved one without trespassing into previous worlds, or even contemporary ones, which s/he has built with others. The threat of exclusion returns and intensifies, only now it is directed at those who love: "But the beloved's gestures, at the very moment they are addressed to us, still express that unknown world that excludes us."[60] The signs of love are not, like the worldly ones, empty and self-referential, but ambiguous and treacherous. There is no love that does not imply, directly or indirectly, the possibility of betrayal. For this reason jealousy, rather than being a pathology, expresses the very truth of amorous signs – their inevitable deceit.

As far as sensuous signs are concerned – and *Remembrance* represents their sparkling stage – they seem to finally transport us into an affirmative universe. There is a reason why they communicate an extraordinary joy, which broadens into an infinite metonymical chain, from one space and one time to another. But be careful. This initially joyous sensation is soon followed by the task, burdensome for thought, of finding the meaning they conceal. This gives rise to an attempt that is far from painless, because it is "at the cost of an effort that always risks failure."[61] It is true that the sensuous signs are affirmative, but they are still material. They therefore elude that which they both contain and conceal, in other words the ideal essence they embody. Ultimately they also fall into a negative register. Despite the flashes they emit, they are exposed, if not even destined, to failure. Only if they are transposed into the world of art can those signs, all signs, worldly, amorous and sensuous, be reconnected to their elusive meaning, which consists precisely of that lost essence that is almost never found again – before it is lost once more. All this – to fill the void, to make up for the lack, to reverse the negative into its opposite – is possible only by detaching oneself from life in favor of art. When one considers the importance that life, understood as immanence into itself, will acquire in Deleuze's subsequent writings up to his last, which is appropriately entitled *A Life* ..., one cannot avoid observing how here it is subordinated to the sphere of art: "Life does not have the two powers of art; it receives them only by corrupting them and reproduces essence only at the lowest level, to the weakest degree."[62]

The gap – which cannot be bridged in these pages – between art and life consists in the fact that, unlike life, art does not rest on the foundation of involuntary memory but on pure thought as the only faculty capable of grasping essences. One should obviously not take "essence" to mean a metaphysical entity of a Platonic type, but rather something virtual, in other words something real that is not actual. The fact remains that we are dealing with dematerialized entities, which for this reason are different from and not translatable into sensuous ones. This gap qualifies a thought that is opposed not only to science, but also to philosophy and to the friendship implicit in its etymon. Both – philosophy and friendship, the same couple that will return in an affirmative guise in *What Is Philosophy?* – appear to the Deleuze of *Proust and Signs* as devoid of contrastive force with respect to a thought that is in continuous tension with its own "non-": "This is because philosophy, like friendship, is ignorant of the dark regions in which are elaborated the effective forces that act on thought, the determinations that *force* us to think."[63] To the spirit of concord, to the will to agreement of philosophy, thought opposes, in the most political sense of the term, the "mark of necessity,"[64] the inevitability of confrontation, the violence of constraint. For the moment Deleuze has not crossed the threshold of pure affirmation. Only a face-to-face confrontation with the negative allows us to rediscover something of the time lost, snatching it from oblivion: "The *leitmotif* of Time regained is the word *force*: impressions that force us to look, encounters that force us to interpret, expressions that force us to think."[65]

6. It is a widely held opinion that Bergson's influence was decisive in the formation of Deleuze's thought. After all, he is the only author to be present in some fashion throughout his entire work. Before the 1960 lecture course on Bergson's *Creative Evolution*, Deleuze had devoted two texts to him, the first of which, *Bergson's Conception of Difference*, contains *in nuce* all the elements that were to be developed in the 1966 book on Bergsonism – a book that in its turn is a prelude to the elaboration of *Difference and Repetition* and *The Logic of Sense*. At the end of his itinerary, in the 1980s, Deleuze will return to Bergson, placing his categories at the center of two volumes on cinema. Therefore the only phase of Deleuze's journey in which Bergson does not seem to appear, except for a few incidental references, is that of the more directly political writings, which he composed with Guattari. Having said this, it would be wrong to assume that Bergson's *dispositif*, largely taken over by Deleuze, *does not* exert any influence on his political ontology. Quite the contrary: Michael Hardt, in his monograph, *does not* hesitate when he affirms that the Deleuzian interpretation of Bergson "reveals at the heart of an ontological problem, a political problem."[66] Except that, later, he concludes that the social theory delineated at the end of *Bergsonism*, as "suggestive as this brief explanation of a Bergsonian social theory might be, it remains in this final section obscure and undeveloped. Furthermore, the rest of Deleuze's work on Bergson does not serve to support this theory."[67]

For what reason? Why, right when Deleuze attempts, in Bergson's name, the transition from the philosophical to the political level, does his conceptual lexicon seem to jam or reach contradictory conclusions? The answer needs to be looked for in the refusal of the category of negation, which Deleuze derives precisely from the Bergsonian paradigm. We need to establish what we mean by this. Not even in Bergson is the negative totally extinguished. As has been noted by one of his most influential interpreters,[68] the duality between the two senses of life – the scientific and the metaphysical, which is reproduced in the dualisms of space and duration, matter and memory, intelligence and intuition – creates a subtle gap, which in some fashion cuts across all of Bergson's monism, just as the finitude of the *élan vital* excavates a void within its own flow, a flow not devoid of negative accents. This negative, however, never assumes any ontological importance. Behind the negative aspects of existence there is nothing that can be assimilated to, or derived from, nothingness – unlike in Heidegger, who from this point of view is at Bergson's antipodes. For the French philosopher, nothingness is a false problem that masks something positive, which one does not accept or whose existence one does not recognize. In this sense what is designated as "non-being" is born from the addition of a being that has been removed and another being, which takes its place in negative form. Negation is nothing but an affirmation reversed into its opposite through a judgment that is not about the thing, but about another judgment. Whether one affirms it or not, nothing exists but affirmation: "*Negation, therefore, differs from affirmation properly so called in that it is an affirmation of the second degree: it affirms something of an affirmation which itself affirms something of an object.*"[69] Deleuze reiterates Bergson's thesis and takes it to its extreme consequences. Far from distinguishing negation from the negative, he unifies them under the same category of "false problem": "This theme is a central one in Bergson's philosophy: It sums up his critique of the negative and of negation, in all its forms as sources of false problems."[70] This concerns not only the "negative of limitation," which consists in an alleged degradation of things, but also that "of opposition," which Kant substitutes for the former. For Deleuze, both notions emerge from the failed identification of differences of nature, which are confused with differences of degree. This is the central argument that Deleuze derives from Bergsonism on the basis of a paradigm of difference that is opposed or extraneous to the paradigm of negation.

If Bergson's polemical objective is, above all, Kant's critical philosophy, Deleuze's is Hegel's dialectic. The entire essay on difference in Bergson is aimed at delegitimizing the dialectical device, both in its weak Platonic version and in its strong Hegelian one. Both end up substituting difference with the negative. Where Plato, while he does distinguish between the concepts of negation and alterity, resorts to an idea of the good that opens up a diaphragm between the thing and its finality, Hegel determines the thing by means of the difference from what it is not, thus superposing difference and contradiction. In both cases, although with different intensities, the negative settles into the heart of difference, pushing into exteriority with Plato and into abstraction with Hegel. This is precisely what Bergson as interpreted by Deleuze contests. His greatest effort "is aimed at a conception of difference without negation, a conception of difference that does not contain the negative."[71]

But what is a difference without negation, a purely affirmative one? In order to define it, Deleuze, as always relying on Bergson, resorts to the notion of a "virtual," which is opposed to the possible and coincides with the real, of which it constitutes an internal fault. The opposition between the two terms, which Hegel interprets as contradiction, is instead no more than the realization of a virtuality that includes both. The virtual, unlike determination, contradiction, and opposition (all, dialectical modalities), constitutes an entirely positive mode of existence because it identifies being and difference, making a continuous process of differentiation out of being. The virtual ends up coinciding with duration, understood not psychologically, as sometimes occurs in Bergson, but in an ontological sense: the virtual is not other than what is, in its perennially differential form. Deleuze's fundamental intent is that of removing Bergson from any form of psychologism, projecting him firmly into ontology in the form of temporal duration. When Bergson uses the term "unconscious" in his definition of memory, he does so to designate being itself, as expressed by a past that pushes into the present and therefore also into the future.[72]

If, when discussing this principle, Deleuze quotes Kierkegaard, it is obvious that his polemical target is now Heidegger. That is whom he is addressing critically when he removes being from all relations with nothingness: "The idea of nonbeing appears when, instead of grasping the different realities that are indefinitely substituted for one another, we muddle them together in the homogeneity of a Being in general, which can only be opposed to nothingness, be related to nothingness."[73] The shift from the explicit polemics with Hegel to the implicit one with Heidegger is marked by the transition – which occurred in the decade that separates the essay on Bergson from the book on Bergsonism – from the issue of determination to that of multiplicity. For Deleuze, to say that being, instead of differing from beings, is difference itself means to recognize its infinite multiplicity, while to talk about being in general, as Heidegger does, means to presuppose an idea of degradation at the end of which there is nothingness; only the idea of multiplicity allows us to snatch being from the negative, inaugurating that affirmative ontology that first Hegel and then Heidegger always missed.

It is precisely the notion of multiplicity – which is not the same as the Many, the dialectical polar opposite of the One – that allows Deleuze, the interpreter of Bergson, to undertake a first move toward political semantics. According to Hardt, since for Hegel the relationship between the One and the Many is the foundation, by analogy, of a theory of social organization, "[t]o attack the dialectical unity of the One and the Multiple, then, is to attack the primacy of the state in the formation of society, to insist on the real plurality of society."[74] The typological distinction between the two kinds of multiplicity – the quantitative one, founded on differences of degree, and the qualitative one, peculiar to Bergson, which pertains to differences in nature – comes back into play. If, in political terms, the former is a multiplicity of order, the latter is a multiplicity of organization. Generated by one differentiation, it produces a further one, without ever passing through identity. What Deleuze delineates is a process that ceaselessly re-creates the presuppositions for new creation. It is another effect of the substitution of the category of the possible with that of the virtual. If the former acts by exclusion – the real as realization of a part of the possible and the exclusion of another – the virtual, since it is already real, proceeds in the form of continuous proliferation. The creative process – also in a political sense – knows no obstacles because it is preemptively sheltered from the presence of the negative, which has been declared false. At this point, however, a fundamental question arises that puts Deleuze's entire political philosophy into question: if politics coincides with the differential character of being, in what sense can it be defined as such? What distinguishes it from ontology? The elision of the negative performed in Bergson's name exposes one to the risk of impeding the reflection on the political as well.

*

The difficulty of a relation with the political experienced by an author who was always involved with it in other ways finds singular confirmation in this conversation with Antonio Negri in 1990. Despite the bonds between the two interlocutors, one could say that Deleuze never responds in kind to any of the questions directed at him, or that he shifts the answer to an area that differs from the political one, to which they refer. While answering the initial question on the genesis of his interest in the political, Deleuze begins by referring to the problem of institutions, and precisely to the difference between the law as a structured complex of laws and jurisprudence as the creative source of the law itself. Only later, around 1968, will Deleuze state he has undertaken "a sort of move into politics."[75] But it is precisely the unsatisfactory denouement of 1968 – which is related to a "minority becoming" and a "nomadic thought [that] always takes the temporal form of instantaneous counteractualization"[76] – that will lead to his fundamental uncertainty about the political, an uncertainty in its turn related to Negri's description in the previous quotation. Deleuze points to an insufficiency of the historical process, incapable of attaining the level of "becoming," as constituting the principal source of this uncertainty. While history limits itself to constituting the negative conditions that make it possible, only becoming, frequently in an unexpected manner, produces the event, which is precisely what May 1968 was. The fact that the outcome was disappointing in the eyes of its protagonists follows from an inadequacy of historical dynamics with respect to the creative power of becoming. One should not confuse – Deleuze states – "two different things, the way revolutions turn out historically and people's revolutionary becoming."[77]

And yet, after this distancing from history made under the aegis of Nietzsche's *Untimely Meditations*, when answering Negri's next question about the political philosophy of *A Thousand Plateaus*, Deleuze responds that both he and Guattari do not believe in a political philosophy that does not "turn on the analysis of capitalism and the ways it has developed"[78] – therefore one that does not refer to a real historical process. After this he points to the three main vectors of *A Thousand Plateaus* as being the lines of escape, the class minorities, and the war machine. The tone, melancholic or tragic, that Negri detects, not without reason, in the philosopher's words derives from the fact that under capitalism there are no means to preserve or produce specifically those becomings that alone could remove us from capitalism's pervasiveness. Hence the impossibility of a political initiative that will not be reduced to pure minority becoming. In response to Negri's next question, namely whether this becoming can ever become majoritarian, Deleuze answers that the minority cannot adopt the model that it intends to fight, if it wants to remain creative. What is important is for minorities to engage in presenting their opinions once again, in taking the floor again – not in support of the current communication, which is functional to the control of society, but a non-communicative floor, capable of breaking or weakening that control. Negri's last question, on the possible forms of political subjectivation, also remains basically without any response – or, better, is shifted onto a plane that it is difficult to define as political: "One might equally well speak of new kinds of event, rather than processes of subjectification: events that *cannot* be explained by the situations that give rise to them, or into which they lead."[79]

*

7. A new breach toward the political, after the impasse caused by Deleuze's conversion to Bergsonism, is opened by the 1968 book on Spinoza. This book is directly connected to the one on Nietzsche and sort of constitutes its enriched and modified continuation, although it does not entail the disappearance of that affirmative fold that had matured during his encounter with Bergson. Quite the contrary, this fold by now constitutes the distinctive bent of all of Deleuze's philosophy, even though there is some variation of emphasis as

regards the determination of the negative, which in its turn is destined to be reflected in the definition of the political. Starting from its title, the book on Spinoza revisits a category – that of "expression" – already used, although differently, in *Proust and Signs*. The concept of "expression" is introduced into the philosophical tradition by Spinoza and Leibniz in a non-superimposable manner. Actually, as Deleuze himself argues, Neoplatonism had already made the topic of the expressiveness of the real into an issue, but Spinoza's closest point of reference is Duns Scotus. To understand his importance, we must dwell on the shift he had introduced vis-à-vis both the negative theology of the Neoplatonists and the theology, at least partly positive, of Thomas Aquinas. While the former implies the idea of emanation, the latter reasons in terms of analogy. Neither of the two conceptions – neither the emanative one associated with negation nor the analogical one tied to affirmation – is followed by Spinoza, because both think of God's nature from the point of view of properties such as goodness, omniscience, omnipotence instead of thinking of his attributes. While properties can at best provide a normative framework of a moral kind, it is only the reference to attributes that entails an affirmative ontology, since it burns its bridges with negation. The attributes as such – not only those of thought and extension, the only ones we can actually perceive – cannot either negate or be negated, because they are expressive of substance. It is from them, and only from them, that we acquire that idea of the univocity of being that Scotus opposes to the negative emanation of the Neoplatonists and to the analogical affirmation of the Thomists. But, Deleuze observes, Scotus continues to remain a theologian and is therefore led to neutralize the univocal character of being within the framework of a creationist principle. If created, being has its cause outside of itself and cannot therefore be perfectly determined within its own concept, as required by Spinoza's system. It is only in the latter that life, in other words being in its perfect expressivity, is absolutely affirmed: "a logic of pure affirmation, of unlimited quality, and thus of the unconditional totality that possesses all qualities; a logic, that is, of the absolute."[80]

And what about politics? In this perspective, to find a passage toward it, one needs to pass through the category of "potential," which is implicit in that of "being." Since the latter, according to the scholastic definition that Spinoza adopts as his own, is essentially productive, this means that the potential becomes its constitutive form. To be and to produce are one and the same thing. For this very reason, the potential to know presupposes that of existence instead of logically preceding it. The two potentials are superimposed in the Spinozist ontology, as is stated repeatedly both in the *Short Treatise* and in the *Treatise on the Emendation of the Intellect* – as well as in a letter to Jelles in which he polemicizes with Descartes: "'The power of thought to think or to comprehend things is no greater than the power of Nature to be and to act.' This is a clear and true axiom, whence the existence of God follows most clearly and forcefully from the idea of him."[81]

This – the perfect parallelism between the two types of potential – assumes an even greater importance in the second book of the *Ethics*, only here the affirmation of the potential of existence is not forced to pass through the concept of God but is expressed in the immanence of existence. That which has the power (in the sense of potential) of self-preservation *does not* need any other cause in order to exist. This is true also of a finite entity like a human being who, even though s/he depends on an external cause, is an integral part of it and therefore participates in the same potential ontologically. The Spinozist conception of being, as reconstructed by Deleuze, therefore assumes an intrinsically political connotation already in this instance; but it simultaneously ends up conferring an immediately ontological qualification to the political, which makes it difficult to articulate it in its specific quality. Since being is in and of itself political, because it is intrinsically productive of potential, any definition of the political in a specific sense ends up being on the one hand redundant and on the other contradictory, given the basic assumption that absorbs it into being. If being is in and of itself political, how can one think of a specifically characterized activity as politics?

This does not prevent a series of attempts to define it undertaken by Deleuze as a reader of Spinoza. The first is constituted by the centrality of the body, unbound from the traditional primacy of the mind and understood according to its autonomous material grain. Seen from this point of view, Spinoza's celebrated passage about a body's capabilities can be interpreted in a directly political sense. It is precisely by means of the encounters, happy or unhappy, between bodies that it is possible to pass from ontology to politics or, more precisely, to grasp the intrinsically political tone of ontology. To do so, one needs to substitute the traditional dialectics between potency and act with the dialectics of active and passive affections. While the bodily need of being affected by something is a given, one can be affected in an active or passive form: in the first case, by expressing the adequate ideas of which we ourselves are the cause, in the second by assuming inadequate ideas that originated outside us: "Therefore our mind ... insofar as it has adequate ideas, is necessarily active – which is the first point. ... therefore ... insofar as the mind has inadequate ideas, it is necessarily passive – which was the second point."[82] The ethical questioning par excellence refers to this alternative between activity and passivity. It is not easy to come up with a specific answer to it, because the relationship between active and passive affections rests on the contradictory definition of the negative, which is simultaneously affirmed and negated. On the one hand all human affections prove to be passive, given that, being finite, human beings have only inadequate ideas. On the other, at the same time, passive affections, unreal in themselves, exist only at the level of the imaginary – not of the real. From this second point of view, it would seem that we need to conclude that only active affections exist, since passive ones are nothing more than our erroneous projection of the former. Deleuze attempts to solve this amphibology by means of the same distinction between actions and reactions he already employed in the book on Nietzsche. Like these, affections are also forces, in one case active and in the other passive. An inversely proportional relationship exists between them – the more intense the former, the less so the latter, and vice-versa. However, only the active forces possess an effective consistency, while the passive ones are constituted by nothing but the absence or the limitation of the former. And yet, already at this point, a difference in the contrastive dynamics that had been theorized in *Nietzsche* can be registered. The conflict, which in that case exhibited a decidedly political force, is now reduced to a disjunction that does not translate into a real collision, because one of the poles – the passive one – is nothing but the opaque reflection of the reality of the former, the only one capable of positively fulfilling the capacity of being affected.

The origins of this incongruence, which precludes a more clearly political outcome of the Deleuze–Spinoza discourse, reside in the reduction of the negative to a simple effect of the absence of affirmation. The paradigm of disjunction is contained and does not reach the intensity of what, in *Nietzsche*, still appeared as a clash of adversarial forces, resolved in that case by a historical victory of the reactive forces. Within a philosophy of absolute affirmation, which is how Spinoza is interpreted using Bergson as a filter, negation takes on a purely phantasmatic trait, as is clear from the handling of the problem of evil. Evil, like passive and sad affections, is but the result of the limitations of our power to act. Even destruction, whether endured or carried out, is nothing more than the decomposition of a positive relationship. It is true that such a conception differs from those of the rationalists who, from Plato to Leibniz, allowed the good to account for all of reality. For Spinoza, there is neither good nor evil in nature. They only acquire meaning in relation to our greater or lesser power to act. This means that "[e]vil is nothing, being in no way expressive. Above all, it expresses nothing. It expresses no law of composition, no composition of relations."[83]

If one defines evil in this way and it does not constitute a real force, to be opposed with an equal and contrary force, why can't we live in the state of nature, as Spinoza admits when theorizing the need for a political state? If, contrary to the transcendence of the law, the right coincides with the potential contained in each body or, even more, with the collective potential expressed by the multitude, what is the purpose of a sovereign placed both above the one and above the other? Spinoza's sovereign certainly differs from the one theorized by Hobbes, because he is not a third party who benefits from a contract of subjection stipulated by other human beings, who thereby become his subjects. Spinoza's sovereign is one with the collective body that expresses him and is formed by the union of the bodies and minds of a multitude that is driven to pursue reason and to produce affections of joy. But why should those who entrust themselves to the *dispositif* of the sovereign conform to such positive behaviors? Either one or the other is true: either they are inclined to do so naturally – but Spinoza denies this, underscoring the extreme rarity of naturally affirmative affections – or they are constrained to do so by a sovereign order, in this case necessarily a transcendent one. The unresolved problem, to which neither Spinoza nor Deleuze manages to provide a convincing answer, remains that of a political ontology marked by the complete identity of the two terms – the political and being. If being is in and of itself political, and if the political is no more than the conscious assumption of the affirmative nature of being, what is the use of the comparison and conflict between different types of political organization?

*

The same question should be addressed to the person who, more than anyone else, has attempted to give Deleuze's philosophy a political content, and who also followed a path that went through Spinoza. In the preface to the French edition of *The Savage Anomaly* by Antonio Negri – that is whom I am referring to – Deleuze identifies its central category in the immediacy of production: "In Spinoza, the forces are inseparable from a spontaneousness and a productivity that make possible their development without mediation, in other words their *composition*."[84] What allows for the immediate development of the productive forces, in Spinoza's case, is the exceptional nature of Holland in his times, determined by "a market as spontaneousness of the productive forces or a capitalism as an unmediated form of the socialization of forces."[85] To the sovereign regime as theorized by the line of philosophers that goes from Hobbes to Hegel, Spinoza builds an ontological and political alternative: a power that needs no power to create society. This is the presupposition of the theory of power that Negri will put forward some years later, in a form that translates Deleuze's ontology into political language. Innervating it with the social and vital contents of the Marxian category of "living labor," Negri makes constituent power into the pivot of a political theory that is directly rooted in ontological production. By removing it from its various juridical formulations, he provides the concept with an important ontologico-political dimension, relying on a heretical line that, passing through Spinoza, connects Machiavelli with Marx. If it is Spinoza who already grasps the ontological character of the political, this is all the more the case today, when "this ontological priority is absolute, because ontology has absorbed the political."[86] That which in a pre-capitalist world could appear to be a utopia, is fully realized today since cognitive capitalism generates the conditions of its own overcoming all on its own. So, via the direct transfer of the category of "production" from the economic to the ontological sphere, the political can do without an institutionally organized form, because it is immediately expressed by the constitutive power of social being. Since it is conditioned by nothing other than its own internal development, the creation of social being requires no institutions, which would only encage the process within a series of conservative mediations brought about by the powers that are being actualized.

As one can see, this is another formulation of the theory of acceleration. Nothing remains for the political (which already inheres in the intrinsic productivity of social being) to do but to accelerate an objective process that is already underway. This is how Negri resolves the problem of a missing articulation between the political and ontological, which was already present in Deleuze, via the integral incorporation of the former within the latter. But has it really been solved? Or brought to a level of further antinomy? In addition to the difficulty, which we already examined, of differentiating constituent and sovereign power, the more fundamental question concerns the indistinct profile of a political subjectivity that is directly inferred from the ontological dimension. Negri and Michael Hardt gave it the name "multitude." But how can one give it political consistency? Laclau pronounces a very clear verdict in this regard: within the theoretical framework assembled by Negri, "[w]hat is totally lacking in *Empire* is a theory of *articulation*, without which politics is unthinkable."[87] This impossibility is based on the closed short-circuit between capitalism's social production and the productive forces by which it itself is produced. From a theoretical point of view, Negri's impasse arises, as it did already in Deleuze, from an entirely affirmative conception of social power, which excludes the negative from the political horizon. As in the case of Marx's proletariat, the multitude is a political subject that is entirely immanent to the capitalist social order. If Laclau can argue, simplifying somewhat, that in Marx "the universality of the revolutionary subject entails the end of politics,"[88] a similar risk is also involved in Negri's multitude. What is missing, within a political ontology of absolute immanence, is not the transcendence of power, but a politically articulated theory of conflict. In its absence, neither the multitude nor its imperial enemy, from which it is generated in contradictory fashion, exhibit the historical determination without which the political loses its characteristics.

*

8. *The Logic of Sense*, far from being a sort of appendix to *Difference and Repetition*, represents instead a sort of textual bridge, within Deleuze's oeuvre, between its most theoretical portion and the part dedicated to the political; this part is represented by the two volumes of *Capitalism and Schizophrenia*, which he wrote with Guattari. We also know, given the previous discussion, that this subdivision does not account for a deeper antinomy, on the basis of which, precisely at the moment in which the Deleuzian ontology develops a more explicitly political character, it seems to shift to a possibly depoliticizing outcome. As I have stated repeatedly, if being, in its differential structure, is already in and of itself political, politics as a specific activity ends up being dissolved into an ontological horizon of pure affirmation. At the conceptual level, this is a consequence of the disappearing tension with the negative, which in its turn is due to the gradual prevailing of the Bergsonian paradigm over the influence of Hume, Spinoza, and Nietzsche. This paradigmatic transition will never develop to reach the clarity of a definitive turning point but seems instead to outline a tendency that is never taken to its ultimate conclusion. *The Logic of Sense*, compared to this affirmative dynamics, represents an element of resistance or of internal distancing that is destined to reemerge, with ambivalent effects, in subsequent texts as well.

The point at which the essay seems to split into two parts difficult to recompose is the thirteenth "series" – as the author calls the subdivisions that articulate the text – entitled "The Schizophrenic and the Little Girl." Up to that point Deleuze continued the anti-metaphysical project he had started in his previous writings. The reversal of the Platonic primacy of the original and the copy in relation to the simulacrum is functional to the centrality that the logic of sense acquires in relation to the logic of truth. Rather than being limited to a formal role, sense embodies the differential process of being in all its dimensions – gnoseological, ethical, and practical. Ideas, actions, passions, bodies: seen from this point of view, they all become machines for the production of sense, disarticulated from the individual consciousness of subjects and, taken as a whole, expressive of a pre-individual and impersonal transcendental field. What most characterizes the circulation of sense, however, is its superficial character, which as such is opposed to any interior depth. It is a circulation that involves what the Stoics defined as "incorporeal" elements, situated in a sphere of being that differs from that of bodies and things. As Émile Bréhier noted in his classic monograph, the Stoic view distinguishes between "on the one hand a profound and real being, force; on the other, the level of facts that occur on the surface of being and constitute an infinite multiplicity of incorporeal beings."[89] The entirety of *The Logic of Sense* is placed at this other level. Sense expresses itself in verbal forms of an impersonal nature – "to grow," "to live," "to blush," "to green" – which translate, in the infinitive mode, the uninterrupted becoming of events rather than the states of things or of subjective entities. If the time onto which they are grafted is not the linear time of *chronos* but the sagittal time of the *aiōn*, the sphere in which they manifest is language. It is language that gives them a voice, making them surface from the depth(s) – not abolished, but instead transformed into a new surface, which underlies the first. All one needs to do is let oneself slide from one surface to the next, to find oneself on the other side of the sheet of paper. In this fashion, connected by the event that traverses them, the two surfaces converge into a single plane of consistency, which is how Deleuze designates what will later become the plane of immanence in *The Logic of Sense*.

The writer Lewis Carroll is the person who used this recursive mechanism of language with the greatest mastery, thereby becoming a paradoxical successor of the Stoics. In *Alice* and in *Through the Looking Glass* he basically deals with nothing other than events that are not reducible to persons or things, because they are placed on a horizontal plane with no depth, which proceeds via lateral movements, transforming depth into width. Events, like crystals, join together on the frame's margins, succeeding one another chaotically, never once raising the curtain of the visible. In this manner each meaning is converted into its own opposite, via a non-sense that confirms it precisely by contradicting it – as happens to Alice, who simultaneously grows and decreases in size. As in structuralism, at the source or origin of each meaning (sense) there is always a non-meaning (non-sense). We should not think of this as a lack of sense, as understood by the philosophy of the absurd for instance, but rather as the "non" of sense. In a manner analogous to Joyce's in *Finnegans Wake*, Carroll invents some portmanteau words that connect two series, intersecting them – for example "to eat" and "to speak" – and the series are destined to branch out into numerous others. This is not a matter of words with multiple meanings, but precisely of the non-sense that traverses the series, articulating the words among themselves.

Suddenly, however, having arrived at the thirteenth series, something unexpected occurs that upsets the equilibrium of the whole.[90] Carroll intersects Artaud, colliding with his modality of writing. Alice is confronted by an event she is not able to sustain. The strange binomial represented by "The Schizophrenic and the Little Girl" disarticulates the univocity of the tale, exposing it to a lacerating alterity. The "and" that unites them immediately appears to be different from the conjunctions that, up to that point, had favored the free circulation of sense. The series' *dispositif* of production jams when confronted by a presence that differs from the others. The border that divides them is overrun by an unmanageable excess. The schizophrenic vortex drags one into depths from which it is not possible to surface again. The skin is ripped apart by the resurgence of a deep body that perforates its surface. Non-sense loses its affirmative role of creator of sense, and becomes its pure destruction.

Deleuze reminds us that this encounter, this clash between Artaud and Carroll, has occurred twice. The first time was when Artaud attempted a translation of *Humpty Dumpty*. Initially Artaud seemed to faithfully follow Carroll, conforming to his way of proceeding. Then, starting with the third verse, he introduced a slippage, which was followed by a collapse of sense. Now everything changes. Carroll's portmanteaus become deformed, as if shaken by a syncope that drags them into another language and another world: this is the harsh and violent world of schizophrenia. The bodies' depth sucks the superficial crust into its vortex. At this point, as Artaud writes in a letter from Rodez, distance becomes incommensurable. Carroll now appears more like a small pervert who *does not* have the courage to go all the way and to stay there: he "holds onto the establishment of a surface language, and who [Lewis Carroll] has not felt the real problem of language in depth – namely the schizophrenic problem of suffering, of death, and of life."[91] So what looked like an extraordinary familiarity turns out to be an irredeemable extraneousness. The two series of bottom and surface, initially adherent to each other, lose all contact and separate into a radical opposition. If the girl always moves on the edge, the schizophrenic plumbs the depths. Carroll's mirror is shattered to smithereens, broken by the bodies' spasmodic suffering. Bousquet's wound event, transposed into the flesh of Artaud, begins to bleed and soon floods the entire scenario. The organism decomposes into a thousand pieces, dragged along by even more maleficent fluids.

That which suddenly returns to occupy the field – of Artaud but, through him, of Deleuze – is the negative, which looked as if it had been expelled from Carroll's surface. A vertical flow penetrates into the horizontality of sense and shreds it, interrupting the proliferation of differences. The Two breaks the univocity of being into an uncontainable bipolarity:

> The duality of the schizophrenic word has not been adequately noted: it comprises the passion-word, which explodes into *wounding* phonetic values, and the action-word, which welds inarticulate *tonic* values. These two words are developed in relation to the duality of the body, fragmented body and body without organs. They refer to two theaters, the theater of terror or passion and the theater of cruelty, which is by its essence active. They refer to two types of nonsense, passive and active: the nonsense of the word devoid of sense, which is decomposed into phonetic elements, and the nonsense of tonic elements, which form a word incapable of being decomposed and no less devoid of sense.[92]

This is the decisive point. Deleuze's entire lexicon folds in a different direction, given how it had been constituting itself, from his first works to *Difference and Repetition*. The univocity of being itself, supported by the plane of consistency, is endangered by this sudden resumption of the negative, expressed by the divergent figure of the Two. The body without organs around which the two tomes of *Capitalism and Schizophrenia* will revolve seems traversed by it from side to side. It configures two polarities, one positive and one negative, incapable of joining together in a single dimension. Carroll and Artaud are much more than two conceptual characters. They represent antagonistic polarities that are destined to clash in radical conflict. And it is here, precisely along this line of fire, that, perhaps for the last time, a conflict between adverse sides flares up again, in a form that not only gives space to the negative pole but seems to actually award it primacy: "For all that, Carroll and Artaud do not encounter one another; only the commentator may change dimensions, and that is his greatest weakness, the sign that he inhabits no dimension at all. We would not give a page of Artaud for all of Carroll."[93]

9. This turning point in Deleuze's itinerary comes with the *Anti-Oedipus*. What determines it is, on the one side, the events that follow 1968, on the other, the encounter with Guattari; in the words of the latter, these two join into a single event of a political nature:

> This collaboration is not the product of a simple meeting of two individuals. Aside from a variety of circumstances, there was a whole political context that led up to it. Initially, it was less of a question of our pooling our knowledge than an accumulation of our uncertainties; we were confused about the turn of events after May '68.[94]

In that period everything seemed to naturally adopt a political tone: "We were under the impression of engaging in politics even when we were talking about music, trees or faces."[95] But, precisely for this reason, the definition of the "political" expands to such a degree as to lose all specificity. Instead of an arena for comparison, or confrontation, between different interests, it ends up coinciding with the plane, defined as that of immanence, of the deployment of desire and its infinite concatenations – not in the weak sense that desire can drive toward revolution but in the more extreme sense that it is itself revolution:

> Desire is not restricted to the privileged; neither is it restricted to the success of a revolution once it has occurred. It is in itself an immanent revolutionary process. *It is constructivist, not at all spontaneist.* Since every assemblage is collective, is itself a collective, it is indeed true that every desire is the affair of the people, or an affair of the masses, a molecular affair.[96]

In order to grasp the extent, and the presuppositions, of this paradigmatic transition, one needs to return to the concept of the body, as elaborated in *The Logic of Sense*. As we saw, starting from Artaud's schizophrenic entry onto the scene, the body's depth emerged as the opposite of Carroll's horizontal surface, part of an irreconcilable antithesis. It is precisely this antithesis that is removed from the *Anti-Oedipus*, as Deleuze himself admits, in an almost brusque fashion, while replying to a question in an interview: "I've undergone a change. The surface-depth opposition no longer concerns me. What interests me now is the relationship between a full body, a body without organs, and flows that migrate."[97] If one considers that that contrast, which has now been removed, was used to preserve a negative nucleus within a horizon that tended to expel it, one begins to draw closer to the heart of the problem. The outcome of the conceptual transition from *The Logic* to *Anti-Oedipus* is on the one hand the extreme semantic broadening of political language, on the other its ensuing loss of specificity. The idea that the political coincides with the affirmative drive of desire, while it does attribute a constituent character to desire, also removes a specific quality from the political, which is identified with the becoming of being. The result is that Deleuze drives the paradigm of political ontology to such a level of integration as to render the two terms – "being" and "political" – reciprocally reversible within the intensity of a desire that incorporates them both. It is this reversibility that fills the distance that, in Artaud's broken semantics, still separated out the depth of bodies in relation to the surface of language. With the closing of this gap, the line of the political no longer passes through the conflictual tension of two contrasting poles, but rather through their superposition at a single level. But, deprived of any point of attrition, the political loses the density of its own dimension. So the transformation of the battered body of *The Logic of Sense* into the glorious body of the *Anti-Oedipus* represents, simultaneously, the implosion and the explosion of a political vector that has become so pervasive as to lose its own contours.

This reconversion, which was at the center of the 1972 work, undergoes a double categorial shift within the concept of "desire" itself. The first, a destructive one, is aimed at discharging it of all those representations that psychoanalysis, both Freudian and Lacanian, had burdened it with: "Destroy, destroy. The task of schizoanalysis goes by way of destruction – a whole scouring of the unconscious, a complete curettage. Destroy Oedipus, the illusion of the ego, the puppet of the superego, guilt, the law, castration."[98]

The entire network that psychoanalysis wove around desire suddenly gives way, faced with its intrinsic productive potential. Far from constituting a subjective, mental, psychic dimension, it is a real machine because productive of reality. Similarly, schizophrenia is not an individual condition, much less a disease, but rather the general form of desire, freed from all external constraints and returned to the affirmative activity of its machines. These, taken together, form an uninterrupted chain, in which each production is grafted onto the preceding, in a continuous alternation of flows and breaks. In other words what the machine produces is nothing more than production. It is true that the body without organs is unproductive in and of itself, but precisely because it constitutes the locus of all production: "The full body without organs belongs to the realm of antiproduction; but yet another characteristic of the connective or productive synthesis is the fact that it couples production with antiproduction, with an element of antiproduction."[99] After all, the contrast remarked upon by Deleuze and Guattari, between a body without organs and desiring machines, is only apparent. It is true that, in its paranoid modality, the body without organs opposes its undifferentiated flow to the machines; but, on its schizophrenic side, it attracts them to itself, identifying with them, since what the body refuses is not the organs, but the principle of the organism.

The second element that characterizes desire is its immediately social character. Although on occasion Deleuze and Guattari speak of parallelism, the two orders, of society and desire, flow along the same plane. One cannot imagine either that one acts on the other – as imagined, in its various versions, by Freudian Marxism – or that a simply metaphorical connection exists between them. One is really dealing with the same flow. Also, when observed from this angle, the influence of Bergson – for whom there is but a single duration, articulated by variable intensities – ends up prevailing over Spinoza's, who, although he relates them to a single substance, preserves the duality that exists between the attributes of thought and extension. Deleuze and Guattari proceed to an integral socialization of desire, in the sense that one *does not* ever desire a single object, but a set whose multiple aspects are interconnected. But it is desire itself, like delirium, that always has a social dimension – and therefore also a historical and political one. Hence the indiscernibility of political and libidinal economies: the libido impacts the entire sociopolitical body, translating it into its own concatenations, as one can conclude particularly on the basis of the Schreber affair. The fact that two different regimes exist – the molar, of a social nature, and the molecular, of an individual nature – should not conceal the ultimate identity of their respective natures. Taken together, they produce an entirely affirmative, vital, salutary dynamic – one which goes well beyond the "small health" promised by psychoanalytical *dispositifs*, seems rather to coincide with the "great health" of Nietzsche, and is placed at the point of contact between body without organs and desiring machines.

But if this is the case, then, once all forms of neurosis have been abolished and the resulting ontogenetic process is fully affirmative, how can the recurring blockages that interrupt it, inverting its direction, be explained? Where do the negative powers that open the crevasses in the surface of history, periodically sucking it into the depths, emerge from? Deleuze's answer relies on two subtly colliding arguments, in which it is possible to recognize a never fully resolved oscillation on the issue of the negative. On the one hand they would seem to arise from the neurotic mechanisms in which we encage our desire, interrupting its flow by means of inhibiting devices – which therefore need to be removed, defused, destroyed. This is the more Bergsonian side of Deleuze's discourse, on whose basis the negative is no more than a subjective error to be corrected, because extraneous to the objectively affirmative flow of the real. A second answer, however, is added to this first one, one that is intertwined with it and that complicates and to some degree contradicts what we have said so far. We are talking about the self-repressive nature of desire itself.[100] Since there is nothing external to it, even that which contradicts it must arise within it: it cannot be something that would transcend the plane of immanence but must be one of its internal folds:

> We do not therefore speak of a dualism between two kinds of "things," but of a multiplicity of dimensions, of lines and directions in the heart of an assemblage. To the question "How can desire desire its own repression, how can it desire its slavery?" we reply that the powers which crush desire, or which subjugate it, themselves already form part of assemblages of desire.[101]

As history demonstrates, ancient and recent catastrophes, fascism in all its macro- and micrological variants included, do not derive from the masses' being deceived by someone else, but from a perverse deviation of their own desire. At its origin Deleuze and Guattari place that will to serve that La Boétie spoke about, the surprising tendency of humans, also noted by Spinoza, to fight for their own servitude as if it were their salvation. This is the unconscious desire for fascism described by Wilhelm Reich; but, while the authors of *Anti-Oedipus* do credit Reich for his discovery, they criticize him for still resorting to psychoanalysis to explain the negative and for not realizing that desire and the field of the social are actually coextensive. For Deleuze and Guattari instead, delirium – which is itself divided between a paranoid–fascistizing pole and a schizophrenic–revolutionary one – is the matrix for all social investment. This – this delirious interpretation of all of history – has a dual consequence: on the one hand, a politicization of psychiatry that goes well beyond the anti-psychiatry of Laing and Cooper, liberating all the flows of schizoid desire; on the other, a psychiatrization of the political that, by unifying opposing fronts, zeroes out their antagonistic potential. The only possible form of politics, in this case, is that of following, or enlarging, the escape lines that open up in all social formations. If desire is revolutionary in itself, the moment it reverses its direction into a paranoid form, the revolution will not be able to have any other figure but that of escape:

> Good people say we must not flee, that to escape is not good, that it *is not* effective, and that one must work for reforms. But the revolutionary knows that escape is revolutionary – *withdrawal, freaks* – provided one sweeps away the social cover on leaving, or causes a piece of the system to get lost in the shuffle.[102]

10. It is fair to state that, in *Anti-Oedipus*, the space in which politics can play out is the one contained between the two terms that provide the work's subtitle – "capitalism" and "schizophrenia." The farther apart these terms are, the more that space increases; the closer they are together, the more it narrows, to the point of disappearing once capitalism and schizophrenia end up overlapping. The authors actually never do consider them as separate poles, one external to the other, but rather as two extremes of a single segment that includes both of them. Although they never completely coincide, schizophrenia and capitalism intrinsically belong to each other, to the extent that one can be seen as the limit of the other. While it is true that this limit is defined by Deleuze as "external," one needs to come to an understanding about the meaning of the term: a limit, if it has an external side, also has an internal one. Otherwise, instead of limit, one would have to talk about an alterity that exceeds the delimited space. But it is precisely this possibility – of excess or transcendence – that is excluded as a matter of principle from the plane of immanence theorized by Deleuze and Guattari. As such, this plane cannot but include both capitalism and schizophrenia within a shared horizon, making the former a contradictory product of the latter. The fact that schizophrenia threatens to lead to capitalism's implosion does not mean that this eventuality, though it has never actually occurred, could develop only from within the capitalist horizon – which thus remains the only space, as well as the only time, in which even its eventual collapse would be situated.

It is certainly no accident that the book's third dissertation, "Savages, Barbarians and Civilized Men," is inaugurated by this recognition of the "universal" character of capitalism. Following what Marx had argued with regard to humans and monkeys, accepting this premise opens up the only lookout point from which it is possible to observe the entire course of the previous history, endowing it with meaning: "Hence it is correct to retrospectively understand all history in the light of capitalism, provided that the rules formulated by Marx are followed exactly."[103] In other words one is admitting the absolutely contingent and discontinuous nature of that history, inclusive not only of its own limit, but also of the possibility of its own end. Provided, precisely, that such a limit, and also such an end, remain their *own* – internal to what they are destroying. Deleuze and Guattari argue along similar lines also with respect to social classes, as compared to the orders, ranks and castes that preceded them. In pre-capitalist formations, in fact, there are elements present that anticipate those that subsequently will become out-and-out classes. For these classes, too, the authors use the term "negative," as they previously had for capitalism – negative not in the sense of something that opposes something else from the outside, but rather like in the negative of a photograph, which preserves the original imprint of what is represented in it. The *reductio ad unum* [reduction to one] that this procedure entails, and that is fully in line with the univocity of being Deleuze is arguing for, also obtains for these very social classes under capitalism that can be reduced to a single one, the bourgeois; and it is inside this class that all the others garner visibility:

> Classes are *the* negative of castes and statuses; classes are orders, castes and statuses that have been decoded. To reread history through the class struggle is to read it in terms of the bourgeoisie as the decoding and decoded class. It is the *only* class as such, inasmuch as it leads the struggle against codes, and merges with the generalized decoding of flows. In this capacity it is sufficient to fill the capitalist field of immanence.[104]

Deleuze and Guattari consequently place the political on a single horizontal plane: only one class moves inside it, and it is impossible to oppose any "negative" alterity to it, since only capitalism and the bourgeoisie are negative in the sense previously explained. Before we ask ourselves about the outcome of this story, however, we need to take a step back in order to reconstruct those transitions that, according to these authors' analysis, have led to this plane. I am referring to the two mega machines that, from a genetic point of view, precede the capitalist one; and, in its turn, the capitalist machine explains these two retrospectively, from a paradigmatic point of view. The first one is the primitive territorial machine, which is tied to and installed on the earth, to be understood as a unique and indivisible entity in which desire is deployed in its savage state. Its principal function is that of codifying the flows of desire, impacting organs and engraving bodies, according to the sacrificial logic that the Nietzsche of *The Genealogy of Morals* and the Kafka of *The Penal Colony* had described with insuperable precision. What it deploys is a veritable theater of cruelty that, when engraving the flesh, enacts a procedure that Nietzsche defines as a "*technique of mnemonics*": "'A thing must be burnt in so that it stays in memory: only something that continues to *hurt* stays in memory.'"[105] The social structure of the savage territorial machine is articulated through indirect lines of filiation as well as through horizontal alliances, organized according to the economic *dispositif* of debt. This is what codifies the flows of desire into an order expressed by the triangular relationship of the voice that speaks, the inscribed body and the gaze that enjoys the pain inflicted on others' flesh.

As acute as this pain may be in the forms that are present in the infinite dramaturgies of public torment, it does not equal the pain imposed by the very harsh discipline of the second territorial machine, barbaric and despotic, which succeeds the first. This second machine differs from the previous one, since it leads to a process of deterritorialization that, in addition to subdividing peoples, subdivides the earth itself, previously undivided, in conformity with imperial or state cartographies. Nietzsche is the author who describes the advent, sudden and unstoppable, of these "founders of states" who, like an irresistible wave, descend on the primitive territorial structure: "they come like fate, without cause, reason, consideration or pretext, they appear just like lightning appears, too terrible, sudden, convincing and 'other' even to be hated."[106] Based this time on direct filiation along a line of descent that goes from god to despot and from despot to heir, the despotic machine proceeds following a double register of destruction and construction: on the one hand it destroys the system of horizontal alliances of the savage socius, on the other it incorporates its principle of debt, applying it to all of existence. What changes in relation to the previous regime is the symbolic center of gravity, which has shifted from the undifferentiated body of the earth to the unique body of the despot, installed at the apex of the imperial pyramid. When contrasted with the codification of the savage territorial regime, as practiced on living bodies, the new machine produces a sort of supercodification that, while it does not exclude the former, redoubles it and extends it to the entire government of humans and things. The dual procedure of fixation of residences and abolition of interpersonal debt serves as a guarantee against the threat of revolutionary deterritorialization, which is outlined at the external confines of the barbaric formation. The despotic regime's greatest fear is an incipient transformation, announced by the advent of the decoded flows of the market and commerce. Against these, imperial power hands itself down, embalming the cadaveric figures that lead it, as Kafka tells us inimitably in *The Great Wall of China*: "Long-dead emperors are set on the throne in our villages, and one that only lives on in song recently had a proclamation of his read out by the priest before the altar."[107]

Too late. By now the largely deterritorialized third machine of capitalism submerges the despotic state with the fluidity of its decoded movements. For this machine to stabilize, it is necessary that the flows of property, money, and workers intersect within the absolute singularity of a contingency that has successfully become a universal principle. The capitalist machine, far from negating the *dispositif* of the state, also makes it its own, functionalizing it for its own economic purposes, as had already occurred in the case of barbarians and savages. This fact attests to the transhistorical permanence of a latent paradigm, that of the *Urstaat* [original state], which both precedes and goes beyond the despotic regime, representing itself, obviously in a modified fashion, in each social formation, including the one that seems to overcome it but is actually absorbing its regulatory effect(s) within its own unregulated order. This is how the capitalist machine can block the otherwise inevitable drift toward total deterritorialization that would consign it to schizophrenia. Returning to what I was saying at the beginning, schizophrenia constitutes its extreme limit, internal or external depending on the perspective from which one looks at it. And yet never as on this point – the role as well as the meaning of "limit" – does Deleuze and Guattari's discourse seem to oscillate, without ever finding a definite center of gravity. Capitalism has schizophrenia as its external limit; as for its internal limit, this is what it itself activates in order to preserve axiomatic control over the flows that run through it from side to side. At the same time, it functions by pushing the first limit continuously forward while simultaneously expanding the latter on an increasingly vast scale. This is how it ends up acquiring the limits it does not have and losing those it does:

> Concerning capitalism, we maintain that it both does and does not have an exterior limit: it has an exterior limit that is schizophrenia,

> that is, the absolute decoding of the flows but it functions only by pushing back and exorcising the limit. And it also has, yet does not have, interior limits: it has interior limits under the specific conditions of capitalist production and circulation, that is, in capital itself, but it functions only by reproducing and widening these limits on an always vaster scale.[108]

Such an ambivalence comes about because capitalism itself is the limit of history, and in this sense its "negative," one that every other socius is simultaneously attracted to and scared by. It is, contemporaneously, the realization and the impediment of desire, which makes it both effective and unfinished. If it did not actually realize desire, capitalism could not survive. But if it fulfilled it, it would be devastated and submerged by it. It is for this reason – just as in the case of the single class that brings it into being – that it cannot have an external adversary, given that nothing exists outside its plane of immanence, which it shares with the very same desire that challenges it. For this reason it can be neither opposed nor brought back to the social conditions that it has irreversibly gone beyond. It can only be accelerated, according to Deleuze's fundamental category, so as to be pushed to an implosion, the result of an excess of the same impulse that produced it:

> But which is the revolutionary path? Is there one? – To withdraw from the world market, as Samir Amin advises Third World countries to do, in a curious revival of the fascist "economic solution"? Or might it be to go in the opposite direction? To go still further, that is, in the movement of the market, of decoding and deterritorialization? For perhaps the flows are not yet deterritorialized enough, not yet decoded enough, from the viewpoint of a theory and a practice of a highly schizophrenic character. Not to withdraw from the process, but to go further, to "accelerate the process," as Nietzsche put it.[109]

What the political might possibly ever become within this horizon remains highly indeterminate, not only because it has been expanded by its own unlimited openness but because its only possibility of development is to strengthen what it would want to oppose. Once capitalism and schizophrenia are not only placed on the same plane of immanence, but reciprocally functionalized one for the growth of the other, political activity does not differ from its own neutralization.

11. The culmination of this antinomic process is reached in the second volume of *Capitalism and Schizophrenia*, published by

Deleuze and Guattari under the title *A Thousand Plateaus*, in 1980. It simultaneously represents the point of fullest deployment of their political ontology and its most problematic outcome. To get there, we should first dwell on another joint effort, a text that in some ways represents its privileged entry point. I am referring to the book on Kafka, which already in its title focuses on "minor literature." Minority – or handicap – is precisely the category the authors deploy to remove politics from all the contradictions, and even regressions, that it underwent in the course of the twentieth century. Even though linguistics – which has generally been oriented toward the major languages – never grasped its political importance, it is in language that Deleuze and Guattari recognize the most disruptive meaning of the minority paradigm. In *Thousand Plateaus*'s fourth plateau, which is devoted specifically to the postulates of linguistics and opposes Chomsky's universalistic methodology, they affirm that there is no linguistic system that is not internally traversed by variations, tensions, and conflicts that test its presumed homogeneity, thus challenging its majoritarian status. This thesis' presupposition is that the process of language unification is essentially political in nature. There is no mother tongue that is not the fruit of a conquest of power exercised over minor linguistic nuclei, which it dominates. But this domination is never complete or definite, because it is continuously contested by linguistic variants that excavate grooves and fractures that are never fully healed. Unlike linguists, who limit themselves to seeing in them only lexical bastardizations and semantic impoverishments, one needs to recognize that they constitute an ellipsis by means of which the variants besiege the constants, weakening their primacy. Strictly speaking, in fact, one ought to say that there are only variants, since the constants are nothing more than the contingent result of the generalization of specific variants. Major and minor, instead of being polar opposites or merely quantitative indexes, are therefore intensive processes that interact reciprocally, modifying the power relationships that prevail at a specific moment in a specific language. A minor language does not tend to replace a major one, nor does it claim its status, but it acts within it, destabilizing it to the point of literally pushing it outside of itself. The role of minor languages consists in the intrinsically political role of this subversive activity or, better, of the processes of linguistic "minorization."

This process occurs in all languages, including those that more than all others exercise an imperialistic role, such as English – inhabited by Anglo-Gaelic, Anglo-Irish, and Anglo-American, which in its turn is modified not only by black English, but also by yellow, red, and broken English. No other language works on concatenations and conjunctions, used as lines of escape to the outside, as much as Anglo-English does. It is unlike French, which always tends to start from a stationary point, or German, which is obsessed with the nostalgia of being, the foundation, the inside: "English on the other hand creates composite words whose only link is an implied AND, relationship with the outside, cult of the road which never plunges down, which has no foundations, which shoots on the surface, rhizome. *Blue-eyed boy* [italics added]: a boy, some blue, and eyes – an assemblage. AND ... AND ... AND, stammering."[110] The American, freed from English heritage, is "the son of a crumbled father, the son of all nations."[111] Inspired by Jefferson, Thoreau, Melville, s/he considers every human being as a brother/sister not because s/he belongs to his/her own community or because of any special qualification, but only because they are human beings. Without peculiarities, *homo tantum*. As Melville writes in *Redburn*:

> You can not spill a drop of American blood without spilling the blood of the whole world. ... We are not a nation, so much as a world; for unless we may claim the whole world for one sire, like Melchisedec, we are without father or mother. ... We are the heirs of all time, and with all nations we divide our inheritance.[112]

But, for Deleuze and Guattari, the most creative case of linguistic "minorization" is the mixture Kafka's language is composed of, situated somewhere between Bohemia's German and a sort of Germanized Yiddish. In order to identify its intensely political semantics, one needs to frame it within the general dislocation induced by the disintegration of the Austro-Hungarian Empire at the end of World War I and by the migratory dynamics it set in motion. In turn-of-the-century Prague, German as the official language of administration, business, and university culture, Czech as the vernacular language of a part of the population, and Yiddish, despised by Germans and Czechs in equal measure, all coexisted and established both mutual relationships and tensions. It is in this framework that the powerful work of linguistic metamorphosis activated by Kafka's writing must be situated. In Deleuze's interpretation, it assumes a function that is more than literary, indeed an eminently political one: not in the sense of a competition between rival languages and not even in that of a dialectal gap, but as a form of creation that is expressive of new forms of enunciation aimed at unhinging official linguistic normativity. This is all the more important as linguistic hegemony is not just one of many possible hegemonies, but is the hegemony presupposed by all the others, without which none of those others could exist. The absolute peculiarity of linguistic minoritarianism must be situated within this primacy. It diverges as much from the universalism of the majoritarian language as it does from the particularism of the minoritarian one, which is tolerated as a subsystem inside the former. Unlike both these systems, Kafka's language works like a foreign presence inside the majoritarian one: "A minor literature *does not* come from a minor language; it is rather that which a minority constructs within a major language. But the first characteristic of minor literature in any case is that in it language is affected with a high coefficient of deterritorialization."[113] Deterritorialized in and of itself, the minoritarian language ends up deterritorializing the majoritarian language as well, inventing a third, which is always transitioning from one to the other. To accomplish this, it is necessary to overcome an initial block that makes any type of writing difficult; this is exactly what happens with Prague's Jews, unable as they are to write in German, in Czech, or in Yiddish. But this is a creative block that, thanks to this preexisting obstacle, opens the way to an escape route that turns the normative system against itself. Like thought, language, to express its full potential, needs to overcome a resistance, to force a closed door.

Its political nature, according to Deleuze and Guattari, consists in this forcing. The violent relationship with his father notwithstanding, what Kafka lived was not an Oedipal phantasm, but a political one. This is so first because in language everything assumes a collective value, then also because, by tampering with the closed system of norms, it acquires an intrinsically revolutionary meaning: "The literary machine thus becomes a relay for a revolutionary machine-to-come, not at all for ideological reasons but because the literary machine alone is determined to fill the conditions of a collective enunciation that is lacking elsewhere in this milieu: *literature is the people's concern.*"[114]

But what people's concern? What people is it that speaks through literature? No existing people, which can be defined as such in identitarian terms and in contrast with, or even to the detriment of, other peoples. It is certainly not "a people called upon to dominate the world. It is a minor people, eternally minor, taken up in a becoming-revolutionary. Perhaps it exists only in the atoms of the writer, a bastard people, inferior, dominated, always in becoming, always incomplete."[115] American literature has produced anomalous writers, capable of making a universal people, made up of emigrants from all over the world, speak in their books. The true writer, after all, never writes to tell us about her or his memories, unless s/he is about to make them the destination of a people to come, renounced or betrayed by those who should have spoken on its behalf – and precisely for this reason ready to be addressed, without pragmatic concerns, by literature. Hence Deleuze's conclusion, which is valid not only for literary writing but also for art and cinema: "The ultimate aim of literature is to set free, in the delirium, this creation of a health or this invention of a people, that is, a possibility of life. To write for this people who are missing."[116]

Kafka takes to its culmination this option for lack. His texts do not "represent" any existing people – be it German, Czech, or Jewish. They do not delineate any reterritorialization, as in the writers of the Prague School, who attempted to enrich German with symbols of other origins. Kafka, on the contrary, empties German, excavating continuous fissures in a language set on a path toward insignificance. He suppresses each symbol, metaphor, signification, designation, literally dragging language out of itself. We are dealing with the same deterritorialization that, in other contexts, produced the extraordinary slivers of genius generated by the explosion of the Austro-Hungarian empire: Einstein in physics, the dodecaphonic composers in music, the expressionists in the world of the image. For all of them it was a matter of decentering, of engaging in something that unhinged traditional representation. The metamorphosis – the becoming animal that runs through all of Kafka's writings – has the same function of removal, excavation, retraction. His human animals or animal humans trace the escape lines that drag away "all politics, all economy, all bureaucracy, all judiciary: it sucks them like a vampire in order to make them render still unknown sounds that come from the near future – Fascism, Stalinism, Americanism, *diabolical powers that are knocking at the door.*"[117] At this point it is not possible, and perhaps it is useless, to attempt to oppose or exorcise them. What can and should be done, especially by writers, is to expose the desire that runs through them. From this point of view Deleuze opposes his interpretation of Kafka to that, either melancholic or tragic, proposed by those who see in his writing the anguish for the incipient catastrophe, or even a line of resistance against it. On the contrary, the political nature of the writer lies in her or his internalizing the catastrophe without opposing to it any polarity that would not have a grip on the smooth flow of desire:

> Only two principles are necessary to accord with Kafka. He is an author who laughs with a profound joy, a *joie de vivre*, in spite of, or because of, his clownish declarations that he offers like a trap or a circus. And from one end to the other, he is a political author, prophet of the future world, because he has two poles that he will know how to unify in a completely new assemblage: far from being a writer withdrawn into his room, Kafka finds that his room offers him a double flux, that of a bureaucrat with a great future ahead of him, plugged into real assemblages that are in the process of coming into shape, and that of a nomad who is involved in fleeing things in the most contemporary way and who plugs into socialism, anarchism, social movements.[118]

Kafka knew these movements but did not join them. His socialist friendships notwithstanding, he did not want to represent either a revolutionary party or a revolutionary project. He practiced his own, very particular revolution within a literary machine of which he was both cog and inventor, victim and functionary. This is because, in the becoming of desire, one cannot distinguish between these roles: "There is no longer a revolutionary desire that would be opposed to power, to the machines of power"[119] – just as it is not possible to oppose power and resistance, revolution and reaction, eros and bureaucracy: "In this sense there is certainly a bureaucratic eros that is a segment of power and a position of desire. And a capitalist eros. And a fascist eros. All the segments communicate with each other through variable contiguities. Capitalist America, bureaucratic Russia, Nazi Germany."[120] By comparison with such contiguity, along the conjoined flows of desire, all criticism, as also all oppositional political activity, would be useless because immersed within the same flow it intends to oppose. The only possibility that remains open according to Deleuze's Kafka, but also according to Deleuze as reader of Kafka, is to multiply the concatenations, to make the series proliferate, to accelerate the speed of the transitions, whatever they may be.

12. The antinomy that runs through the entirety of Deleuze's political ontology already emerges in these passages of *Kafka*. Once it is inscribed in the minoritarian escape lines, the political is identified with the ambiguous flow of desire that gives rise to it, thus losing all autonomous consistency. Internal to the process of "minorization," it ends up vanishing, no differently from the forever absent people toward which it gestures. But this becoming minor is only the first

form of derealization of the political. It is followed by a second one, which returns to the theme of the "war machine," which is elaborated, in the form of a treatise on nomadology, in the concluding section of *A Thousand Plateaus*. One must immediately add that, like many of Deleuze-Guattari's concept terms, "war machine" should not be understood in a historical sense, but rather in a paradigmatic one – as a sort of diagram that the authors themselves describe as "abstract" because situated outside a specific time or space. As we saw with the *Urstaat*, the war machine also possesses a transhistorical dimension that traverses all the areas of experience, mobilizing them, from thought to technology to art, but in a direction that is frontally opposed to that taken by the state. Not only is the war machine extraneous to the state *dispositif*, but it is irreducible to both of the dimensions that express it, power and the law.

Deleuze insists on this exteriority – directed toward an outside that the state always attempts to internalize – because the political significance of the war machine resides in it. It is not the specific terrain on which the war machine operates that is political, but the antagonistic relationship that sets the war machine in opposition to the logic of the state in all fields. In each one – from epistemology to game theory to philosophy – an unbreakable line separates the nomadic modality of the war machine from the sedentary one of the state's organization. While the former deterritorializes, the latter reterritorializes by tracing borders that enclose the smooth space outlined by the war machine, striating it. Deleuze and Guattari explain that, to be able to fully think this through, one needs to avoid two errors of perspective, both of which can be referred back to a sovereign perspective. The first is that of interpreting the war machine from a negative perspective, as if there could be nothing positive outside the state *dispositif*, instead of treating it as an entity with a specific origin, nature, and form. The second error, which is even more widespread, is that of placing the machine along an evolutionary line that is destined, after an immature phase, to be completed within the horizon of the state. This is the hermeneutical risk that Pierre Clastres also incurs – even though it is to him that one owes the first theorization of a society without a state – from the moment when he studies war machines independently from, instead of in opposition to, state order. If one considers the two regimes as being autonomous but not conflicting universes, one is inevitably led to fall back into the evolutionary paradigm, which presupposes their succession. The thinker who instead best grasps their radical incompatibility is the greatest theorist of the Leviathan, Hobbes, when he sees war as the antonym of the state. What the war machine opposes is precisely the state, which in its turn has been instituted to put an end to it: "Hobbes saw clearly that *the state was against war, so war is against the state*, and makes it impossible."[121]

In this fashion, however, by opposing state and war machine, Deleuze consciously opens up a fissure in his argument. If state and war machine fight each other ceaselessly, they end up sharing precisely what should divide them, namely war itself, fought by one against the other. But then, if even the state fights the machine, just as the machine fights the state, what differentiates them? In order to be able to make war against war, the state must appropriate the very *dispositif* it intends to defeat, just as the latter, in order to defend itself, needs to reproduce the same logic as the state. This is exactly what happens when the state, attacked by the war machine, incorporates its procedure, reproducing it within itself and using it for its own ends. Deleuze is aware of the problematic nature of his reconstruction and asks himself the questions that inevitably ensue: "is the battle the 'object' of war? But also, is war the 'object' of the war machine? And finally, to what extent is the war machine the 'object' of the state *dispositif*?"[122] The answer he himself provides, in order to avoid the aporetic consequences of identifying that which he intends to oppose, is that war is not the war machine's true object, even if at times, to defend itself against the war that the state launches against it, it is forced to engage in it. After all it is a well-known fact that guerrilla warfare tends to avoid, until it is possible, any frontal engagement, aiming, if anything, for the non-battle. In this manner the originary configurations of the two antagonistic polarities tend to exchange places with each other symmetrically. While the object of that which has indeed been defined as "war machine" is not war, the state, which originally was extraneous to war, practices it against the very machine that besieges it. At that point, in an indissoluble chain of consequences, even the war machine, threatened in its very survival, cannot but respond to the state's attack, assuming war as its direct object.

The truth is that, despite the proclaimed exteriority of war machine and state, they end up being inextricably intertwined, as soon as one passes from the paradigmatic level to the historical one, and so much so that one can actually speak of a single reality, viewed from two opposite angles. After all, on the plane of immanence as established by Deleuze, nothing can transcend anything else, given that no negative exists that is not the reactive reverse of an affirmative power. It is for this reason that the striated is nothing more than the opposite of the smooth, the sedentary the opposite of the nomadic, and the identical the opposite of the different. At the ontological level, there is nothing but the war machine, which the state, in order to exist, must appropriate, modifying it to its own ends. Except that, once appropriated, that very same war machine becomes a *dispositif* that is internal to the state, corrupting itself to the point of reversing its creative power into a violence destructive of what is other than itself, and ultimately destructive even of itself. It is this slippage of the escape lines into lines of abolition and death that constitutes the false (double) bottom, always waiting to reemerge onto the surface, of Deleuze's political ontology. Once the alternative between machine and state has disappeared – an alternative in which the possibility of the political resides – only a single process remains at the historical level, and it is a process that dissolves both. Hence the second modality of the derealization of the political, a modality both ulterior and specular in relation to the one that is implicit in the becoming minor. It is war that now sucks the political up into the vortex, as can be seen from the falling away of their respective borders; and this leads to their being fused into a single negative block in which one is the instrument of the other.

Those events and processes that unfolded after the failure of 1968 and that Deleuze sees coming to fruition in a Europe still divided by the Berlin Wall realize the indistinction between state and war machine, in a nefarious exchange of characteristics. If, up to a certain moment, which can be situated in the first decades of the twentieth century, it was states that had appropriated the war machine, functionalizing it to their goals, now it is the war machine, transformed into a machine of global destruction, that incorporates the states as instruments of its own planetary deployment. Two phases succeed each other, concatenated in a deadly drift. First comes fascism, which instrumentalizes war for its own expansion. Then comes capitalist domination, which, having vanquished fascism, engages in speculative profiteering during a peace poised precariously between terror and survival. By now even the deterritorialization that the primitive war machine opposed to the state's striations is reversed into a mega machine aimed at integrating war and peace into a single horizon: "The war machine reforms a smooth space that it now claims to control, to surround the entire earth. Total war itself is surpassed, toward a form of peace more terrifying still. The war machine has taken charge of the aim, worldwide order, and the states are now no more than objects or means adapted to the machine."[123]

This is where von Clausewitz's famous formula, according to which war is the continuation of politics by other means, is effectively inverted into its opposite – in the sense that the states, after having appropriated the machine, are captured by it in their turn, in a subjection of politics to a war that was not always hot but that for precisely this reason was even more total:

> Doubtless, the present situation is highly discouraging. We have watched the war machine grow stronger and stronger, as in a science fiction story; we have seen it assign as its objective a peace still more terrifying than fascist death; we have seen it maintain or instigate the most terrible of local wars as part of itself; we have seen it set its sights on a new type of enemy, no longer another state, or even another regime, but the "unspecified enemy."[124]

Although, due to the developments of capital itself, the possibility of activating new minoritarian, popular, revolutionary war machines *does not* disappear, the dynamics that are actually unfolding don't lead one to imagine that this could happen. There is no space for the political from this side either, introjected and annihilated as it is by the global war machine.

*

The suicidal drift of the war machine is not circumscribed only to the relationship with the state. This is the risk that underlies all of Deleuze's vitalist ontology, because of, and not despite, its affirmative articulation, the negation of the negative that it antinomically proclaims. At the center of a life that is affirmed absolutely there is the dark point of death: a death instinct that haunts Deleuze's entire oeuvre, and perhaps even his very biography, if only subterraneously. David Lapoujade, in a lucid analysis of his philosophy, makes exactly this argument in *Deleuze: Les mouvements aberrants*.[125] The thesis it puts forward is that it is precisely these movements that end up giving Deleuze's works their ultimate orientation. Traversing matter, life, thought, they express a force that not only accelerates but also perverts real processes. The figure of the pervert is tied to that of the schizophrenic in Deleuze: it is both intertwined with it and central to his philosophy – it is in fact its phantasmatic double. After all, the procedures involved in perversion always imply a sort of duplication; one extracts a double from the original so as to go beyond its limit, grabbing it from behind to the point of inverting its sense. The death instinct haunts the vital power, reproducing it, strengthened, even though it does not coincide with it. Lapoujade warns against the risk of confusing the aberrant movements with their possible self-destructive outcome. One needs to be careful not to attribute to Deleuze a fascination with death that was always alien to him. Death is not a transcendent power that challenges life from the outside, but the ultimate outcome of its unlimited acceleration. It is what frees life from its personal ties, exposing it to the power of the impersonal. Even if elevated to a transcendent principle – in the distinctive sense that Deleuze confers upon the term – the death instinct never exceeds the plane of immanence. If anything, it represents its most extreme expression:

> The death drive does not attest to a mortuary kind of thinking, to a being-for-death, it is the affirmation of the powers of life, without regard for whoever the subject bearing them might be, in the sense that it undoes anything that prevents the, continuously renewed, distribution of these powers. ... Loss, pain, suffering are the self-destructions that life traverses in order to set new powers free.[126]

Unlike Freud – who views Thanatos as that which sucks life into the indifference of matter – Deleuze relates it back to the work of difference: *Thanatos is that which, by exposing it to its finitude*, prevents the ego from becoming fully one with itself.

In *A Thousand Plateaus* the death instinct, which has been moved to the collective plane of aberrant movements, acquires an even more dramatic tone. It remains immanent in desire, but can also provoke its explosion, inverting the desire of death into the death of desire. If such a dynamic involves all the three social stratifications of savages, barbarians, and civilized people, it especially concerns the latter – and therefore us. The *dispositif* that enacts it is precisely that of the war machine. Once it has been captured by the state, it is separated from its own liberatory essence and turned against itself. Here the transition from affirmative to negative destruction appears in full light. The war machine is a machine of destruction, but of positive destruction, because it destroys that which is opposed to the free circulation of multiplicity: to the extent that it is destructive, it is eminently creative. But once it has been captured by the state and coincides with it, it inverts its affirmative destructiveness into a negative destructiveness. It is destructive even of itself, like all flows that become absolute. Since they cannot be concatenated to others, they can only turn against themselves, thus turning from destructive into self-destructive. This is the tragic outcome that, behind the surface glitter, is at risk of taking hold of Deleuze's entire ontology. When, in our times, the war machine becomes the grand security *dispositif* that claims to secure the peace, it is reversed into a machine of pure abolition, transforming even the living into living dead.

*

13. And what about the political? Compressed in a pincer movement, having to opt between becoming minor and becoming war, after *A Thousand Plateaus* its centrality diminishes in Deleuze's subsequent works. Their prodigiously inventive richness notwithstanding, one

cannot claim that the books on cinema and painting bring any new elements to his political ontology. There is one significant exception: the 1986 volume on Foucault.[127] It allows us to conclude the hermeneutical itinerary we have outlined so far and brings us back to the question we started from: the comparison between Deleuze and Heidegger. In the almost twenty years that separate this work from *Difference and Repetition*, the distance from the German philosopher broadens and deepens. The most significant element, however – also because it questions the issue of the political for the last time – is that the distance from Heidegger now passes through a passionate proximity to Foucault. Immediately after having reminded us that "[b]eing itself is political," almost as if wanting to reiterate the ontologico-political nature of his argument, Deleuze admits that, more than a monograph on Foucault, what he wrote is a book about his own relationship with him: "I'm not, in this book, trying to speak for Foucault, but trying to trace a transversal, diagonal line running from him to me."[128] When, responding to a question like "what does thinking mean?," Deleuze cannot answer without comparing Foucault to Heidegger, he does so only to underscore their difference, placing the former well ahead of the latter: "Yes, thinking – as a perilous act, he says. It's definitely Foucault, along with Heidegger but in quite a different way, who's most profoundly transformed the image of thought."[129] And he even says: "Foucault's more thoroughly philosophical than anyone else in the twentieth century, probably the only philosopher."[130] In this manner an unusual triangle is created between the three thinkers, by means of which it is almost as if Deleuze meant to close his accounts with Heidegger via this intermediation. By identifying with Foucault – to the extent that it is not always easy to understand whether he is reconstructing Foucault's position or speaking in the first person – Deleuze distances himself ever more sharply from Heidegger, following a critical orientation that will be taken to its extreme in *What Is Philosophy?* It is true that Foucault himself had always declared that he was fascinated with Heidegger's philosophy, but also that he could understand it only by way of Nietzsche, and especially the "political" Nietzsche, of force and power: "It was necessary to recover force, in the Nietzschean sense, or power in the very particular sense of the 'will to power.'"[131]

But what is the conceptual figure that, all differences notwithstanding, connects Foucault to Heidegger on a terrain that Deleuze himself shares? It is the "fold" – which is also the title of Deleuze's book on Leibniz that he wrote at about this time: both Heidegger and Foucault, like Merleau-Ponty, work on the fold of being. Just as in Heidegger ontological difference, more than a differential relation "between" being and beings, is the fold (*Zwiefalt*) that is constitutive of being, so Merleau-Ponty's "flesh" is the fold by means of which one's own body twists on itself, everting itself. Foucault adopts the same procedure, but with a decisive difference by comparison with both Heidegger and Merleau-Ponty – a difference that definitively distances him from the phenomenological perspective they both remain tied to in different ways. While, still according to Deleuze's not always persuasive interpretation, Merleau-Ponty does not succeed in emancipating himself from the category of intentionality, in a "savage" configuration of experience that allows the thing to be facing consciousness, Heidegger activates an ontological reflection that relates being and beings within the fold of difference. But he thinks of the fold according to the modality of the open rather than that of the outside, which is instead what Foucault does. Hence a non-mediatable difference between the three philosophers. While both Heidegger and Merleau-Ponty superimpose the plane of seeing onto the plane of speaking, thereby remaining within the horizon of intentionality, Foucault opens a fault line between them, one into which intentional consciousness plummets. If the object of sight differs from that of speech, there cannot be a unique single subject capable of transitioning between one and the other. To make the fold into the zipper of the open instead of the constantly escaping line of the outside means that one establishes a shared belonging across the modality of seeing and the modality of speaking that prevents any disjunction between them. But in this manner the turn from phenomenology to ontology attempted by Heidegger remains incomplete: Dasein and world continue to correspond to each other in an originary opening, which unites gaze and word in the same interior light. Foucault's radical novelty in the history of thought consists in the rupturing of this continuity. According to him, one does not see that which one speaks of and one does not speak of that which one sees: "The light-Being refers only to visibilities, and language-Being to statements: the fold will not be able to refound an intentionality, since the latter disappears in the disjunction between the two parts of a knowledge that is never intentional."[132]

What does this mean vis-à-vis the political? Nothing in terms of content, but a great deal from the lexical point of view. What Foucault's texts outline – and what makes them much more timely than those of Heidegger and Merleau-Ponty – is not only a distinction between the universes of enunciation and visibility but an out-and-out clash between them. More than a simple splitting or doubling, in

Foucault the fold assumes the configuration of a divergence. Nothing resembling the peaceful consonance of Heidegger's "between" or of Merleau-Ponty's "chiasmus." When Deleuze writes that "[t]he Heraclitean element has always gone deeper in Foucault than in Heidegger, for phenomenology is ultimately too pacifying and has blessed too many things,"[133] he is alluding precisely to the conflictual tension that enlivens Foucault's writings. Certainly, in Foucault too there is relation, interweaving, mutual interpenetration. "But this interlacing is in fact a stranglehold, or a battle between two implacable foes who are the forms of knowledge-Being ... [it] is the audiovisual battle, the double capture, the noise of words that conquered the visible, the fury of things that conquered the articulable."[134] It is about the comparison, and in fact the confrontation, between two irreducible dimensions, which battle for prevalence, for one's domination over the other. If in *The Archaeology of Knowledge* the line of language prevails over that of sight, in *Discipline and Punish* the relationships of sight, in their turn, prevail over the linguistic ones. The sinister figure of the panopticon, around which the entire book revolves, does not relate to the syntax of enunciation, but to the plot of visibility. It is wrapped in a beam of light that, before making it a stone building, makes it the point of intersection of infinite gazes. A hiatus opens between the visible and the enunciable that generates two orientations, and these not only are radically divergent but compete for primacy. And yet this disjunction in the order of being is no more than a first line of horizontal clash, destined to be cut across by another vertical fold, which opposes the form of knowledge to the force of power.

It is as if, inside a first line of conflict, an even deeper division were engraved that is internal to the play of forms and concerns this time the field of forces – the factory of power, which Foucault develops between *Discipline and Punish* and *The Will to Knowledge*. It is the transition from the archive to the diagram, the machine of power that undergirds the stratifications of knowledge, traversing them from side to side. If what characterizes the modalities of knowledge – visibilities and enunciations – is their reciprocal exteriority, what qualifies the forces is an absolute exteriority that refers to an irreducible outside:

> We must distinguish between exteriority and the outside. Exteriority is still a form, as in *The Archaeology of Knowledge* – even two forms which are exterior to one another, since knowledge is made from the two environments of light and language, seeing and speaking. But the outside concerns force: if force is always in relation with other forces,

> forces necessarily refer to an irreducible outside which no longer even has any form and is made up of distances that cannot be broken down through which one force acts upon another or is acted upon by another.[135]

This is a further intensification of the political dimension that Deleuze recognizes in Foucault's text. The transition from the stratified context of knowledge to the diagrammatical one of power, while it does not annul their relation, subordinates it to the predominance of force over form. Just as in Nietzsche's universe there is nothing that escapes the impulse of the will to power, so Foucault's world is entirely traversed and mobilized by the confrontation between conflicting forces. If in the Nietzschean genealogy a reactive force responded to every active one, in Foucault's a resistance responds to every power – sometimes even preceding it, if not even constituting it. This – the precedence of resistance to power – is simultaneously the cause and the effect of the absolute exteriority of the forces in play. The fact that the diagram, unlike the archive, comes from the outside means that the future reverses the relations of priority with the past, backtracking on it. In this sense any exertion of force presupposes a contrary force that opposes it by resisting it:

> Moreover, the final word on power is that *resistance comes first*, to the extent that power relations operate completely within the diagram, while resistances necessarily operate in a direct relation with the outside from which the diagram emerges. This means that a social field offers more resistance than strategies, and the thought of the outside is a thought of resistance.[136]

In these pages Deleuze's writing, chasing Foucault on his own terrain, adopts an intensely political manner – potential, force, power, resistance. At the center of the clash, as in the great Foucauldian essays of the mid-1960s, there is life, itself continuously resisting the pressure of death. Quoting the extraordinary pages of *The Will to Knowledge*, in which life is understood by Foucault as the stakes in political struggles, Deleuze seems to adopt that inversion of biopower into an affirmative biopolitics in which "life as a political object was in a sense taken at face value and turned back against the system that was bent on controlling it."[137] It is one of those moments in which Deleuze's political ontology seems to gather strength even as it sees in life that point of tension through which power can be faced, and also sometimes defeated: "When power becomes bio-power resistance becomes the power of life, a vital power that cannot be confined within species, environment or the paths of a particular diagram. Is not the force that comes from outside a certain idea of Life, a certain vitalism, in which Foucault's thought culminates? Is not life this capacity to resist force?"[138]

14. But this is not Deleuze's last word on Foucault. After having reconstructed his itinerary from the archaeology of knowledge to the genealogy of power, at a certain moment Deleuze identifies a breaking point – not a new fold, similar to the one that separates the enunciable from the visible within knowledge, or to the more pronounced one that articulates the archive to the diagram. Up until then, Foucault's philosophical itinerary, for all its metamorphoses and through them, had continued to grow without dramatic turns. But then something different occurs – a profound rift, which tears apart the philosopher's life, together with the weave of his thought. According to Deleuze, this explains the interruption of the *History of Sexuality*, of which *The Will to Knowledge* was supposed to be the first element, and the prolonged silence that followed. Certainly, at the biographical level the setbacks incurred by the prisons movement and the disillusionment regarding the outcomes of 1968 could have weighed on him. But Deleuze ties Foucault's crisis to something more internal to his work, something that concerns the issue of power: "What happened during the fairly long silence following *The History of Sexuality*? Perhaps Foucault felt slightly uneasy about the book: had he not trapped himself within the concept of power relations?"[139] This is not merely a matter of philosophical dissatisfaction, Deleuze continues; it is about the impasse that power inscribes in the life of someone who analyzed it in all its folds. This is the "blind alley" into which, at the end of the 1970s, Foucault goes. Up to that moment he has investigated the formations of knowledge and the mechanisms of power, exposing the hybrids that are born of their intertwinement. Then, with *The Will to Knowledge*, he has reconstructed the modalities with which they impact the enunciations of sexuality, which are also ultimately dependent on the dynamics of power – until, at the end of the journey, crushed by the intensity of his discovery, Foucault is at risk of losing himself:

> But I think he must have come up against the question of whether there was anything "beyond" power – whether he was getting trapped in a sort of impasse within power relations. He was, as you might say, mesmerized by and trapped by something he hated. And it was no use

> telling himself that coming up against power relations was the lot of modern (that is, infamous) man, that it's power that makes us speak and see, it wasn't enough, he needed "some opening." … He couldn't stay locked in what he'd discovered.[140]

It is true that for Foucault power is never absolute – rather it functions by producing points of resistance that contest and relativize its dominion: but both the genesis and the status of such resistances remain opaque in his eyes. Not only: they are never protected from a regression that is destined to solidify them into new power blocks: "But what happens, on the other hand, if the transversal relations of resistance continue to become restratified, and to encounter or even construct knots of power?"[141] The same question intersects the issue of truth. If it is power that produces it, as Foucault has always theorized, how can their relationship be inverted, looking at power from the perspective of truth? Foucault's answer, at the time of his writings on biopolitics, should be sought in a form of life capable of turning the *dispositifs* that power activates to control life against power itself. But it is precisely the relationship between life and power, as it is thought of in the category of "biopolitics," that does not convince Deleuze. There is something in it that creates a blockage in Foucault's thought, and ends up immobilizing it. Foucault finds a first line of escape, with respect to this interdict, in that bundle of perspectives that converge in the hermeneutics of existence – which, in the final phase of his production, took the place of the analytics of knowledge and of the genealogy of power. Deleuze underscores the fact that the "government of the self," which the last Foucault is concerned about, should not be understood as a sort of retreat into interiority or, even less, as a restoration of the category of the subject. The power of the outside, theorized in the political writings, does not give way. It rather exerts itself on itself, making the subject the outcome of a process of subjectivation that is born outside it. The "inside" is always an operation of the outside. And in fact it is the result of such an extreme exteriorization as to fold it toward its opposite. The outside is not conceived of by Foucault as a limit, but as peristaltic matter, composed of folds and wrinklings that continuously tend to twist on themselves, turning the most extreme outside into the deepest inside – "they are not something other than the outside, but precisely the inside *of* the outside."[142]

But all this is not sufficient. The reference to the Greek *ēthos* [character] does not solve the problem Foucault is facing. Because it is precisely this projection of the outside into its opposite that obsesses him, like a specter that continually reemerges to the surface. We are dealing with the ghost of the double, constituted on the margin of the joint between splitting and doubling: "the theme which has always haunted Foucault is that of the double. But the double is never a projection of the interior; on the contrary, it is an interiorization of the outside. It is not a doubling of the One, but a redoubling of the Other."[143] According to Deleuze, Foucault never managed to shake off this obsession, to the extent that, in the final phase of his existence, he lost himself in its play of mirrors. Power is the channel of this negative energy, the machine that functions so well that it dragged its theorist into an uninhabitable void – that absolute exteriority capable of introjecting even the inside that it generates at its external boundaries. Driven by dissatisfaction with what he himself had theorized, at a certain point Foucault feels the need of cutting the knot between power and life, driving himself into an outside that is even more extreme than the one he had encountered up until then. This time he is not withdrawing toward the inside but driving it to implosion. This is the direction, the reverse of that oriented toward the "government of self," that he took in the text on infamous men[144] – faceless beings, only recognizable in the instant in which, absolutely at the mercy of power, they slide into the depths of existence, never to reemerge to the light of day. To cross the line of power to the point of passing to the other side, toward a place from which it is impossible to return – this is what attracts the philosopher at the moment in which he loses any control of himself: "Perhaps Foucault had the feeling that he must at all costs cross the line, get to the other side, go still further than knowledge and power. Even if it meant reconsidering the whole project of the *History of Sexuality*. And that's just what he's telling himself in the very fine piece on infamous men."[145]

This is where, according to his interpreter, Foucault must have seen a crevasse. Once the extreme threshold of the outside has been traversed, sucked into its space of deployment, "what tells us that this outside is not a terrifying void and that this life, which seems to put up a resistance, is not just the simple distribution within the void of 'slow, partial and progressive' deaths?"[146] This is the same direction taken by captain Ahab in his becoming whale, or the one followed by Van Gogh until his death. These are the forms of vertigo one experiences when one chases lines that go nowhere – beyond knowledge, beyond power, in a voyage with no return. The impasse into which Foucault has slid does not contemplate any ways out. There could be one "only if the outside were caught up in a movement that would snatch it away from the void and pull it away from death."[147] In this case, a new axis could have been delineated, in addition to those of knowledge and power – but one that Foucault could have experienced only by distancing himself from it, risking in this way to fall back into the other two. Nothing remains, then, but to ride the escape line, even if it can always transform itself into a line of death and devastation: "you may be heading for death, suicide, but as Foucault says in a strange conversation with Schroeter, suicide then becomes an art it takes a lifetime to learn."[148]

At this point what it means for Deleuze to follow Foucault to the end, accompanying him, together with Blanchot, to an outside with no conditions, is no longer clear. And it is not even clear up to what point Deleuze is following Foucault or, on the contrary, drawing him toward himself, situating him on his own lines, making him speak his own language. What is clear is that, in a letter written to his friend and published posthumously, Deleuze distances himself from the author of *The Will to Knowledge*, returning, this time in an explicitly critical fashion, to the topic of power. Once one has assumed the heterogeneity, but also the reciprocal immanence, of a macro and a micro level within the *dispositifs*, is it still possible to use the notion of power as Foucault continues to do? "The notion of the state is not applicable at the level of a micro-analysis since, as Michel says, the issue is not to miniaturize the state. But is the notion of power any more applicable? Is it not also a miniaturization of a global concept?"[149] In its place, retrieving a central term from his own political ontology, Deleuze places desire. Like all of politics, power is nothing but an effect, an affection, of the concatenations of desire – not its opposite, as Foucault wanted. Deleuze agrees that removing the category of repression from the paradigm of power, as Foucault does, is the right move, but without losing sight of the fact that, while taking second place to desire, power's *dispositifs* do in any case have repressive consequences for its lines of escape. These, as has been seen, are not in and of themselves revolutionary. In fact they can always be reversed into lines of destruction and death. However, by codifying and territorializing them, power's *dispositifs* in any case exert an inhibiting effect on them, even where resistance momentarily prevails over power, since it is itself generated by power and reproductive of it. Therefore politics, the only one that Deleuze conceives of, does not pass through conflict with, or resistance to, power, but rather through its reintegration into the flow of desire:

> I myself don't wonder about the status resistance phenomena may have, since flight lines are the first determinations, since desire

> assembles the social field, power arrangements are both products of these assemblages and that which stamps them out or seals them up … I therefore have no need to posit the status of resistance phenomena if the first given of a society is that everything escapes from it and everything is deterritorialized.[150]

If everything escapes and gets deterritorialized in Deleuze's univocal ontology, there are no forces that can reciprocally oppose one another. There is nothing but a single plane of immanence, or a body without organs, "as biological as it is collective and political." Nothing but the body without organs itself, in its opposition to "all strata of organization, the organism's organization as well as power organizations,"[151] can be political.

3

Instituting Thought

1. The third ontologico-political paradigm, following those of Heidegger and Deleuze, can be tied to the name of Claude Lefort. His degree of influence on the contemporary debate is naturally greatly inferior to that of the first two: by comparison to theirs, knowledge of his work has remained limited to a relatively restricted group of readers. Nothing comparable, therefore, to the enormous influence exercised, even outside of the philosophical field, by Heidegger and Deleuze. However, and perhaps for this very reason – because it has remained in a sort of latency – his perspective contains an untapped meaning potential that can still be put to use, while other paradigms begin to exhibit a certain amount of exhaustion. For the time being, let us ask: How can the limited diffusion of Lefort's work be explained? Why did it not give rise, as one would have expected, to a series of studies comparable to those dedicated not only to Heidegger and Deleuze, but also, to remain within the confines of political philosophy, to Rawls, Habermas, Foucault, and Arendt?[1]

A first answer to this question, which involves the argumentative complexity of his conceptual *dispositif*, does not seem to be fully convincing. One cannot argue that, when compared to the philosophical writing of Heidegger and Deleuze, which are both among the most elaborate in twentieth-century thought, Lefort's, while sophisticated, is more hermetic. A second reason, which pertains to the heterogeneity of his cultural universe, seems more to the point. He was influenced, already since his years in high school, by his encounter with Merleau-Ponty's phenomenology; and Lefort also enriched the Marxist framework he used as his starting point with the languages of sociology, ethnology, and anthropology. It was these languages, together with his phenomenological foundation, that moved him away from Marxist scholasticism during his years of political militancy in the groups of the French radical left. The result was, however, that after a series of interactions with these languages, Lefort explicitly distanced himself from them, turning instead to political philosophy. What no longer satisfied him in the protocols of the human sciences was on the one hand their tendency to separate the point of view of the interpreter from that of the object of research and, on the other, the acceptance of sectoral perimeters of specialized forms of knowledge, that were uninterested in an overall view of the phenomena they were researching. Hence his critique of an analytical framework that presumes to master its object of inquiry from on high, according to the modality of gaze that Merleau-Ponty defined as *survol* [flying over]. Lefort was repelled by the positivist illusion, typical of a certain kind of sociology, that a knowing subject, even if placed outside the horizon of a social phenomenon, is able to grasp its objective reality.

While he did move away from the terrain of the social sciences in the direction of political philosophy, Lefort did not let much time pass before also formulating a series of reservations about it; within the confines of political philosophy he did not find a stable location either, as is clear from his hesitant reply to those who wanted to place him in the philosophico-political domain.[2] What didn't convince him about this discipline, at least in its more usual acceptation, was its tendency to employ certain political categories without preemptively discussing their presuppositions. Hence a hermeneutical deficit with regard to the depth of the underlying problems, which could not be reached by means of a superficial gaze. Although Lefort was less inclined toward the specialization of the social sciences, in his eyes political philosophy also ended up reproducing a sectoral perspective from the moment in which it adopted political categories without articulating them into a meaningful underlying grid. This is the reason for a certain diffidence with respect to the philosophico-political lexicon that he had chosen but never completely acclimated to. So, after having abandoned the publics of sociology and anthropology, Lefort did not acquire any in political philosophy, situating himself in a sort of no man's land that, owing to the breadth of its horizon, we can relate to a problematic of an ontological character. Rather than specific conceptual contents, what is at issue is the instituting role of political divisions in any type of society. Unlike in perspectives that frontally oppose order and conflict, for Lefort social unity becomes understandable because of the conflictual threshold that divides it into opposing parts. This instituting effect of division, however, which is present in all political regimes, is not recognizable as such except with the help of the light from an ontological horizon, in other words with the help of certain symbolic characteristics. The relations between the political, the economic, and the juridical, between public and private, or between legality and legitimacy, while they are important, remain opaque so long as they stay outside a fundamental question that concerns the symbolic framework they are situated in. Whoever practices or thinks about the political presupposes a particular relationship with her or his "being" in time and space, in nature and history, in life and the world.

The very starting point of Lefort's research already underscores the absolute singularity of a thought that is irreducible to either the social or the political sciences, both of which are blind with respect to the ontological weave from which they emerge and onto which they are grafted. It is inscribed in the inevitable gap between the plane of reality and that of the symbols that make it identifiable to itself and others, separating it from its surface image. In the political there is something that is not interpretable politically, because it presupposes a series of metapolitical meanings that exceed its domain, giving it sense. As we are taught by the founder of modern politics to whom Lefort dedicates his principal work, "the horizons of political thought are not themselves political, [so] that the relationship of the prince with power is a figure of the relationship of man with time and Being."[3] It is this complex conception, which addresses the specificity of the political but also of that which goes beyond it, that makes situating Lefort's thought within the contemporary philosophical landscape so difficult. It also helps explain the inadequate diffusion of his work: since it is external to the statutes of both the social and the human sciences, but also eludes the canons of the philosophico-political tradition, it activates an ontologico-political paradigm whose full potentiality, also by comparison with the much more familiar paradigms of Heidegger and Deleuze, has not yet been grasped.

Lefort occupies a position that one could call transversal with respect to their paradigms – not external to the problems they both pose, but oriented in such a manner as to face them along a different perspectival axis; while it is not devoid of references, both implicit and explicit, to Heidegger's philosophy,[4] Lefort's conceptual lexicon remains substantially alien to it. What their thinking does share is the refusal to reduce phenomena to an ontic dimension, by compressing them into their merely objective sense. Lefort believes, just as Heidegger had, that the reference to the originary opening of being inscribes the trace of difference in phenomena; but both his notion of "being" and his notion of "difference" differ markedly from those in Heidegger's lexicon. According to Lefort, being has not withdrawn into an unfathomable abyss but is the manner in which relations between humans are manifested; difference is therefore not the one, of an ontological kind, that separates being from beings, but is rather a division that society instituted and that exposes it to the test of alterity. Just as, ultimately, being is always social, so difference coincides with the conflict that traverses it from time to time, giving it meaning. The result is a series of divergent consequences, which affect the way Lefort conceives of both the political and the relationship with modernity – which for Heidegger was decidedly negative, while for Lefort it is fundamentally positive. For the French philosopher, the political, as an instituting form of the social, expresses itself fully only within that very modernity that Heidegger sees instead in the light of the domination of technology. In a 1986 lecture devoted to Leo Strauss's book *Natural Right and History*, Lefort situates the outlines of his perspective along the margins that differentiate it from other interpretations of the modern.[5] After having pointed out the aporias of Weberian sociology, he proceeds to a critical examination of Strauss's position, relating it to those, just as anti-modern, of Arendt and Heidegger. A series of significant differences notwithstanding, they share the joint presupposition of depoliticization as the mark of modernity. Whether this depoliticization is the result of technical machination, as it is for Heidegger, of the primacy of labor, as it is for Arendt, or of the philosophy of history, as it is for Strauss, the conclusion that their perspectives lead to is a drastically negative image of modernity when we compare it to the Greek beginnings, whose restoration is wished for:

> Starting with the end of Greek democracy (Arendt), of Platonic and Aristotelian philosophy (Strauss), of Presocratic philosophy (Heidegger), history is characterized by an ever-growing concealment which reaches its culmination in modernity. Our age therefore represents a moment of vacillation in which humanity is ready to sink into the abyss or, as a consequence of the intensity of this concealment, once again find the meaning of action (Arendt), the measure of human nature (Strauss) or the meaning of being (Heidegger).[6]

Well, if there is something that Lefort clearly refuses, that is the interpretation of modernity as the age of depoliticization: on the contrary, he views it as the era in which the political emancipates itself from all transcendent foundations. This does not mean that it is placed on a plane of absolute immanence, as Deleuze believes – who is as distant from Lefort as he is from Heidegger. If that were the case, if the political were entirely immanent in itself, both the function and the very possibility of the conflict that traverses it would vanish. Certainly, being is rendered constitutively political by the infinite proliferation of its differences, if one follows Deleuze's lead as well; yet it is precisely the diffuse coincidence of ontology and politics that Lefort questions, on the basis of the insuperable gap that separates the symbolic from the real. What, for Deleuze, is the univocity of a being that is always said in the same way is, for Lefort, the heterogeneity of social forms differentiated by a peculiar symbolic relation with being.

From this point of view, one could say that Lefort inscribes his thought on the very line that divides Heidegger's and Deleuze's perspectives. Lefort's perspective, like theirs, exhibits the deeply rooted traits of ontology. The triangular relationship between being, difference, and the political plays out in his ontology too. But his interpretation of difference modifies the relationship between ontology and the political, preventing both a radical divergence and a complete superposition. There is neither Heidegger's irreducible distance nor Deleuze's absolute superposition between the political and ontology – one instead finds a conflictual tension that simultaneously connects and distances them. This involves giving up both Heidegger's destitution and Deleuze's constitution in favor of something we can certainly define as "instituting thought." For Lefort, difference does not play the role of deactivating a political work incorporated in technical machination, as in Heidegger, but it is not the inexhaustible power of becoming imagined by Deleuze either. It is the caesura that the political impresses on a social being still unaware of its originary division. Vis-à-vis the Heideggerian paradigm, difference is not that which separates the ontological level from the ontic, or the impolitical from the political. Nor is it the infinitely repeated proliferation of a being that coincides with its own becoming, as conceived of by Deleuze. In Lefort's thought, difference is the political institutionalization of a society that is always separated from itself. As in the other two paradigms, here too we are within a post-foundationalist horizon.[7] In this instance, however, it does not have dissolutive consequences for the political – neither by default, as in Heidegger, nor by excess, as in Deleuze. On the contrary, it is precisely society's lack of foundation that determines the need for its political establishment. Since it is not founded on a substance that endows it with a presupposed identity, social being needs to be politically instituted.

2. But how? And, even before that query, what does Lefort mean by the term "to institute"? To answer this question, which is crucial for his political ontology, one must first clear the field of an authoritarian conception of institution that has been around since the category was formed. It goes back to the proto-juridical lexicon of glossators and canonists, most especially to the concept of *persona ficta* or *repraesentata* [legal or juristic person, created under the law (lit. fictitious person, represented person)] introduced by Sinibaldo dei Fieschi and relates to *voluntas superioris* [the will of a higher authority], which was in force not only at the origin of *institutio* [institution] but during the entire course of its existence. Unlike the corporation, which is based on the personal element of *collegium* [fellowship], and unlike the foundation, which is functional to the preservation of a collective good, the institution, in its original meaning, relies on a transcendent authority, of which the institution's organs are mere executors. Something of this authoritative semantics remains in the modern tradition up until Weber's systematization, which is then adopted by almost all subsequent sociological and politological formulations. What seems to characterize the institution – and it is no accident that the "movements" will come to oppose it – is a tendency toward the conservation of norms that emerged from rigidified social equilibria. This conservative, if not reactionary interpretation of institution is taken for granted not only by anti-modern philosophies but also by progressive ones. Profound lexical differences notwithstanding, different authors such as Searle, Bourdieu, and Foucault – and actually already Sartre in *Critique of Dialectical Reason* – converge on this conservative interpretation of the institution, understood as that which neutralizes the innovative drives from society, in order to legitimize existing powers. At bottom it recalls, even though with a different intent, both the Marxian idea of the necessary extinction of the state and the Freudian one of the process of civilization used to repress instincts. According to this conception, instead of being oriented toward social inclusion, institutions have a selective and perhaps even exclusionary function vis-à-vis citizens. As both Gehlen and Goffman believe, this is accomplished by protecting us from the outpouring of the instincts, but also

by exonerating us from complex thought: institutions channel our behaviors into repetitive and automatic protocols, which preclude a creative release.

As we have seen, in his first works Deleuze proposed a more dynamic interpretation of the institution, connecting it precisely with the expression of instincts. While it does not indulge them directly, if favors their development, stimulating their growth: Deleuze adopted a thesis he derived from Hume and argued that, as opposed to the law, which is imposed from above, the institution presupposes the social utility of those it represents. This does not mean that the transition between instincts and institutions is fluid and linear. On the contrary, it passes through a bottleneck that selects for the naturalness of tendencies, subjecting it to conditions and objectives that are historically determined. In this phase, far from removing the "negative," Deleuze made it the necessary conduit for institutional functionality. While the law, which is expressed in obligations and prohibitions, is the negation of an affirmative behavior, the institution is the affirmation of a constraint that is functional to its realization. In sum, institutions are the negative filter that provides social demands with the necessary articulation to ensure their endurance by distancing them from their immediacy.

While Lefort does not directly refer to Deleuze, his instituting thought moves in a similar direction. In order to reconstruct its elaboration, which developed over the course of time, one needs to trace it back to the phenomenological tradition, which goes from Husserl to Merleau-Ponty, in a crescendo of theoretical intensity and political radicalness. The initial point of departure can be identified in Husserl's *Stiftung* [foundation], which is transposed by Merleau-Ponty himself into the French *institution* [institution]: in making this choice he differs from Levinas, Ricoeur, and Derrida, who, diminishing its semantic depth, translated it either with *formation* [formation] (Levinas) or with *fondation* [foundation] (the other two). But, in view of the political twist that the concept will take in Lefort, it is even more important to note the categorial transition it undergoes when passing from Husserl's original formulation to Merleau-Ponty's. In Husserl, who actually never proposed a systematic definition, *Stiftung* points to the intentional consciousness' process of objectivation, which is directed toward giving consciousness a certain stability within experience, thus providing it with continuity over time – a status that reaffirms what is born of statutes or rules destined to preserve it. Already in this version, in the connection between birth and consolidation, *Stiftung* assumes a dynamic importance, strengthening the meaning of the corresponding verb in relation to that of the noun. The institution is only an intermediary station in an "instituting" that both precedes it and follows it. Rather than blocking its temporal dynamics, it ensures its flow, protecting it from the entropy that threatens it. Situated at the point of intersection between nature and history, it opens a new situation, without breaking its ties with its genetic conditions. Husserl translates this movement into the circular path that goes from *Urstiftung*, the originary institution, passes through *Nachstiftung*, the reinstitution, and arrives at *Endstiftung*, the end institution. Just as the first, from the very beginning, refers to the third by means of a sort of prefiguration, this last one refers recursively to its own genesis, relaunching the originary impulse in a new configuration. In this retrospective projection the institution, far from compressing the new onto the cast of what has already occurred, finds in it the spring for its future creativity.[8]

This does not mean, however, that this dynamic, even if oriented toward objectivation, still pertains to intentional consciousness. What institutes sense by means of this dual movement of advancement and feedback is still the apperceptive activity of the ego, even if placed in an intersubjective kind of ontological narrative: hence its impolitical and even, tendentially, ahistorical tenor. Merleau-Ponty intervenes precisely on this configuration, forcing its subjective semantics.[9] As Lefort himself reminisces in his "Foreword" to Merleau-Ponty's 1954–1955 course at the Collège de France,[10] Merleau-Ponty's interest in the topic of the institution dated to the mid-1940s, and in particular to his first philosophical essay, *Cézanne's Doubt*, in 1945.[11] The same movement, which on that occasion was examined in conjunction with the concatenation of antecedences that are impressed into the work of art, returns in the 1952 contribution *Indirect Language and the Voices of Silence*, where the painter's work is interpreted as the conversion of use into institution. The fact that even the greatest painters elaborate their own styles of painting within grooves already left by others and by themselves makes "a sort of provisory eternity"[12] out of the expressive operation, which is not only metamorphosis but "also a response to what the world, the past, and the completed works demanded":[13]

> Husserl has used the fine word *Stiftung* – foundation or establishment – to designate first of all the unlimited fecundity of each present which, precisely because it is singular and passes, can never stop having been and thus being universally; but above all to designate that fecundity

> of the products of a culture which continue to have value after their appearance and which open a field of investigations in which they perpetually come to life again.[14]

In the chapter "The Algorithm and the Mystery of Language," published in the posthumous volume *The Prose of the World*, Merleau-Ponty also recognizes in mathematical thought a recursive process, which opens up to a new meaning in the unprecedented organization of elements elaborated in preceding structures.[15] All these conceptual elements converge in the 1954–1955 course, within an overall framework that gives them the traits of a real theory of institutions. As is well known, the lessons from those courses – collected by Lefort's students and published under his direction in the form of "notes" – are synthesized by the author in a summary that does not do justice to their full depth. It is nevertheless sufficient to provide the overall direction of his argument, which represents a clear step forward by comparison with Husserl's reflections on *Stiftung*. The decisive transition with respect to those resides in an emancipation of the institution from the philosophy of consciousness and, more particularly, from the separation between subject and object that is implicit in it. Even though Husserl does not admit it, in phenomenology objects remain the objective reflection of acts of consciousness that were initially autonomous. This subjectivist twist has a dual inhibitory effect, in both historical and political terms. On the one hand, the relaunching of the past into the present, and therefore into the future, is in fact impeded by a fracture that interrupts its transit; on the other, this vertical interruption determines a second horizontal caesura, which blocks the interaction between subjects enclosed in their own individuality. It is regarding this double impasse that Merleau-Ponty distances himself from Husserlian phenomenology, marking the difference between constituting power and instituting thought, which is related to the different role that the negative plays in each case: in the first an exclusionary role, in the second an inclusionary one:

> If the subject were taken not as a constituting but an instituting subject, it might be understood that the subject does not exist instantaneously and that the other person does not exist simply as a negative of myself. What I have begun at certain decisive moments would exist neither far off in the past as an objective memory nor be present like a memory revived, but really between the two as the field of my becoming during that period. Likewise my relation to another person

> would not be reducible to a disjunction: an instituting subject could coexist with another because the one instituted is not the immediate reflection of the activity of the former and can be regained by himself or by others without involving anything like a total recreation. Thus the instituted subject exists between others and myself, between me and myself, like a hinge, the consequence and the guarantee of our belonging to a common world.[16]

For Merleau-Ponty, then, the negative becomes the filter through which each human experience can identify itself only by distancing itself from itself and by exposing itself to its own alterity. This is true for any activity, public and private – in art and in thought, and even in love, whose alleged purity is at risk of being reversed into absolute negation, as Proust infers from the "signs" of separation and jealousy that we already discussed. Far from being opposed to affirmation, the negative constitutes its internal articulation, which expresses its historical and symbolic depth. Anticipating one of the central vectors of Lefort's thought, Merleau-Ponty finds the same tension that connects unity and division in the relationship between past and present:

> Now this working of the past against the present does not culminate in a closed universal history or a complete system of all the possible human combinations with respect to such an institution as, for example, kinship. Rather, it produces a table of diverse, complex probabilities, always bound to local circumstances, weighted with a coefficient of facticity, and such that we can never say of one that it is more true than another, although we can say that one is more false, more artificial, and less open to a future in turn less rich.[17]

*

The difference between institution and constitution that Merleau-Ponty grasped has recently become the topic of a chapter in Pierre Dardot and Christian Laval's *Common*.[18] The two terms, which come from the same root – the Latin verb *statuere* [to set, establish, decide] – are distinguished by their prefix: *in-* for institution and *con-* < *cum* for constitution. While the second term mostly has the meaning of a founding carried out by a subject equipped with sovereign attributes, the former, especially if understood in its verbal usage, has a more ample and varied meaning. It refers at the same time to establishing, undertaking, and teaching, but also to qualifying things in a specific manner. While the concept of constitution is used mostly in a juridical context – in addition to the biological, naturally – that of institution exhibits greater semantic elasticity, lending itself to different lexical uses in sociological, anthropological, and linguistic contexts. These distinctions notwithstanding, the two concepts often end up being confused in an inappropriate manner, which runs the risk of clouding the meaning of both. This happens to some degree also to Hardt and Negri, who, while they intend to oppose constituted to constituting power, end up attributing some of the characteristics of instituting praxis to the latter – for instance the capability of self-transformation – in such a way as to recognize the same "will to institute and to constitute"[19] in revolutionary processes.

The person who returns to the practice of distinguishing the two concepts, following lines of thought that are not too distant from Lefort's, is instead Cornelius Castoriadis. One could say that he establishes a relationship between instituting and instituted that resembles the one that others have drawn between constituting and constituted – but shifts it to a different level. Following the practice of the proponents of constituting power, Castoriadis also looks at the phenomenon of instituting from the point of view of the instituent rather than from that of the instituted. While he never severs the tie between them, he contests the sociological reduction of the institution to the instituted and points to the instituting act as the only one capable of creating a social bond. In this sense, the instituting activity has a political dimension, in addition to a social one – namely that of instituting society via the practice of what Castoriadis calls an "instituting imaginary."[20] It is precisely this attitude that distinguishes the semantics of the institution from that of the constitution, as the author states in a passage also quoted by Dardot and Laval: "For the fundamental 'power' in any society, the prime power upon which all the others depend … is the *instituting power*. And unless one is under the spell of the 'constitutional delusion,' this power is neither locatable nor formalizable for it pertains to the instituting imaginary."[21] This has a much more ample and widespread scope than the sovereign punctuality of constituting power, such as to get disseminated throughout the entire arc of experience – from language to customs, to practices, to ideas. Therefore, "behind *constituting* power, one needs to recognize the exercise of *instituting power*."[22]

These are the two fundamental elements, ably identified by Dardot and Laval. The first is the distance of the instituting process from the theological notion of *creatio ex nihilo*, to which the idea of constituent power remains instead attached. It is Castoriadis who already distinguishes creation *ex nihilo* [from nothing] from creation *cum nihilo* [with nothing]; and he distinguishes it even more from creation *ex aliquo* [from something], in the sense that, far from being absolute, instituting creation is always conditioned by constraints and given situations that channel its action into a course that has at least partially been already excavated. But "conditioned" does not mean "determined," because the meaning that has been created cannot be fully explained by the preexisting one. It is the concept of "emergence" that allows one to identify a possible point of equilibrium between the sovereign decision of absolute creation and the decision, mediated by the instituted, of the new institution. Something emerges from something else without being determined by it and in fact transforming it – as for instance occurred with psychoanalysis relatively to the science of the period: transforming, that is, not only what is already instituted, but the very instituting subject itself. This is the other element that characterizes instituting praxis, differentiating it from constituting power. While in the latter the subject precedes the constituted object without being modified by it, in the instituting process the subject does not preexist its own praxis but comes into existence together with it, modifying it and simultaneously modifying itself.

*

3. Lefort takes back his own conception of "institution" to precisely this tension. What differentiates it, moving it well beyond both Husserlian *Stiftung* and Merleau-Ponty's *institution*, is its radical politicization. Certainly Merleau-Ponty, by inscribing it into the "flesh of history," has already placed an obvious metapolitical imprint on the institution. Once emancipated from the philosophy of consciousness, it opens up a pre-subjective space, or an asubjective one, which cannot be related to an individual separated from others, but is allowed, and in fact constituted, precisely by their relationship. In Merleau-Ponty, however, this metapolitical articulation still appears to be more a consequence of the phenomenological project than its center of gravity. We have to wait for Lefort to see this second scenario unfold, starting with the moment in which he conceives of all of politics as a social institution. As the institution is always political, so the political is always instituting. But one should not misunderstand. To argue that, in Lefort's work, reflection on the institution coincides with reflection on the political to the point of making it into political thought on the institution does not mean that he examines political institutions as a sociologist or a political scientist might. It means rather that he thinks of all politics in the form of instituting power: "The issue posed by the phenomenon of power – Lefort writes in an article devoted to exactly this issue – therefore brings us back to the topic of the *institution* of the social. I no longer use this term [social] in its conventional sense, but in a sense that preserves all the force of the verb 'to institute.'"[23] What Lefort means, shifting the argument from the noun to the verb, is that the expression "institution of the social" should not be understood in the weak sense of political institution situated in society but in the strong sense that society is instituted by the political.

To grasp this statement in all its scope and complexity, it behooves one to start from a text entitled "Sur la démocratie: Le politique et l'institution du social," edited by Marcel Gauchet on the basis of a course held by Lefort at the University of Caen in 1967.[24] It is as if Lefort's entire philosophical itinerary – from the analysis of archaic societies to investigations into modern politics and up to the comparison with totalitarianism – were condensed in the problem of the political institution of the social. The relationship between the political and the social is not, therefore, one of the many topics Lefort addressed, but the pivot around which all his thought rotates. It is for this reason that it should be examined by giving the utmost attention to each of these terms separately, as well as to the set that they form – outside which neither is entirely comprehensible. Let us start with the political. It is not an outcome or an expression of economic dynamics, as the Marxist vulgate believes. But it is not a horizontal subsystem of the social system either, as functionalist sociology and generally political science would have it. It is instead the vertical form of the institution of the social. In this manner Lefort does not refer to a transcendent element that intervenes on society from the outside, modifying it – or, even less, to something that precedes it, enabling its birth. In that case a causal relationship would exist between the two elements – the social and the political; and this is completely alien to his perspective. The political is unimaginable outside its relationship with the social. If there were no society, there would be no politics either, since politics is necessarily oriented toward relations between human beings. But the reverse is also true: without politics what we define as society would not be such, in other words a whole that is recognizable both from inside itself and from outside itself. The meaning of a society does not arise from its natural properties and not even from empirical circumstances – from the bare facts, which remain isolated and mute if isolated from the horizon in which they inhere. Certainly societies exist in and of themselves, but they are not understandable before a politics "forms them," giving them precisely that identity that differentiates them from others, both contemporaneous and preceding. The philosophical questioning of the political is directed precisely at this dynamic:

> It is guided, from its inception, by the intention of understanding what the fact that human beings live in society means, by the intention of finding a small number of *forms of society* among the diverse human contexts that are organized around the idea of a common identity and autonomous will, by the intention of discovering the criteria that underlie this distinction and of identifying what the best kind of life or the best regime are, both in an absolute and in a relative sense.[25]

This, naturally, is also true of classical political philosophy, above all as regards the definition of the best regime – a matter alien to Lefort's interests also because it would imply the adoption of that *survol* gaze that is available only to those who place themselves outside the framework being analyzed. What characterizes the instituting power of the political over society is rather another element, one that can be found in the division that traverses it from the moment of its emergence but of which it is not initially aware. The role of politics is that of making it aware – of revealing to society itself the principle that "forms it": and this principle is the conflict between opposite parties. This is true of all societies, which are always traversed by conflict – but differentiated from one another according to the way in which they relate to it: by neutralizing it, by canceling it, or, in the case of modern democracies, by recognizing it as inevitable and productive. The political is nothing more than that – the answer, the name, that different societies give to the "fact" of their separation. In this sense, far from being an external element, it is always immanent in them.[26] It is the consciousness of their partiality, of the impossibility of conceiving of oneself as a whole by amalgamating the opposing perspectives of those who inhabit it. But this immanence of the political in society also, simultaneously, has the form of an exteriority, without which society would coincide with itself, losing sight of the gap that constitutes it in the form of its own disunion. If society forgot the split that divides it, it would lose the symbolic principle that makes it what it is, distinguishing it from the others. Unity and separation are therefore inseparable in it:

> Such a division does not reach the point of being able to actually split the social into parts that are alien to one another: through it the social relates to itself, distancing itself from itself and acquiring its identity. It appears as such. Open in its being to its own present–absent foundation, the social is a *continuous gifting and instituting of itself*.[27]

That society can relate to itself only by distancing itself from itself, testing its own exteriority, means that the institution does not have the shape either of a decision – much less an *ex nihilo* one, as occurs with constituent power – or of a self-institution. What decides it is neither a presupposed subject nor itself, its own self-productive power. If it had a stable foundation at its base, as classical ontology would have it, there would be no need for institutions – it would be sufficient, in order for it to define itself, to follow the foundation's directives or to search for a "new beginning," in case the first had been lost – which is what Heidegger, Strauss, and Arendt actually do, albeit in different ways. If, vice-versa, society could institute itself by producing itself, as a postfoundationalist perspective would have it, one would be following the immanentist path of Deleuze or, at least in part, that of Castoriadis. But this self-institution, as defined by Castoriadis, would be "imaginary" – in the sense that the distinction between real and symbolic, which is decisive in Lefort, would vanish. It would be another way for society to negate conflict, thus erasing the political, in the hallucinatory pretense of coinciding with itself. This would also mean overcoming the distance from its origin and making it its own. But in this case the genealogical relationship with the originary, which can be experienced only as the inconceivable limit of the temporal process, would be lost.

The non-appropriability of the origin, which differs both from a foundation and from a transcendental a-priori, expresses the need, for society, to know itself via a movement of exteriorization – directing itself to a sort of "internal outside," something necessary for its own intelligibility. This internal outside, this "immanent transcendence," is power – understood by Lefort as the manner in which society knows itself and its positioning in being with respect to knowledge and the law: "As a consequence of the splitting of power and society, a dimension of *exteriority* is born as a dimension of the identity of the social. Society relates to its own outside via power."[28] Since it is necessary for the institution of all societies, obviously power assumes different forms each time. If in archaic and *ancien régime* societies power is constituted in a purely transcendent dimension, situating itself in a place that is separate from and external to social conflict, in modern societies it is that which results from the outcome of such a conflict. Democracy is the only regime to recognize the absence of foundation, institutionalizing it. In democratic societies power is a hollow structure, one not appropriable in a definite fashion, because it is continuously contested by contrasting interests and values instead of being impersonated by fantastic entities or by the mystical body of the sovereign. This results in a society whose identity is in permanent transformation, a consequence of the power relationships that are generated by its contrasting parts, or parties. Power is both expression and governance of this dialectic. Its place "cannot be occupied" – Lefort concludes – "in the sense that the impossibility of taking up residence there proves to be constitutive of the socialization process."[29]

*

If Lefort inscribes his theory of institutions in the framework of the phenomenological tradition, one should not, however, overlook Maurice Hauriou's influence on all the French culture of the period. Deleuze is well aware of him and anthologizes one of his texts in the collection *Instincts and Institutions*; and Hauriou enjoyed widespread international fame, to the extent that he was recognized as a teacher, alongside Santi Romano, by the likes of Carl Schmitt.[30] In the analytical context, his influence can be found even in the neo-institutionalism of MacCormick and Weinberger.[31] What is the reason for the widespread fame of a jurist who was not technically impeccable – and from this point of view much inferior to Santi Romano? Most probably it is his eclecticism, which leads him not only to modify his conception of the institution over the course of time, but also to hybridize it with motifs of heterogeneous origin. Influenced by Tarde and Bergson, but also by Claude Bernard, he takes a critical position toward the two dominant juridical traditions of his times. While he distances himself from the German subjectivism of Gerber, Laband, and Jellinek, which traces the entire normative system back to the will of the legislator, he also contests the French objectivism of Durkheim and Duguit, who make the individual subject into a mere vehicle of social consciousness, just as clearly. By defining the institution as "an idea of a work or enterprise that is realized and has juridical staying power in a social environment,"[32] Hauriou connects law and society, norm and life, idea and action in a form that, instead of opposing one to the other, aims for their mutual implication.

The same occurs when dealing with the relation between subject and object. On the one hand the idea of work, spread throughout the social environment, has an objective existence that preexists the subjects who enact it – they, more than creating it, find it or meet it, "just as the miner meets the diamond."[33] On the other, in order to be realized, the idea of work must incorporate itself into, or impersonate, specific subjects who will become its carriers, raising to consciousness the socially subconscious elements that move below the subjective will. Hauriou, by mixing elements of different origin – juridical, sociological, biological – confers upon the institution a vitalist dimension that removes it from both positivism and normativism. Just as human beings are represented as a conglomerate of cells unified within the same person by the biology of the period, the institution is considered a corporate plexus organized around a guiding idea. Hauriou actually distinguishes between the phenomena of incorporation and personification, which are both necessary to the continuity of the institution over time, but the former in an objective form, the latter in subjective terms.

The French jurist pushes this difference to the point of placing person-institutions and thing-institutions side by side. He does state that he is especially interested in the former, while almost neglecting the latter, but this *does not* take anything away from the importance of the distinction, which contributes to the dissolution of the binding constraints between institution and juridical personhood. Paolo Napoli, in a keen essay on the topic,[34] observes that the category of juridical personhood itself, in its

Roman formulation anything but a living body, is a technical construct that is functional to the juridical determination of interhuman relationships. Hauriou's reference to institution-things, even though not elaborated, opens onto a discourse that, finally freed of the mythology of the person, contributes to leading the instituting praxis back to a materialist horizon.

The impossibility of deriving the concept of institution from that of person – or of reducing it to it – is also supported in a different way by Paul Ricoeur. Developing the Husserlian dialectic between *Stiftung* and *Urstiftung* [original foundation] in a text from the 1970s,[35] he starts from the observation that, just as no one can inaugurate a language, so no one can found an institution from scratch, since such a foundational act is always preceded by something that is already instituted. We are dealing with that element of passivity, also mentioned by Merleau-Ponty, that cuts across the structure of intersubjectivity, withdrawing it from any grasp: it precedes all attempts at instituting it from the outside, thus rendering them vain. We can act only within intersubjective forms that are already given, however much they may conceal their own historicity, presenting themselves as rootless. The realization of freedom always passes through a constraint, which makes an immediate relationship with the other impossible. For two freedoms to be able to cross without mutually destroying each other, they necessarily need to pass through a neutral term that would channel their relationship within specific margins. This term is the institution, which is tied to the production of freedom with an indissoluble knot. Just as all vital institutions establish a free space, so freedom, in order not to be reversed into its opposite, needs to be fashioned within the perimeter of institutions. Nobody can jump over one's own shadow, adhering immediately to oneself and to others.

This explains the failure of all attempts to derive the political, or even the social, from the personal relationship between "I" and "thou," without passing through the mediation of the "third person" – the impersonal one. Unlike those philosophies that look to dialogue as the archetype of all possible social relationships, even face-to-face interactions are made possible only by the presence of institutions aimed at protecting them from an excess of immediacy. One does not pass immediately from I to you, from one to the other, without transitioning through the "non-person," which relates them via impersonal institutions. As post-Weberian sociology is well aware, only a minimal part of intersubjective relations is susceptible of personalization – since the majority of them are institutionalized within roles, services, artifices. On the other hand we have seen how the same juridical idea of "person" was born in Rome with this external or objective connotation; the "person," in the sense of juridical personhood, is something one "has," not something one "is."[36] Nobody, not even the most expressive of actors, fully adheres to the character they interpret. This is the impersonal dynamics that Hegel defines with the expression "objective spirit"; personal liberties, in order not to be annihilated in the "fury of destruction," need to be mediated by those filters which we call "institutions." As much as we attempt to internalize them – or, as Hauriou puts it, to impersonate them – they always exhibit an irreducible exterior facies, destined to remain outside us. Naturally, as Ricoeur – following Freud – concludes, this means that culture and alienation coincide, or at least have a common segment. This is exactly what Lefort argues: contrary to the projects of self-production of the social, each appropriation necessarily passes through an alteration that prevents the full immanence of society to itself. The political name for this instituting alterity is "power."

*

4. It has been said that politics institutes a society that is initially unaware of the division that traverses it. This misrecognition, which aims to cancel the fractures that divide the social, is defined in Marxism by the term "ideology." Why, therefore, does Lefort not adopt its concept instead of distancing himself from it more and more, to the point of replacing it with that of the "symbolic"? This question is so critical as to get situated at the center of his itinerary, marking the complex relationship he entertains with Marx's thought. While in the 1950s Lefort agrees with Merleau-Ponty's inclinations and is still engaged in freeing Marx's thought from economistic interpretations that diminish its philosophical depth, starting from a specific phase, which corresponds to his exit from *Socialisme ou barbarie*, his critical posture increases, ultimately reaching the point of questioning the very presuppositions of Marxism. The fact that Lefort continues to refer to Marx, and continues to make use of some of his categories even after the symbolic turn, does not diminish the distance he establishes from the latter's basic framework. At that stage, denouncing the bureaucratic configuration that all communist political organizations adopted – as Lefort did for a whole decade, side by side with Castoriadis – will no longer suffice, if one is not able to recognize the inevitable outcome of an intrinsically totalitarian logic of this trend. In the 1979 preface to *Éléments d'une critique de la bureaucratie* he writes, taking the self-criticism he had already formulated in the 1971 edition to the point of no return: "At one point I thought I could see the outlines of a revolution carried out by the oppressed themselves and capable of defending itself from those who lay claim to directing it. ... That was how I represented the path of truth in History to myself. Today I know I was wrong."[37]

What is rejected is not only revolutionary praxis, with all that it induces in terms of the relations between leaders and militants, but the very idea of revolution, in other words of a constituent power that is the creator of an entirely new reality. The myth of an undivided society, entirely transparent, is not simply an error of perspective, but the necessary outcome of a philosophy of history that is destined to be disproved. From that point on, having turned to the analysis of democracy and its totalitarian degenerations, Lefort realizes that "the development of class struggles, the logic of their expansion, are not revealed except in the register of the symbolic."[38]

But how exactly does this register differ from the Marxian *dispositif* of ideology? It should be said that, in reconstructing its genesis in the works of Marx, most particularly in *The German Ideology*, but already in the *Critique of Hegel's Philosophy of Right* and in *The Eighteenth Brumaire*, Lefort does not undervalue its heuristic scope at all – first of all because, unlike those who attribute ideology to any social group, Marx confines it to the bourgeoisie, situating its origin in capitalist society, but also because, far from reducing it to a simple reflex, he recognizes how it functions in the negation of the triple division that traverses bourgeois society: between capital and labor, between state and society, and between knowledge and reality. Marx therefore grasps not only ideology's element of mystification, but also its power to express a reality it reproduces in reverse: by negating social division, ideology ends up redoubling it, because it hides what it reveals and reveals what it hides. What Marx, however, does not undertake is the next step, in other words the recognition of the symbolic space in which the exchange between reality and imagination takes place. He realizes that modern society translates the real into the imaginary, making the imaginary into something real. But, instead of referring this intertwinement back to the social institution from which it emerges, he considers it to be a simple effect of capitalist division. In this way Marx derives social division from ideology rather than the other way around. At the basis of such a perspectival exchange is the illusory idea of an undivided society that must be restored in order to fill the gap between reality and ideology that the capitalist mode of production has produced. Only in this fashion – that is, by revolutionizing social relationships – would one be able to overcome both the real and ideological divisions, simultaneously.

But Lefort observes critically that postulating such a possibility means to situate one's point of observation outside the dynamics one analyzes, presuming that one can dominate the entire process. And this is exactly what Marx does, once he assumes ideology as the object of a knowledge that aims to substitute it with science. In this fashion, by presuming to be able to overcome the partiality of a socially conditioned point of view, he makes his own discourse on ideology ideological and exhibits an analogously opaque gaze. It is precisely in this attitude that Lefort identifies the seed of that conception of *survol* that Merleau-Ponty had criticized and that thinks it stands above the real, ignoring that it is conditioned by it. Marx confused the ideological level with the symbolic. Instead of seeing ideology as the effect of a more general symbolic *dispositif*, he referred the latter back to the former. Hence also an erroneous conception of the relation between economics and politics. Marx intends to derive power, knowledge and the law from the relations of production, whereas in reality the latter become intelligible only on the basis of the articulation of the former. One cannot interpret power, in other words the instituting source of the social, as an effect of economic relationships that, on the contrary, emerge from it. What Marx fails to distinguish, homologizing them into a single block of meaning, is the empirical division of society and the division that is politically instituted, or otherwise the plane of material production and that of its representation – which comes down to the same thing. The symbolic system, although it emerges from it, always exceeds real dynamics, preserving a protrusion that feeds back into them. In spite of appearances, power has more to do with discourse – in other words with its representational construction – than with the economic relations within which it is instituted. Lefort completely reverses the cause and effect relationships between economics and politics, as well as those between subjectivity and representation. Subjects do not consciously open up a new symbolic field; it is the field that makes them subjects, inscribing them within specific social practices. The state itself is not understandable, except in relation to the set of symbolic presuppositions that explain its genesis. It is not enough to move from the social to the political level or, reversing direction, to return from the latter to the former, since neither fully coincides with itself but both presuppose something which precedes them – in other words the process of their own institution. Marx's error cannot be attributed to a lack of awareness of the social, or even historical dimension, but rather to the illusion of being able to enclose all human reality within the confines of society and history.

This is not about a subjective error in his interpretation. It is about the limit that all ideologies reach, once they no longer manage to govern the contradiction that generates them – that of attributing a general configuration to a particular phenomenon. The wall against which, at a certain point, it inevitably bangs its head is the fact that, by ignoring the bond with the regime that institutes it, it cannot describe reality without exposing its exteriority from it. Hence its doubly mystifying nature. Ideology masks not only the reality of the relations of production but also the horizon of sense from which they emerge. What is removed, once this is modified, is not ideology as such, but *that* particular ideology, which is destined to be substituted by another one, suitable to the new symbolic order. Each new ideology takes hold from the failure, or at least the blind spot, of the one that precedes it, as occurred with the genesis of totalitarian ideology from within bourgeois ideology – before it was replaced in its turn by a new ideological formation, which Lefort defines as "invisible" and in which we still find ourselves. Its greater capacity to endure, by comparison with other ideologies, resides in its diffuse adhesion to the real. And yet it is right now, when the social seems to coincide without residues with itself, that a different ontology, as yet undefined in its own contours, outlines itself at its external margins. The need for a new instituting thought is beginning to make itself felt from inside the closed space of ideology.

*

5. Lefort works on the elaboration of an instituting thought from the early 1950s, when his relationship with Marx is far from broken. It goes without saying that his degree of awareness at that time was a function of the conceptual maturing of the category of the "symbolic" and its gradual replacement of the category of "ideology." Lefort is, above all, led to distance himself from the Marxian paradigm as a result of his dealings with the French anthropology of the period, from Mauss to Lévi-Strauss, but also with American culturalism, from Kardiner to Bateson, and finally with the British functionalism of Malinowski and Evans-Pritchard. The Maussian notion of a "total social fact" constitutes, from Lefort's perspective, a first approximation of the concept of the symbolic as an articulation of power, knowledge, and law. What begins to be outlined in his anthropological essays is the antinomic link, never contemplated in Marxism, between socialization and division: in other words the idea that no society, not even the most primitive, can ever fully coincide with itself, but is rather structured by the conflicts that traverse it and that therefore highlight the instituting relation between the political and negation. The political institutes the social, not directly, but passing through the negative. If it unifies human beings by decomposing their immediate relationships, this means that instituting processes always deal with an alterity that eludes empirical analysis and belongs to what is really an ontological domain. As Lefort argues in

the preface to the volume in which his political anthropological texts are collected,

> We continue to think that no sociology is worthy of this name if it does not carry the seeds of a question on the being of the social within itself, if it does not attempt to decipher, whatever the object of its analysis, the phenomenon of its institution, the manner in which a humanity is differentiated – in other words, more radically, is divided – in order to exist as such, the manner in which it avails itself of symbolic references in order to represent that which escapes it: its origin, its nature, time, being itself.[39]

The first of these essays, published in *Les temps modernes* in 1951 under the title "Exchange and the Struggle between Human Beings," aims to go beyond the rationalism of Hegel, Marx, and also Husserl by referring to the anthropological horizon opened by Mauss. Like the young Marx, Mauss, too, asks himself about the actual relationships that bind human beings above and beyond the ideologies and rules they give themselves. And, like Husserl, he addresses "the social things themselves, as they are, concretely."[40] But he does so not by establishing cause and effect relationships between phenomena of a different nature, but instead by aiming to recognize the overall meaning generated by their intertwinement. In order to grasp the most disruptive consequences that the shift brought about by Mauss had on traditional sociology, it is necessary to rescue his thought from the logico-mathematical interpretation – defined by Lefort as symbolic, in a very different sense from the one he himself will later confer on the expression – that Lévi-Strauss provided. What characterizes Mauss's "total" method is the tension that the phenomena of exchange give social relationships. Once the traditional genealogy has been rejected, even one of Marxian origins, which sees barter as the most ancient form of exchange, Mauss focuses his attention on the logic of the gift. Its most singular trait consists in the fact that, although this form of exchange is not made up of useful goods, it is not free, but is in fact regulated by a series of constraints that make it de facto obligatory. Those who, within the logic of this domain, abstain from giving gifts, or refuse to accept gifts, not only situate themselves outside the social circuit, but are considered a true "enemy." Malinowski also notes that in the Trobriand Islands clans challenge one another, attempting to subdue their adversaries by means of gifts. The custom of the potlatch itself – which so struck Georges Bataille, who was also constantly engaged in a dialogue with Mauss[41] – in which the giving of sumptuary gifts is replaced by their destruction, is enacted in order to "annihilate, 'quash' the adversary."[42] This antagonistic element is not exclusive to the Native Americans of America's Northwest but is present in all societies that engage in a gift economy.

What does Lefort derive from this, as regards the instituting paradigm? For starters, that the exchange of gifts has a plurality of meanings that are irreducible to a theory of primitive exchange and more generally to the economic system; but also that the gifting economy does not arise, as argued by Mauss, from a merging tendency but, on the contrary, from a principle of separation. Hence the far from peaceful character of the gift. It is "a threat" – something that, for Malinowski, "clasps," or "bites," and with respect to which partners consider themselves "adversaries."[43] As one can gather from the ambivalent meaning of the term "gift," both present and weapon, both cure and poison, it reveals an antithetical relationship with the other: something that it is dangerous to accept, but also not to return; a mutual dependence but also a death threat. This is a powerful testimony that Lefort finds, on the terrain of anthropology, for his theory of the political institution as the division of the social, which he is still developing:

> In other words, the more human beings feel reciprocally dependent, the more they feel the urge to keep their distance in order to avoid the risk of breaking the bond that unites them. Further on we shall see how this risk is an indication of a greater danger, which does not concern the individual as such, but the social or human truth that s/he represents. For the moment it is sufficient to establish that exchange is an act that separates the humans and places them face to face.[44]

To place themselves "face to face," one facing the other – no differently from in the challenge to the death between servant and master in Hegel – human beings must first separate themselves from one another. What is at stake is not the thing that is exchanged, gifted, and reciprocated, with a surplus that can make one think of usury, but the subjectivity of the donor, increased or decreased by the disproportion between gift and countergift. Until s/he *does not* reciprocate it with a surplus, the recipient is alienated from the thing received, which becomes in some ways her or his inanimate master. In the exchanging of gifts, recognition does not have the soft traits of a comparison, but the harsh ones of a clash: "The *potlatch* should therefore be described like a war: for the Kwakiutl, the knife on top of a cudgel is its symbol; for the Tlingit, who use the same designation for the *potlatch* and for the war dance, it is the raised spear. For both war is the way to be 'recognized' in one's full autonomy."[45]

From this point of view, the relationship between sociality and separation could not retrace a more significant genetic matrix. If even the most archaic societies are so deeply marked by it, this means that it is situated at the center of the instituting paradigm. One institutes by dividing – or, better, by bringing the originary division that has always cut across social space to symbolic expression. One also institutes by negating. Division is also negation – of unreflective social unity. But the practice of the potlatch also confers another meaning on negation, an even more intense one, bringing it to its apex: that of destruction – not as an end in itself, but functional to the affirmation of the donating subject: "The *potlatch*, however, is not only self-affirmation on the part of the donor, but also negation of things, destruction of the wealth 'offered.'"[46] But why destroy or, as the Haida literally express themselves, "kill" wealth, property? The first reason is that to destroy one's gift places those who receive it in the impossibility of reciprocating, and thus defeats them even before one has their answer, *negates* their answer – unless the recipient of the destruction responds with a destruction analogous or superior to the first, thus negating in turn what s/he has *not* received. But negation also has a second motivation, addressed not to the other, but to oneself. Notwithstanding the tendency of humans to identify with what they possess – or, better, precisely because of this tendency – by negating things, humans negate themselves: "Humans undo their appearance and posit themselves saying: 'I am not all this.'"[47] The second reason is even stronger than the first, because – according to Lefort – the purpose of the potlatch is not only, or not so much, the submission of the other but the submission of nature, following the necessarily artificial character of instituting logic. Certainly, not every gifting takes the form of a potlatch. Nor do all negations entail destruction, but the potlatch does no more than bring to its point of culmination an antagonism that, in essence, is present in any gifting. In each one – insofar as they are constitutive forms of social relations in primitive societies – the opposition between human beings and nature is added to that between human beings. But, once one has highlighted the intensity of the negation or division, one should also take care to recognize the figure of socialization in it. By avoiding any dialectical recuperation of the negative, one instead has to see the other face of the conservation of life in negation, its very expression. Without the symbolic – in other words, without the angle that the negative impresses on each experience – we would be crushed by the unbearable pressure of the real, inevitably translated into the imaginary: "In solitude the individual feels that s/he is overwhelmed by reality; lost in that which belongs to her or him."[48] The gift allows us to break this suffocating adherence to reality, the oppressive bond that unites us with things. But this is possible, the operation succeeds, only if the other recognizes it and reproduces it, multiplying the negative in a play of mirrors whose outcome is sociality. *Not* being things reestablishes human beings in their mutual relationships in the only possible form – that of their conflictual division. The distance from Marx that Lefort achieves, thanks to anthropological discourse, could not be greater: by negating nature, or rather by acquiring a reflective knowledge of their relationships with it, at the extreme confines of archaic societies, human beings conquer the dimension of history.

*

If anthropology plays a relevant role in Lefort's development – particularly where the division within the institution of the social is concerned – one should not lose sight of the role, more discreet but just as decisive, of psychoanalysis, especially Lacanian. After all, Lefort's introduction to the French edition of Abram Kardiner's *Individual and His Society*,[49] is placed precisely at the intersection of anthropology and psychoanalysis; and Kardiner himself was both an ethnologist and a psychoanalyst. In it Lefort distances himself somewhat from the criticisms that Kardiner directs at Freudian psychoanalysis from a point of view that is still influenced by a behaviorist methodology. Lacan's name appears only once in Lefort's text, but in a strategic position,[50] relating to Kardiner's inability to keep the symbolic plane distinct from that of the real. In his effort at articulating individual and social psychology, he ends up considering both the individual and society as real terms, united by an empirical causality rather than by a symbolic relationship.

According to Pauline Colonna d'Istria, an analogous distinction between real and symbolic can also be retraced in Lefort's formulation of the division of the social. Against the current interpretation, which only looks at the influence – in itself indubitable – of Machiavelli, this idea would seem to also come to Lefort from Lacan.[51] They knew each other, read each other, especially via the mediation of Merleau-Ponty: he had met Lacan in Kojève's seminars on Hegel, before attending Lacan's own, together with Lefort. Lacan, in his turn, had attended the public defence of *Machiavel* as a *doctorat d'État*. This contiguity does not allow for any undue superposition. Lacan's clear opposition to any attempts to politicize his discourse is well known. This does not mean that it is not possible to find more than one lead for political reflection within the folds of Lacanian psychoanalysis. At its center is the articulation between law and desire, which Lefort recalls in his introduction to Kardiner[52] by way of a reference to Laplanche and Pontalis' interpretation: the *Oedipus* should be understood as the "negative" that blocks access to immediate satisfaction, thus articulating desire with the law. The social division instituted by politics – and, more generally, the semantics of the institution – has the same negative function of precluding society's immediate coincidence with itself. Hence the need to ensure that the symbolic nature of the conflict is kept firm. It can never be reduced to a simple clash of opposing interests but expands to the horizon of meaning in which different political regimes are inscribed.

Without confusing different theoretical *dispositifs*, one should note that there is an obvious assonance between Lefort's instituting division and the *clivage* [rift] that splits the subject in Lacan's conception. What is at stake in both cases is the distinction of the symbolic not only from the real, but also from the imaginary. Although the latter term never assumes a definitive configuration in Lefort's work, it in any case does remain tied to the paranoid project of healing the symbolic wound that splits the social. While the symbolic order preserves the experience of the loss with which it ultimately coincides, the imaginary is obsessed by the ghost of suture. Hence the chiasmic relation between the political, as Lefort thinks of it, and the order of psychoanalytic discourse. At the individual level the ghost of the erasure of the limit leads to foreclusion, at the political level it leads to totalitarianism. From this point of view those who believe that, if it is not possible to derive any political indication from Lacanian psychoanalysis, this is no reason to exclude an interest by the political in Lacan's thought,[53] are right.

*

6. Lefort's second anthropological essay, published in 1952 under the title "Société 'sans histoire' et historicité" ["Society 'without History' and Historicity"], is devoted precisely to the issue of history – its range and its meaning. In this case as well, the polemical targets are Hegel, Marx, and Husserl – criticized this time for their, albeit different, philosophies of history. If for Hegel history proper is born with the state, and it is thanks to the state that society acquires consciousness of itself, Marx on the one hand affirms the historical continuity of the human species while on the other he introduces a vertical fracture into this history represented by class struggle; and it is only from this fracture that "true" history would be generated. Finally, according to Husserl, the universal development of European reason leaves at its margins a residual humanity incapable of contributing to the spiritual progress of the species in a non-subaltern manner. In each of these cases, ultimately, outside the groove of

western civilization, there would seem to be a society without history or prior to history, removed from becoming, and blocked in an eternal repetition. But what can such a society ever be like? If it does not *become*, a society *is* not, since each human organism, singular or collective, is constitutionally temporal. We are dealing with an antinomy that is expressed, especially in Hegel, by the presence of worlds that are both historical and non-historical, situated outside and within history, presupposed by its emergence and expelled from it, as for example India and China. While they inaugurate true history, they remain formally excluded from it, following an enigmatic figure that marks the entire system of Hegel's philosophy of history.

Anthropological culture has addressed this issue, attempting to dominate its contradiction with the help of the concept of "stagnant societies": although internal to the horizon of history, they slow its course, halting it in its first steps. But, even if they tend to slow it, stagnant societies still are located along the mobile line of historical becoming. As a consequence, Margaret Mead adopts a diachronic perspective, attempting to find the deep web of human experience within institutions' succession. Kardiner's studies on the "basic personality" – to which Lefort devotes more than one work[54] – go in an analogous direction, conferring a temporal dimension to all cultural phenomena: social reality, especially if viewed from a symbolic perspective, is never enclosed in the circle of the present, it always implies something that pushed it beyond itself. Even the most static social organisms always reveal, upon closer inspection, the signs of imperceptible movement, to the extent that Lévi-Strauss and Evans-Pritchard tend to identify ethnology and history. This does not mean, however, that there are no differences between stagnant and dynamic societies. Every community entertains relationships with its past, and therefore, inevitably, with its future. But the perception of time, in other words the evaluation of change, can vary quite markedly. In order to grasp this difference it is necessary on the one hand to insert the so-called stagnant societies fully into the circuit of history, overcoming the impasse of nineteenth- and early twentieth-century philosophies of history, and on the other to identify their distinctiveness vis-à-vis those models of societies that are aware of the need for their own development. Ultimately one needs to determine what kind of historicity societies that were once considered without history actually exhibit.

An important contribution in this direction comes from Gregory Bateson's studies on the society he himself defined as immobile ("steady state"), located in Bali.[55] Its uniqueness is due to the fact that in it all conflicts are overcome, or contained, with the goal of preserving the initial social equilibrium. They are preemptively neutralized by rules and devices that tend to avoid the explosion of these conflicts or soften their impact, for example by giving fines to those who, having quarreled in the past, still talk to one another, or by fortifying the territories of rival groups so as to discourage them from the idea of fighting one another. The rigid division into castes does not allow for individuals of different ranks to come into mutual contact. To this end, even communication is fragmented into separate segments, instead of flowing freely. Even music and dance are kept under control, and any form of "crescendo" is avoided. The flow of time itself is separated into blocks, one external to the other, so they can never enter into any reciprocal relationship. In this way the past, no different structurally from the future, never transitions into it but instead continuously folds onto itself. Analogously, space is cut into separate areas without reciprocal contact. The general purpose that organizes Bali's universe is that of not superimposing individual experiences, of making them flow in non-communicating orbits.

But what does this very peculiar conception of space, time, and being mean – what does it lead to and what does it presuppose? And what is its relation to Lefort's political ontology? And to a conception of power that institutes the social through that very division that seems to be forbidden in Bali? His answer centers precisely on that prohibition: on the effort, recognizable in all kinds of Balinese activities, to eliminate, or at least reduce to the minimum, the possibility of conflict; on the attempt, using every means at one's disposal, to prevent it from going from being potential to actual, from latent to real, from cold to hot. This neutralizing strategy on the part of Bali's inhabitants presupposes the conflict it wants to avoid, which is thus situated at the center of their world, in a form that does not differ from Lefort's argument: "Their refusal of conflict is no more than the remarkable and extreme effect of this representation of the world: conflict would entail risk, the possibility of putting facts back into discussion, something that is not compatible with the needs of attachment to their environment."[56]

But – the philosopher continues – one needs to be careful not to confuse this manner of opting to confront conflict with a natural attitude, when it is instead an artificial option and therefore, ultimately, a political one. Bali is in no way a harmonious, homogeneous society devoid of oppositions. On the contrary, it is traversed by all kinds of rivalries, tensions, and contrasts. So, the very same society, stagnant and immobile, that, according to the interpretation of a certain kind of anthropology, could or should have invalidated Lefort's thesis of a conflict institutive of the social, if looked at from the opposite side, constitutes its most exemplary confirmation. At the base of all the neutralizing behaviors of the Balinese is the same division that institutes modern societies. Obviously with the decisive difference that, while the latter assume the instituting presence of conflict as their own historical driving force, Bali's community instead attempts, in vain, to exorcise it in order to halt the rhythm of history. When read from the perspective of instituting thought, stagnation is revealed as a form of historicity – of confrontation, even if negative, with history – that does not differ from the others. What is contested is that principle of non-comparability that keeps history and anthropology in two diverging horizons, incapable of communicating with one another. Nature and history, order and conflict, association and division are not opposite poles but complementary borders of the same hermeneutical framework, which absorbs strength from their tension. Not only is a stagnant society not the opposite of a historical one, as postulated in nineteenth-century philosophies of history; it is even a mechanism internal to it that, in its very deformity, contributes to explaining it.

Already in these first essays Lefort masters a method that he will develop in an increasingly productive manner in his subsequent works. His fundamental thesis of the institution of the social via division is confirmed by it – in an affirmative fashion for modern societies and in a negative one for preceding ones. Relation and difference, one reflected in the other, constitute the bipolar axis of a single point of view, defined precisely by its tension. There is a reason why, at the end of the essay, after having highlighted the comparison between stagnant and dynamic societies, Lefort recalls what continues to differentiate them, and does so in a form that he will reuse and expand upon in subsequent texts. I'm talking about the relationship with alterity. In both kinds of society, according to the symbolic register that all regimes are subjected to, identity cannot be conquered except via alteration. But this is a structurally different alteration. If the alteration that traverses modern societies traverses them internally, separating on the one side the political and the social, and on the other the groups that struggle for power, the alterity that identifies archaic societies is situated outside them. While the modern division passes through the relationships between human beings and things, the division of stagnant societies situates the Other in an unreachable place, because it is beyond not only history but also nature.

7. If, rather than *without*, stagnant societies turn out to be *against* history – and therefore, for this very reason, necessarily historical – something similar can be said about those that appear to be devoid of a state. This issue is addressed by Lefort in a dialogue with Pierre Clastres, an anthropologist who was particularly close to him, author of *La société contre l'État*.[57] Indeed "Dialogue with Pierre Clastres" is the title given to the essay he dedicated to his prematurely deceased friend. The hermeneutical procedure that Lefort adopts in it does not differ that much from the one adopted in the essay we just examined. Just as the apparent absence of history in archaic societies allows the traces of their historicity to shine through, albeit negatively, the vaunted absence of the state reveals, analogously and contrariwise, the politicalness that traverses it: "Clastres brought together facts that a number of ethnologists had described without relating them to each other, and he shed light on them, showing, beyond the singularity of various behaviors or institutions, an intention common to all primitive societies, a political intention."[58]

Of course, "political" is said here in a very different sense from the one we are used to giving the term. More than any other anthropologist, Clastres shows how the primitive world is irreducible to the modern; and he institutes a radical extraneousness between the two. While modernity accepts change, real or at least possible, the primitive universe uses any means at its disposal to prevent it. In this fashion, however, albeit negatively, it confirms its centrality. In order to oppose it, it must necessarily presuppose it. Instead of being extended to the entire historical dynamic, the refusal of change is focused on one specific trait – the one thanks to which the power of the state separates itself from the society it emanates from. What is even more important in Lefort's interpretation is the circumstance that opposition to the state, far from excluding the political dimension, represents a specific version of it:

> The question he [Clastres] was articulating – or, to say it better, discovering – at the heart of primitive society was the question of the political. As he was to state with vigor, primitive society is a political society, for, whatever might be the mechanisms [*mécanismes*] that assure that humanity is constituted beyond the reign of animality, there exists, under one form or another, only political society.[59]

This is an inevitably political society, which has a precise objective: that of impeding not the constitution of power as such, something that is unavoidable in all social organisms, but of a power that is autonomous from its own social matrix. Such an outcome is sought by means of four *dispositifs*, both divergent and convergent: the interdiction, for those who occupy a dominant position, of ruling; the initiation ritual, cruelly impressed on the bodies young people, which certifies, by means of an indelible mark, a condition that is equal for everyone; the limitation of goods to those that are necessary for immediate consumption, a measure aimed at preventing the accumulation of wealth; the maintenance of individual groups' identities by means of continuous wars designed to prevent mutual integration. Unlike other approaches, which are unable to provide a unitary interpretation for this heterogeneous set of behaviors, Lefort links them to a political intention. That which appears to be the result of casual practices has a unitary motivation: to defend the social group's control over its own form of life. Within this dynamic Lefort finds a confirmation of his own thesis that only an ontological analysis of the political, or a political conception of ontology, allows one to overcome the hermeneutical impediment that prevents Marxism and the social sciences from grasping their object of analysis in its deepest foundations. Societies are distinguished from one another through specific "moldings" of individual and collective relationships that are centered on a specific representation of power – in other words, the different ways in which political division joins and at the same time differentiates nature and history, symbolic and real, internal and external.

In this sense Clastres, far from situating his own research within a polarity opposed to that of Lefort, claims a hidden contiguity with his perspective. Although this might appear to be the case at first, even though he talks of "undivision" (*indivision*), the anthropologist never claimed the existence of a society without power, therefore devoid of internal fault lines, but rather only of societies hostile to a power that was autonomous from its own social bases. That which "societies without a state" want to avoid at all cost is an exercise of power that is removed from their control and potentially turned against them. This interpretation, however, far from configuring a harmonious society that adheres to itself, reveals its constitutive articulation. Clastres never gave in to the Rousseauian myth of the good savage. His writings, very crude, on the practice of torture, as well as those on continuous war, expose a scenario that is traversed by harsh divergences – not only between power and society, but also between symbolic and real. Power, however one defines it, cannot be confused with any of its empirical manifestations and tends rather to be located in a sphere that is unreachable by a purely sociological gaze, because it belongs to a horizon of meaning in which the relationship of human beings with the symbolic conditions of their existence comes into play.

But this fundamental agreement with Clastres does not exclude a divergence that is just as clearly marked, that Lefort does not avoid mentioning and that he expressed most forcefully in a different interpretation of a text by Étienne de La Boétie, the *Discourse on Voluntary Servitude*.[60] What is at stake is not only what appears to Lefort to be an excessively clear-cut distinction between statist societies and societies that are against the state, but something that concerns the essence of the political. Clastres posits a radical rupture between that which precedes and that which follows the state, interpreting the latter's advent as an irreparable "misfortune" (*malencontre*), in conformity with La Boétie's theses. It is true that he is far from imagining that, in history, one can go back, regressing to the "good society," the one that precedes the encounter with the "cold monster." Nevertheless, Clastres's tendency to bracket the entirety of history, separating it into two blocks, that of freedom and that of servitude, remains – and it is one that Lefort *does not* feel he can support, and in fact clearly rejects. This *survol* gaze presupposes the idea, anarchist in origin, that the state is in and of itself a *dispositif* of coercion that puts an end to the reign of liberty – almost as if voluntary servitude were a constant, at this point unmodifiable, of all modern societies. Modern political regimes, all equally corrupt, would seem to be distinguished only by their degree of oppression, in such a manner as to deprive the conflict between adversarial parties of meaning. This possible anarchist drift of Clastres's argument involves a dual risk: that of freeing the "societies against the state" of any contradiction, and that of consigning all statist societies to an undifferentiated negative drift, erasing all differences between legal power and arbitrary power.

As far as the first point is concerned, Lefort focuses on a decisive element that seems to escape Clastres. As we observed previously, for Clastres non-statist societies, in fact anti-statist societies, refuse the separation instituted by the state. It is an attempt, on the part of those societies, to avoid the eversion [*estroflessione*] of power into an autonomous organism. The very rites of inscription onto the bodies themselves would therefore bear witness to a tendency toward the incorporation of the signs of power, oriented toward including command within a socially undivided horizon. But this should not let one think, as in some sense occurs with Clastres, that there is a full immanentization of power in these "societies without a state."

This is because one should not lose sight of the fact that similar rites are based on the belief in invisible powers located outside the reach of human beings. These are transcendent forces, originating from an immemorial past, which exercise an absolute and uncontrolled power on society. In this fashion the very "undivision" theorized by Clastres presupposes an even more originary and drastic separation than that experienced by statist societies, because it is located outside them:

> Of course, he talks about the terrifying cruelty of the rite, whose virtue would be to inscribe the nonseparate law into a nonseparate space, that of the body. But he *does not* noe that this mode of inscription presupposes the primary idea of a law that lies at a distance from men, so that it swoops down upon them from the outside. ... Far from the writing of the law on the body making itself the sign of a consubstantiality of the one with the other, there is an interiority that bears on its flip side an absolute exteriority.[61]

While law in modern societies, even in its separateness, is still internal to them, as a sort of transcendence within immanence, the dominion of the powers to which the rites of inscription on the bodies of human beings address themselves is situated in a dimension that is not only separate but alien to society – a dimension to which society is subjected without having any form of shelter.

8. Lefort states on many occasions that his distancing from Marxism was caused on the one hand by his analysis of archaic societies, which we just reviewed, and on the other by the study of Machiavelli, which he started at the beginning of the 1960s and never abandoned.[62] As is well known, its most conspicuous result, both at the qualitative and at the quantitative level, is the large volume published in 1972 under the title *Le travail de l'oeuvre Machiavel* [*Machiavelli in the Making*]. But, in order to identify the genetic moment of his distancing from Marx, which runs parallel to the discovery of "planet Machiavelli," one needs to step back more than a decade, more precisely to the 1960 essay "Sociological Reflections on Machiavelli and Marx: Politics and the Real," in which Lefort compares their two models of realism, starting from the general question "What is realism in politics?." And, more precisely, what is it, in works such as those of Machiavelli and Marx, that – although they are very much influenced by their respective socio-historical contexts – gives one access to the real? According to Lefort, to answer this question, instead of looking at their areas of agreement, one needs to look at their areas

of disagreement. For the comparison to be feasible, it is necessary to start from a presupposition that the two authors share – in other words, from the idea "that *empirical reality*, as it is made by the history of human beings, is accessible to knowledge and that it in turn may find grounds for adequate action."[63] But how are the two segments of this proposition connected, those that concern knowledge and action? How is it that, from the recognition that the real is nothing more than itself, both Machiavelli and Marx derive the need for its transformation? How can a reality that fully coincides with itself contain the conditions, in fact the exigency, of its own overcoming? The answer to this apparent paradox lies in the fact that reality is understood by both as praxis rather than as an immobile block. It is this interpretation that reveals the true meaning of the celebrated Marxian thesis according to which, although the philosophers have done nothing but interpret the world, now one needs to change it. This is not a question of a purpose that is added to the task of knowledge, replacing it, or of an impossible revolt against the real. Instead, the issue revolves around the circumstance that, since reality is praxis, the philosophy that is rooted in it objectively tends to transform it. In this sense, it is possible to affirm that realism, more than an attitude about the real, is a process of realization through which human beings affirm their own sociality.

Although very distant from Marx, Machiavelli anticipates his logical architecture. Convinced that in all ages human nature presents significant series of invariants, he believes it is realistic to apply to the present situation solutions that have demonstrated their validity in the past, avoiding the errors previously incurred in the process. Since both human passions and the conflicts triggered by them are constant, the realist will be the person who, without aiming to change reality's terms, can order them in a manner favorable to her or his aims. Like Marx after him, Machiavelli derives the tools to restore living substance to the real from the real itself. Hence a series of affinities that connect the two thinkers, although the latter are placed in historical situations that are not at all comparable: breaking with the cultural traditions of their time, claiming history as the only field of knowledge, refusing to superimpose an ideal model onto concrete passions and interests, diffidence in the face of a moralism that, while claiming to defend values, opens the field to the most arbitrary violence, and criticism of Christian religion. But then, starting from similar presuppositions, how does one explain the very clear differences between the two authors' political projects?

To answer this question, Lefort introduces the thinker who is placed at the point of intersection between Machiavelli and Marx, using Marxism to understand Machiavelli and using Machiavelli's works as a lever to rethink Marxism. I am obviously speaking of Gramsci, to whose *Brief Notes* on Machiavelli Lefort devotes the densest pages of his essay; these pages were then reused and developed in *Machiavel*. At issue is not only the content of the *Prince*, but even its addressee. Regardless of the subject whom he intentionally addresses, Machiavelli reveals the mechanisms on which political life is based and thereby provides an analytical key for all social groups that intend to defend and reinforce their own positions. One obviously needs to situate his arguments in the proper framework and identify the progressive class of the period in the bourgeoisie, which was allied with the monarchy – or even, under specific conditions, with a "new prince" – and opposed to the residual feudal forces. The "prince," therefore, more than a historical character, is a political myth that, like the Communist Party, inscribes the people's intentions into the real. In this sense, for Gramsci, Machiavelli's works prefigure subsequent history by elaborating a "popular realism" that anticipates the philosophy of praxis. It is within this dialectic between Machiavelli's *Prince* and Marx's *Manifesto* that the analysis of the real can become one with the practice of its transformation.

But here is the question, not formulated up to this point, that gives Lefort's analysis a more critical tone: Is the Gramscian interpretation capable of grasping the peculiar meaning of Machiavelli's works? Or does it not instead reveal a blind spot in Marxist theory, even in its version as philosophy of praxis? Does the interpretation of reality as praxis, attributed to Machiavelli himself, not sacrifice the most intrinsic features of his oeuvre? One of these features is the complex relationship between the *Prince* and the *Discourses*, which Gramsci does not discuss, thus losing sight of some decisive questions that will be at the center of Lefort's reading. The problem is that, by making Machiavellianism into a moment of its own story, Marxism flattens and distorts its historical and theoretical specificity – just as, by superimposing practice and theory without residue, he ends up losing the role of both. The problem, which Gramsci does not seem to realize, is the impossibility of incorporating Machiavelli's thought, without residue, into a different conception, erasing its internal tensions, for instance those that exist between the *Prince* and the republican perspective of the *Discourses*. The oppositions between nobility and the *popolari*, republic and principality, tyrant and legislator, rather than being hermeneutical obstacles to be overcome, lie at the heart of Machiavelli's oeuvre. Not only should they not be nuanced in order to safeguard the author's vaunted coherence, but they should instead be valorized as the expression of a discourse immersed in the contrasts of the time. Machiavelli reproduces this conflictual dynamic, intensifying it, so as to make reality reemerge in all its complexity. Returning to the initial question, realism cannot be reduced to the representation of the real as a single force field. It consists not only in describing a given situation by tracing its causes and effects, but rather in subjecting it to a series of questions that do not always have an answer. Machiavelli's greatness lies precisely in this awareness – in the indeterminacy in which even his clearest theses are set, allowing their irresolvable problematic nature to emerge.

To these concluding reflections of his essay, Lefort adds a series of much more emphatic criticisms of the entire Marxist framework in the chapter "Machiavelli in the Making," which is devoted to the Gramscian interpretation of Machiavelli. Gramsci legitimizes the disjunction between class and party, which breaks the unity of the political subject, on the basis of a point of view – that of the philosophy of praxis – that considers itself capable of embracing the entirety of history in a single gaze. Understood in this manner, this point of view would constitute a place of mediation that is destined to suture, thanks to the party's role, the fracture between knowledge and power, theory and praxis, past and present. But in this fashion, although he overcomes the rigidity of traditional Marxism, Gramsci restores the idea of the exteriority of the object with respect to the interpreter, analyzing it under the guise of a mediator capable of occupying all the positions – of theory and practice, of party and class, of politics and history. It is precisely this organicist presupposition that produces the closure of that horizon that Machiavelli had freed up, erasing the vital contradiction that his work allowed to emerge. Instead of allowing the Machiavellian text to speak, Gramsci exercises an effect of mastery over it, occupying the place of alterity, to which that text remains vitally exposed. By placing himself in the position of the Other, the interpreter not only occludes the dilemmatic nature of Machiavelli's text but erases the necessarily problematic nature of her or his own discourse when reconstructing the traditional modalities of the Marxist conception.

9. It is not only Gramsci who experiences this hermeneutical limit. To a different degree, such a limit involves all the great interpretations of Machiavelli, to whom Lefort devotes almost half of his book, reconstructing them in extraordinary analytic detail

both as to their presuppositions and outcomes. Their undoubted merits notwithstanding, none of them convinces him. This is not due to a lack of scientific rigor vis-à-vis their object of analysis; on the contrary, it happens precisely because of it – because they consider it an object that needs to be investigated in its completeness by a subject capable of penetrating it fully. The more Machiavelli's text is reconstructed "objectively" by its interpreters, while they are seeking its incontrovertible truth, the more it escapes them, it withdraws from them – at least as long as this same withdrawal is not understood as the movement from which the text arises and draws its vital lymph rather than as an unbreakable limit off which interpretation bounces. While the need for a dialogue with the interpretations of the past remains strong – a dialogue in whose absence the new interpretations would remain flattened onto themselves – one should not let oneself be trapped by the web of determinations that they weave around the work, since it is precisely the space of its internal oscillation that restores it to us in its most intimate essence. If the purpose of criticism is the elimination of all blind spots in favor of an integral visibility, it condemns itself to failure by not comprehending that this indeterminacy is not the opaque background against which the text's contours get lost, but its most intrinsic mode of being. This indeterminacy is communicated from the work to its interpreters, exposing them to the trial of the enigma and involving them in the same vacillation of meaning that it generates. Hence the dialectic that, according to Lefort, connects work and reader in a knot that it is impossible to solve, since the existence of both derives from it: if without a work there would be no reader, reading constitutes the only space in which the work lives and produces its effects. The instituting circuit, which is at the center not only of Lefort's political reflections but of his entire oeuvre, is outlined in this fashion. Just as the work institutes the reader, so the latter institutes the former, in an incessant exchange, which finally takes on a dimension that is collectively instituting. This is a further, peculiar meaning that Lefort attributes to the term "institution":

> Convinced that the oeuvre only gives itself to us on condition that we give our thoughts to it, I am also persuaded that it never had any other existence than in an open exchange, that is, an existence of such a nature that the answer does not cancel out the question but requires new ones – by the institution of a collective discourse, at the heart of which the words of each are intertwined or articulated while at the same time mutually governing one another's advent; and thus – in

> questioning the exchange, that *institution*, at the very moment when my work in turn brings me to participate in it – it is already the oeuvre that I question.[64]

If this is true of all the great works of the past, it is especially true of Machiavelli's. His unique power of establishing things is proven by the effect that reading his work has on one's experience of time. The way this work reaches us, addressing us with a force that cannot really be compared to any other, is due to the tension that lives within it: from the past, it takes it to the present, projecting it toward the future. This is not all: by continuously superimposing Florence and Rome, Sparta and Venice, France and Spain, this temporal difference also reveals itself as spatial difference. So Machiavelli's works, although they are certainly not ahistorical, do not belong to only one age, just as they do not belong to only one space, but, transitioning from one to the other, express a dynamic that, across five centuries, makes his horizon intersect with ours.

Lefort does not derive this hermeneutical register, recognizable in all his essays, from any of the interpreters of Machiavelli whom he assembles in his book – not even from Leo Strauss, whose extreme interpretive subtlety he nonetheless recognizes. The author who instead emerges from these pages is the master to whom Lefort owes his own philosophical approach: Merleau-Ponty. It is to him that the very notion of indeterminacy can be ascribed, both as an elevated subject's impossibility of embracing the totality of an object and as the body's non-coincidence with itself – of the active with the passive, of touching with being touched, of seeing with being seen. As for Heidegger, though in other respects, for Merleau-Ponty, too, being is given only in the movement of its own removal, and this makes any retracing of a path to the origins of experience impossible. It is from this chiasmic nature of the real that the necessary co-implication between interpreter and work – on which Lefort insists – derives, too. The work presents itself also as lack, a lack that concerns him, involving him in a hermeneutic circle similar to a vortex from which both reading and reader reemerge transformed. What allows for their contact to occur is not so much the ungraspable nature of the work as its absence – the "non-" that traverses and suspends it from a regime of continuous alteration. The negative, in this case, unlike any dialectical *dispositif*, is not a moment of the process destined to be overcome by a subsequent affirmation but its dark side – the difference that prevents the real from closing on itself, with exclusionary effects on to what is not.

Merleau-Ponty's presence in Lefort's analysis of Machiavelli is not only indirect, tied to the phenomenological method that Lefort had learned back in his high school years. It is also direct, since it is precisely to Merleau-Ponty that we owe one of the first attempts, at least in France, to remove Machiavelli's oeuvre from the ambit of the traditional "Machiavellian" interpretation, as well as of the nationalistic variant activated in fascist Italy during the preceding decade. In addition to the various quotations one finds in subsequent works up to the "Preface" of *Signs*, in 1949 Merleau-Ponty devotes to Machiavelli a brief but a particularly dense "Note on Machiavelli"; in it one can recognize a first sketch of that *ontologie nouvelle* [new ontology] that would later be elaborated in the unfinished pages of *Le visible et l'invisible* [*The Visible and the Invisible*]. It is striking not only for its incisiveness but also because it synthetically anticipates the two dominant vectors of what would become Lefort's interpretation of Machiavelli – that is, the politically decisive role played by appearance and by the non-extinguishability of conflict – grasped in their reciprocal relationship. As far as the first vector is concerned, Merleau-Ponty, anticipating a constitutive trait of contemporaneity, observes that, especially in the *Prince*, political space is structured as an appearance that coincides with being, because it is productive of effects that are just as real:

> Or as mirrors set around in a circle transform a slender flame into a fairyland, acts of authority reflected in the constellation of consciousness are transfigured, and the reflections of these reflections create an appearance which is the proper place – the truth, in short – of historical action. Power bears a halo about it, and its curse (like that of the people, by the way, who have no better understanding of themselves) is to fail to see the image of itself it shows to others. So it is a fundamental condition of politics to unfold in the realm of appearance.[65]

When Machiavelli writes that "[m]en in general judge more by their eyes than by their hands, because seeing is given to everyone, touching to few" (*The Prince*, ch. 18),[66] he inaugurates a sort of political phenomenology in which bodies, starting with the prince's, seem to reflect themselves in a play of mirrors, at the intersection of convergent gazes.[67] What is seen in them, whether it corresponds to the truth or not, in any case determines the real power relations embodied in historical events: "What he means is that even if the leader's qualities are true ones, they are always prey to legend, because they are not *touched* but *seen* – because they are not known in the movement of the life which bears them, but frozen into historical attitudes."[68]

Hence the second vector, inevitably tied to the first, of the ineluctability of conflict that Merleau-Ponty had already discussed in *The Adventures of the Dialectic*: in addition to being originary, conflict is endless. Since political reality, rather than being a given, is constructed each time from different and often opposite perspectives, its natural condition cannot but be one of perpetual clash, which is rendered even more insoluble by the prevalence of contingency and the irrational. So, "[c]onsidering this history where there are so many disorders, so many oppressions, so many unexpected things and turnings-back, he sees nothing which predestines it for a final harmony."[69] However – and this is a crucial point that we will come across again in Lefort's interpretation – this does not mean that a political order is impossible. It only means that, far from being opposed to political struggle, it derives from it in an always provisional and mutable form, one destined to be modified in its turn, on the basis of new power relations. Even more, at the culmination of his analysis and sometimes in contradiction with its cornerstones, Machiavelli recognizes a "principle of communion" in his republic that makes room, within the clash of particular interests, for a collective interest oriented toward a defense of "free living":

> But Machiavelli nowhere says that the subjects are being deceived. He describes the birth of a common life which does not know the barriers of self-love. Speaking to the Medici, he proves to them that power cannot be maintained without an appeal to freedom. In this reversal it is perhaps the prince who is deceived. Machiavelli was a republican because he had found a principle of communion. By putting conflict and struggle at the origins of social power, he did not mean to say that agreement was impossible; he meant to underline the condition for a power which does not mystify, that is, participation in a common situation.[70]

*

The relationship between order and conflict has by now become a topos in Machiavellian scholarship; its stake is not only the interpretation of Machiavelli's text but his sagittal relationship with us.[71] That is what presents itself periodically as the "Machiavellian moment," even if in a variety of tonalities. Already in 1951, only two years after Merleau-Ponty's

"Note on Machiavelli," Eric Weil, in a text entitled "Machiavel aujourd'hui" ["Machiavelli Today"], recognized the presence – in addition to erudite phases characterized by historico-philological research – of "moments" of the ontology of actuality within this secondary literature, moments that "give new life to someone who up to that point was only one author among many: it is to him that the passionate questioning on the being of politics is addressed, one engages in discussions with him as with a contemporary."[72] *The Machiavellian Moment* is the title of an influential book by John G. A. Pocock that inaugurated a new interpretive line, situating Machiavelli in the republican tradition that, starting from Florentine humanism, reaches American revolutionary ideology through the mediation of Harrington.[73] More recently, it was Miguel Abensour who gave the subtitle *Marx et le moment machiavélien* [*Marx and the Machiavellian Moment*] to a study in which he opposes democracy to the state with the intention "to rediscover a political realm [that was] lost."[74] The theme was lost in a certain respect by Marx himself, notwithstanding its latent presence in some of his youthful texts – most particularly in the *Critique of the Hegelian Philosophy of Right* of 1843 – and resurfaced once more at the time of the Paris Commune.

Abensour's book is particularly important for my research because, by prefiguring, in the name of Machiavelli and Lefort himself, an "insurgent democracy" against the state, he raises the issue of its relationship with the institution.[75] Against those who accuse him of having interrupted this relationship by blocking the "passage from negativity to institution,"[76] Abensour identifies an original connection between the two terms in accordance with the 1793 constitution, which recognizes people's right to insurrection. Although immediately suppressed and at this point erased from the democratic imaginary, this right expressed the "Machiavellian" desire of the people not to be dominated. But this is not the only issue. "Insurgent democracy" addresses the institution in another sense as well, one that concerns the relation, which is also at the center of Machiavelli's oeuvre, between instant and duration, present and past: "Just as insurgent democracy can bring about an interaction between insurgence and institution, it can also set in motion a circular flow between the present of the event and the past, insofar as this involves encounters among emancipatory institutions holding out a promise of liberty. Here, the people rose up against the liberating institutions' lack of a present, demanding that these institutions be respected."[77] On the whole, insurgent democracy is not an alternative to the logic of institutions to the extent to which it is capable of selecting those institutions that actively favor freedom from any type of domination.

At this point Abensour, reiterating the opposition between laws and institutions that had been theorized by Saint-Just in his *Fragments on the Republican Institutions*, refers to a youthful text by Deleuze that views institutions as an anticipation capable of generating emancipatory customs and attitudes.[78] While Abensour does argue along these lines, he *does not* attempt to hide a fundamental difficulty. Once insurgent democracy has been deployed against the most durable of institutions, in other words the state, is it possible to recognize an institutional and, more generally, a political profile in it? Abensour provides a dual answer to this question, which he himself had posed, in a fashion that seems to be somewhat hesitant. To begin with, he reminds us that non-statist and anti-statist political communities have existed in the past, for instance those identified by Clastres in archaic societies. To break the Hegelian identification between politics and the state, as is done by the Marx of 1843, does not necessarily mean to slide toward Buber's anarchism, which dissolves the political into the social. Second, Abensour refuses to identify durability with immobility, understanding it rather as a "base" or "launching pad" for change. In order to do so, one needs to distinguish a fluid and multiple dimension from another, which is static and uniform within duration itself, and privilege the first. Up to this point we have examined Abensour's critical and interpretive thesis. Is it a convincing proposal? Does it accurately render the meaning of Lefort's thought, to whom Abensour refers more than once? If his intention is to state that not all institutions are equal for an "insurgent" or "savage"[79] democracy, then one can without doubt agree with him. But in what institutional space insurgent democracy would be deployed, once removed from and opposed to the state's space, that still needs to be explained.

*

10. Many times people have insisted on the relevance of the interpretation of Machiavelli for the development of Lefort's political ontology. It is as if he were searching in Machiavelli's work for intimations of that conception of democracy that would increasingly become his focus, also as a result of the comparison with totalitarianism. Lefort was obviously too conscious of the discontinuity between the periods he and Machiavelli lived in to superimpose intellectual experiences that were so different and distant at both the historical and the lexical level. His Machiavelli has nothing of the democrat, and even less of the revolutionary. The distance he established from Gramsci is also intended as a reagent against undue and deviant actualizations, which have not been lacking over the course of the years. Machiavelli is too immersed in the dynamics of his own age to be projected, with a leap of more than three centuries, onto the scenario of late modernity. However, even given the historical distance, Lefort perceives a paradigm in his writings that is destined to take shape much later and that, to a certain extent, is still with us. Without being able to follow *Machiavel*'s sophisticated analyses in detail, I am going to try to concentrate on the issue that I am most concerned with. According to Lefort, the culmination of the

Machiavellian discourse, which seems to traverse time's demarcations and reach us, is situated at the intersection of the two vectors identified by Merleau-Ponty, the productivity of appearance and inevitability of conflict – naturally within a much more elaborate analytical framework, which shifts the emphasis from the phenomenological onto the ontological plane. The celebrated passage from the *Prince*, according to which "in every city these two diverse humors are found, which arises [*sic*] from desire neither to be commanded nor oppressed by the great, and the great desire to command and oppress the people. From these two diverse appetites one of three effects occurs in cities: principality or liberty or license" (ch. 9), contains its principal elements in condensed form – inexhaustibility of conflict, symbolic primacy of representation, importance of the negative.

Let us start from the first vector. We should not forget that the other author whom Lefort – together with Merleau-Ponty – continues to bear in mind, although increasingly distancing himself from him, is Marx. The political centrality of conflict derives from him, to the extent that, with a noticeable degree of terminological approximation, the author of *Machiavel* does not hesitate to define the social clashes in Florence as "class struggle." But, if Marx is the greatest modern thinker of conflict, he is also the one who forecasts its future exhaustion in a communist society. This is exactly the point regarding which Lefort completes his detachment from Marx via the Machiavellian paradigm. For Machiavelli, conflict is not only originary, but also insuperable. It is originary, in other words instituting, because it is not preceded by anything – not even by classes, which, rather than the cause, are its effect. In this sense Machiavelli's ontology, unlike those derived from an Aristotelian matrix, is unfounded, not only because it is exposed to absolute contingency, which bars it from any teleological temptation, but because at the base of society there is no foundation, let alone the foundation of the One – if anything, a binary *dispositif* that is irreducible to unity. But even in this case one cannot talk of foundation: if there is no society prior to conflict, there is also no conflict prior to society. They are co-originary. The social is divided from the very beginning, and the division has forever been social. Therefore, if contained within the confines of politics, antagonism is not destructive of sociality – it is rather its most intrinsic expression. It is the form that coexistence assumes. Only through conflict can society relate to itself, recognizing itself as such – one and binary simultaneously. It is for this reason that it cannot be the result, as Hobbes would want, of a contract between individuals who choose to exit the conflictual state of nature in order to enter the social one. First of all, since society is originary, there is no state of nature that precedes it; second, the social state, far from excluding conflict, is instituted by it.

Naturally, Machiavelli, too, believes that, in order for society not to degenerate into civil war, the clashes must be kept within the bounds of pacific coexistence. It is precisely to this end that politics is organized – not to abolish conflict, but to regulate it. How? Through a third power, installed at the margins, which both separates and conjoins the parts into a single society. As is well known, Machiavelli does not characterize it in a univocal manner. Depending on circumstances, it can be occupied by republican magistratures or by a prince. What counts is that it maintains the forces in balance, putting a brake on the tendency of the *grandi* [nobles, magnates] to oppress the *popolari* [simple folk], as well as on any excessively radical tendencies of the latter. The separation, which does cut across society, should never be disjoined from the bond that unites it. Rather separation and bond should be considered two faces of the same instituting *dispositif*.[80] Lefort insists on the symbolic character of such an institution. The conflict, embodied in the opposed desires of the social partners, should not be compressed onto the bare materiality of interests. Given the implication of reality and appearance discovered by Machiavelli, it has an eminently symbolic character, in the sense that it responds to an exigency that is representative of mutual recognition. What connects the desires of the two social partners, in their asymmetry, is the exigency of each to be recognized by the other. Even the proper functioning of the relation between prince and subjects requires a one-to-one dynamic that takes both points of view into account – since "to know well the natures of peoples one needs to be a prince, and to know well the nature of princes one needs to be of the people" (*The Prince*, Dedication). If this bipolarity is removed, coagulating only into one of the poles, power loses the symbolic capacity of representing the entire society, folding back onto itself in a self-referential manner. When this occurs, the symbolic, which always involves a relationship with the other, slides into the imaginary, with a complete loss of connective capacity. It is true that the prince unifies the social body by means of the glorious image of himself he projects – but only if he himself does not identify with it as well. For if, fascinated by it, he gets reflected in it without mediations, mirroring himself in his own reflection, then the symbol is broken, shattering the social body.

But, for Machiavelli, the seat of power is not necessarily occupied by the prince. This only occurs when all the other options are exhausted – most particularly the republican one. In republics the void that separates the conflicting parties is occupied not by a single individual, but by the law. The most virtuous example of such a dynamic, reconstructed in the history of the Roman republic, is the institution of the tribunes of the plebs. In no other case does such a close bond tie an institution to the conflict from which it derives and that it reproduces. Contrary to the Hobbesian presupposition, which opposes them, the law is born from within social conflict. Obviously this is not always the case. Conflict can always get out of hand, shatter the contours of the institution, thereby exploding in a destructive fashion, as occurs precisely in Florence when the conflict first goes from bipolar to tripolar – with the division of the *popolari* into *popolo grasso* and *popolo minuto* – then is pulverized into ungovernable fragments. The desire for freedom can also be reversed into a will to dominate, as history demonstrates with a wealth of cases. This occurs not only when the primary division splits into further decompositions, but also when it is negated in the name of *reductio ad unum* [reduction to one]. The bulwark against this tendency consists of the institution itself and, even more effectively, of the instituting process in its entirety, which includes the negative that it necessarily incorporates. This productive role of negation, implicit in instituting logic, is foregrounded by Lefort. Institutions, starting with the tribunes, serve to contrast power rather than to augment it: they provide instruments of resistance vis-à-vis those whose aim would be to centralize it. Unlike the desire of the *grandi* to oppress, the desire of the people is certainly to *not* be oppressed. But the tribunate, within the institutions of republican Rome, represents the very place of negativity:

> Henceforth Machiavelli forbids us to think that the institutions of the Republic play no more than the role of a third party in the class struggle: the tribunate in which the power of the law is expressed has the effect of impeaching the occupation of power by one person – whether of the prince or of oligarchs – and in this sense it is only effective as the organ of negativity.[81]

One should remember, and emphasize, that the category of the "negative" runs through Lefort's entire production like a common thread, starting with the 1951 essay *Sur l'expérience prolétarienne* – in which he argued that the progress embodied by the working class "is only inscribed negatively on the image of the exploiting society."[82] There is one difference, however, namely that, while he then identified the way to definitively overcome the conflict in the class's negation of its own condition, now he sees in negativity, as represented by the tribunate, that which keeps it alive. For Machiavelli, as for his interpreter, the negative, situated within the heart of the institution, constitutes that which prevents it from handing itself over to the always resurgent power of the strongest, guarding the exigency of continued renewal. As is the case with the "flesh" of the social that Merleau-Ponty talks about, the negative represents the moment of exteriority in the interior of being – that which, by differentiating it, pushes it beyond itself. Precisely because it constitutes the pole of non-power, the people's class is the driving force of the instituting process: "The desire of being and negativity in action, these are the reasons why society's being exceeds all of given reality."[83]

11. We already spoke of Machiavelli's relationship, certainly not historical, but rather paradigmatic, with modern democracy. If the second term – "democracy" – is entirely outside the Florentine republic secretary's perspective, the second is much more contiguous. For many interpreters, Machiavelli is the founder of modern political thought, even though in a modality that differs greatly from Hobbes's. But even his relationship with modernity, at least in its fully deployed form, is far from linear,[84] in the sense that, between Machiavelli and what Tocqueville calls "democratic revolution," there is a long period of absolutism. Lefort does not devote any specific treatment to absolutism, except to measure the distance that democratic society has traveled in moving away from it. The *ancien régime* is analyzed, not so much in itself, but as that which modern democracy puts an end to – albeit without completely getting rid of its lexicon and even by incorporating a not inconsiderable portion of it that pertains to the phenomenon that Lefort himself describes in the terms of a political theology. And in fact "Permanence du théologico-politique?" ["The Permanence of the Theologico-Political?"] is the title of one his more enlightening texts on the entire complex of his production.[85] At its center is the ambivalent nature of a secularization that, rather than entirely consuming its sacred nucleus, translates it into a different conceptual lexicon, simultaneously determining both its overcoming and its permanence. It is as if, in this case, continuity and discontinuity, rather than being opposed, intersected each other in a chiasmus that sees one installed inside the other, without erasing either. The same relationship of differential implication exists

between politics and theology. They are not confused with each other, to the extent that what defines modern politics is precisely its detachment from the theological matrix. But in this case, too, they do not lose contact with this matrix; they even reproduce some of its traits in a different modality, which pertains to the different role that the symbolic form of power assumes in it. While in premodern societies, both of an archaic and of an *ancien régime* kind, that form is situated outside of the historical process – in the sphere of nature and in that of transcendence, respectively – in modernity it is situated within the dynamics of history, to the extent that it constitutes its instituting principle.

But how and when does such a transition take place? By means of what *dispositif* does the political become autonomous from the theological, even if it does not take a definitive leave of absence from it? To answer this question, one needs to look at another text by Lefort, one devoted to Dante's *Monarchia*. This is a work that constitutes the decisive junction in which one transitions from a medieval universalist conception to modern political philosophy. It is well known that Dante was not at all interested in the absolutist states that were in the process of being formed, but instead identified the empire as the only political subject destined to guarantee peace to humankind. Developing the classic presupposition according to which humanity approaches divine experience when it takes on the form of the One, he views the figure of the emperor as the person who best embodies it historically: "The true name of the emperor is the name of the One."[86] As is typical of the theologico-political machine, the One is the exclusionary modality in which the constitutive binariness of the political is condensed.[87] And in fact, for Dante, the paradigm of sovereignty is split between a political government ruled by the emperor and an ecclesiastical government represented by the pope. Humankind, united in a common *civilitas* [citizenship], refers to both, in a manner that does not subordinate the first to the second but gives them full autonomy within their own order. It is precisely this theologico-political device – which splits the One into two, or incorporates the two into the One – that transitions from the imperial to the monarchical regime at the end of *respublica christiana* [the Christian republic]. This is the reason why, even though all reference to empire is abandoned, the theorists of state sovereignty refer to Dante's *Monarchia* as a prototype of extraordinary conceptual rank. Dante's oeuvre, like Machiavelli's, works in a direction that diverges in part from its author's intentions, becoming a reference for those monarchical states whose legitimacy the empire had long denied;

even more, it also opens the doors to civic humanism, including one of a republican inspiration, which finds in Machiavelli one of its sharpest representatives.

For this theologico-political device to be able to function, however, one needed to cast it within a symbolic space capable of giving it, simultaneously, both compactness and articulation. What responds to this need is the body metaphor, which in its turn was transposed from Adam to the body politic. The latter, already in the late Middle Ages, had been subjected to that process of splitting between the personal body of the sovereign and the institutional body of the kingdom; this is admirably reconstructed by Ernst Kantorowicz in a book that Lefort could not have missed.[88] In it the theologico-political splitting between mystical body and political body, which in its imperial formulation goes back to Dante, becomes the central *dispositif* of absolute sovereignty. The monarch's authority, still tied in the medieval period to a series of reciprocal obligations with local powers, becomes absolute, configuring the reign as a single body in which the king, as God's representative on earth, constitutes the head, while the subjects, divided into classes, are its limbs: hence its dual legitimation, secular and theological, one within the other. In this fashion the reign, into which liturgical authority flows, appears to be formed by a body made up of many little bodies, following a process of dual incorporation still recognizable in the image that adorns the cover of Hobbes's *Leviathan*. Each individual is identified via her or his own body, and they are all reunited in that of the state, of which the king is simultaneously part and whole, head and body. So, even if its source of legitimation remains external, once incorporated into the sovereign's body, power unifies the entire society, which is itself being conceived of as a body.

This "regime" – a term understood by Lefort not only in its constitutional sense, but as the symbolic marker that allows each society to represent itself as such – lasted for a particularly long time, which in a certain sense even outlasts itself, and remained alive after its substitution by the democratic regime. This explains why, once secularization has been completed, Christian religion continues to interpellate politics, even after they have been formally separated. In order to understand this situation, rather than taking theology and politics as two different areas considered each time either jointly or separately, one needs to think of them from the very beginning as connected by their reciprocal implication – in other words in the intertwining of an already politicized theological sphere with a politics that has already been elaborated in theological terms. There is a reason why even the revolutionary transition, which seems to break every thread of contiguity between religion and politics, is recounted by one its greatest interpreters as a religious event that draws a good part of its lexicon precisely from theology.

This is because Michelet's criticism (for I am speaking of him) of the *ancien régime*, from the point of view of the revolution, ends up using precisely the theologico-political categories it intends to free itself from, with an apologetic twist for modernity's benefit. By combining the teachings of Guizot and Ballanche – one aimed at recognizing the uselessness of a monarchy that has been overtaken by the society over which it continued to reign, the other convinced that the spirit of Christianity had permeated social institutions in an irreversible manner – Michelet attempts to hold together the contradictory instances of religion as human beings' insuperable horizon and of the law as the ultimate instrument for their emancipation. Hence a dual image, simultaneously political and religious, of France, viewed as the heir to the Roman Empire. It is the French people's salvific mission, a people formed by the dual drives of material interests and spiritual values, to bring heaven to earth. It is the same people that, during the revolutionary process, confirmed its sacred orientation by going from the theological denomination of "the anointed of the Lord" to the political one of "the anointed of the Revolution." Michelet's history of France therefore reveals profound differences from the other history authored at about the same time by Tocqueville. While the latter, preoccupied with analyzing the decomposition of French aristocracy, loses sight of the symbolic level, Michelet outlines a symbolic architecture that does not differ too much from that of the medieval period. At its center is the unconscious representation of society that is embodied in the king, a society that is "not simply ordered in accordance with a 'carnal principle,' but whose members are so captivated by the image of a body that they project it onto their own union, that their affects are precipitated in an amorous identification with that body."[89] It is precisely this erotic relationship with the king that will make the decapitation of his mortal body, after the deposition of the political one, an unpardonable error from Michelet's point of view. Once generated by the theologico-political *dispositif*, the people's love for their king is not only not erased by his death but, on the contrary, reaffirmed at the sight of blood that gushes from a body that has been identified with that of the nation for a period of time too long to be able to completely detach itself from it.

12. But how can one explain such an obviously theologico-political language from someone who contributed more than anyone else to nourishing the myth that put an end to the *ancien régime*? The question acquires an even greater importance if one considers that Michelet is not the only one to experience this contradiction. One can say that, although starting from different presuppositions, all those who reflect on the revolutionary transition – from Quinet to Guizot, from Tocqueville to Lorroux – recognize the constitutive role of religion in a society that still attempted to free itself from it. The question, posed in problematic fashion by Lefort, of the permanence of the theologico-political at the time of its retreat, returns. At the heart of political immanence, established by the democratic revolution, an element of transcendence resurfaces. The search for the autonomy of the social, driven to paroxysm by the execution of the king, reproduces a remainder of heteronomy. The past, precisely when it is renounced most vehemently, seems to take hold of the present once more and to keep it with itself. But how should this persistence of the past in the present be interpreted? As the survival of something that had never disappeared, or as a defeated power's return to the field of battle? Is this simply a ghost destined to be dissolved in the folds of the new society, or is it something deeper, internal to the movement of history and expressive of its dynamics? So, must we think that the machine of political theology is still functioning, or "that a new experience of the institution of the social began to take shape, that the religious is reactivated at the weak points of the social, that its efficacy is no longer symbolic but imaginary?"[90]

Lefort does not provide a conclusive answer to this fundamental question, which is decisive for the interpretation of his entire work, and oscillates between two different hypotheses without taking a definite position in favor of either. Even though apparently opposed, the two hypotheses – that of the exhaustion of the theologico-political paradigm and that of its resumption – are not mutually exclusive, but seem to be articulated with each other. It was precisely the violence of the rupture with the preceding regime that produced a sort of rebound that, although it did not reestablish its overall structure, did repropose one of its segments, which pertains to the difficult relationship between the symbolic, the real, and the imaginary; but it did so in a form that prevents any kind of superposition. While in premodern societies the symbolic coincides with an alterity that is situated outside of society – in nature, or in divine transcendence – in modern society it is internal to it, constituting the fault line that separates it from itself. As I said, at the origin of this process there is the dearticulation between the locus of power and the body of the king, which, under the preceding regime, occupied it. Since the monarch contemporaneously represented both the body and the head of society, his decapitation, both symbolic and real, shatters the entire *dispositif* of the *ancien régime*. With its collapse, it is as if the entire society exploded, disintegrating into infinite fragments constituted by individuals who passed from the status of bodies internal to a more comprehensive body to the status of numbers, to be counted by universal suffrage. The difficulty with which the latter was accepted – not only by conservatives but by liberals as well – gives one the measure of the fear that surrounded the institution: numbers stir even more fear than the masses, because they seem to deprive society of its living substance, exposing it to the loss of the symbolic dimension. This first disintegration is followed by other, no less disquieting ones: on the one hand, that within state – no longer represented by the king's body – and society, which is pulverized at this point; on the other, that within the orders, previously mutually imbricated, of power, knowledge, and the law, now situated on different planes and mutually independent. Even within knowledge itself, its different sectors – political, economic, technological – once they have been autonomized, are subdivided into the different branches of the social sciences; hence a general atomization, to which a series of counterweights correspond that seem to restore the previous order, but that are really the index of its defeat. The bourgeois cult of order, fatherland, and family corresponds to the need to compensate, via new forms of sacralization, for the absence of body that connotes democratic society: "democratic society is instituted as a society without a body, as a society that vanquishes the representation of an organic totality."[91]

The emphasis is on the verb "to institute," insofar as this is the praxis specific to democratic society. What distinguishes it from the past as a praxis with no precedents is the fact that, instead of being instituted on the basis of criteria of a natural or supernatural kind, it institutes itself in accordance with its own principles. This does not mean, however, that it does so completely autonomously, establishing a regime of pure immanence, or that is capable of appropriating its own origin and its own destiny. Were that to occur, if its trajectory were perfectly recognizable, it would lose its relationship with the contingency of events. But above all it would restore the totality from whose disintegration it was born, reconstructing the logic of the lost foundation. Since this is not possible, since it is never perfectly present to itself, to institute itself, democratic society must pass through an alterity – which is what separates it from power or, even better, makes of power the space of its internal separation. It is in this sense that the formulation repeatedly adopted by Lefort – namely that power, once dearticulated from the king's body in which it once inhered, is *empty* – must be interpreted. One could say that democratic society is a vortex that rotates around an empty point. While this occurs unconsciously in all kinds of society, in the democratic kind this dynamic acquires awareness, presenting itself for what it is. The void is no longer hidden or masked, but recognized in all its symbolic power. This does not mean that, in actual fact, power is not exercised by those who, each time, gain it, to then cede it to others. The exercise of power, rather than a positive good to be appropriated, gathers its force from the lack of its exercise by others. It carries within itself the void from which it is born and in which it installs itself. Lefort repeatedly underscores this *negative* dimension of democratic power, without ever losing sight of the difference between the planes of the symbolic, the real, and the imaginary. If power were stably occupied by someone, this would imply the preemptive exclusion of a part of the citizenry. This is what occurred even in the Greek *polis*, where a large number of subjects were excluded from the group of those who participated in the city's government. Its recurring formulation, that power resided "in the middle," reflected the imaginary self-representation of a social group, self-proclaimed as the only holder of political sovereignty. But the contrary thesis, that no one should exercise power – translating the symbolic register of the void into the real one of absence – ends up destituting the meaning of democracy, transforming it into anarchy, with a consequent elision of the political.

To guard against this double risk of identifying the symbolic with the imaginary or of compressing it onto the real, modern democracy is the only regime in which the gap between the symbolic and the real keeps power being available for a continuous exchange between the ones and the others. Instituting praxis, as the specific form of democratic politics, reacquires its centrality. It neither creates nor dissolves power – it is neither a constituent power nor a destituent one – but makes it circulate within institutions that are destined by their very function to be renewed. In this sense, contrary to a widespread thesis, modernity is, in principle, the only age in which politics is revealed as possible, because it is the only one that holds fast to the distinction between the symbolic, the real, and the imaginary – the void in which power is inscribed each time. But what does it mean, more precisely, that the seat of power is empty? It means that it can be continuously contested by different parties via the democratic practice of political conflict. This is the crucial presupposition of Lefort's political ontology. In democracy, what fixates the relationship of the political with space, time, and the world is neither the One nor the Other, but the Two. By avoiding the materialization of either the Other, as practiced in archaic societies, or the One, as practiced in *ancien régime* ones, modern power coincides with the dual division of society, from itself and within itself: "Nor can power be divorced from the work of division by which society is instituted; a society can therefore relate to itself only through the experience of an internal division that proves to be not a *de facto* division, but a division that generates its constitution."[92]

This dual division, situated at the heart of modern democracy, allows one to penetrate more deeply into the concept of "institution" as a key category in all of Lefort's thought. To argue that power constitutes its subject is not exact. What should actually be said, in line with Machiavelli's teachings, is that it is not power that institutes conflict, but rather the opposite: "The institutionalization of conflict is not within the remit of power; it is rather that power depends upon the institutionalization of conflict,"[93] since it is only the outcome of the conflict that decides who should exercise power each time, on the basis of the juridical *dispositifs* that regulate political struggle. In this sense, instituting activity comes to coincide with the very meaning of political praxis. Removed from both the sovereign logic of constituent power and the messianic deactivation of destituent power, the instituting act makes conflict the continuously renewed principle of the political order:

> Not less worthy of note, however, is the fact that the delimitation of more properly political activity results in the institution of a *stage*, on which the conflict is represented for everyone's eyes to see (since citizenship is no longer a privilege reserved for the few), insofar as it is necessary, irreducible, legitimate. It does not matter much that each party proclaims its calling to defend the *general* interest and realize *union*: the vocation this antagonism gives credit to instead is that of society for division.[94]

*

It has been said that democratic society is self-instituting because it does not search for its symbolic codes elsewhere, but within itself. But it also does not do so "autonomously," establishing a regime of pure immanence. This is a not unimportant specification, which distinguishes Lefort's perspective from that of the thinker who, in other respects, is closest to him, and not only from a biographical point of view: Cornelius Castoriadis. For Castoriadis as for Lefort, instituting praxis does not create something *ex nihilo*, but always *ex aliquo*. Society has always already been instituted, but it is also the object of a generative process that ceaselessly transforms it. If the two authors agree on this presupposition, what is the source of the dystonia that, from the years of *Socialisme ou barbarie* until the posthumous evaluation of 1968, does not cease to characterize their positions, not only political but also theoretical?

In an ample monograph devoted to Castoriadis's political ontology,[95] Nicolas Poirier identifies the center of gravity of this dissymmetry in the different meaning that the two thinkers attribute to the term "self-institution" – which in Castoriadis refers to autonomy and in Lefort's to heteronomy. What separates them is, so to speak, the relation between the same and the other. Both authors relate the instituting process to continuous alteration – in other words, to the modification of what is already instituted. But, while Castoriadis identifies the subject and the object of the alteration, making society both the subject and the object of itself, for Lefort the two terms never completely coincide. Society cannot be considered an object, not even of its own work. If this were the case, it would have the same relationship with itself that an engineer has with that which s/he produces. But this would lead to the condition of full immanence that has been established by totalitarian regimes, which imagined that they were creating the new human. Obviously Castoriadis is very far from these constructivist temptations. He is quite aware that the origin is unattainable, that each knowledge of itself, on society's part, always has a remainder of opacity as a residue. And yet the project of self-creation, if radicalized, is at risk of sliding toward that idea of community as a product of itself, whose dangers we have learnt to be wary of.

It is this risk of immanentism that Lefort intends to avoid when, exposing himself to a series of criticisms, in truth not completely devoid of merit, he connects the concept of "alteration" as change to that of "alienation" as an inevitable degree of heteronomy that is implicit in every self-institution. This margin of heteronomy coincides, ultimately, with the symbolic pole of power as a necessary means for any instituting transition.[96] Castoriadis talks about power too, as the coercive capacity of the "political" to impose injunctions and sanctions. But he excludes it from the horizon of "politics" as invented by the Greeks. It is an outcome that distances him from Lefort. If it is possible to imagine a perfectly self-instituted society – in which the political is dissolved into politics – then what articulates society will no longer be division, as Lefort would have it, but the union between all its members. Castoriadis does not explicitly criticize Lefort; but he *does not* hide his distance from him, identifying the division theorized by his friend with domination. The difference between the two authors is even more clearly exhibited in their views on the symbolic, specifically on its relationship with the imaginary. Both Lefort and Castoriadis use both terms, but the former does so by separating and almost opposing them (the imaginary is the compression of the symbolic onto the real), the latter by articulating them – to the point where he ties the imaginary to the process of instituting even in the title of his book, *The Imaginary Institution of Society*: an expression Lefort would hardly have used.

I already mentioned the relationship, mediated by Merleau-Ponty, between Lefort and Lacan. The empty point – the non-appropriability of power – around which the democratic *dispositif* revolves provides the occasion for a closer examination, which has the institution as such for its object. In a series of texts collected under the heading *Il vuoto centrale* [*The Central Void*],[97] Massimo Recalcati proposes "a psychoanalytic theory of the institution" that produces an effect – unintended, I imagine – of unusual juxtaposition with Lefort's perspective. Starting from the Lacanian doctrine of the four discourses discussed in Seminar XVII, *The Other Side of Psychoanalysis*[98] – the discourse of the master, of the hysteric, of the university, and of the analyst – Recalati relates them, all of them and all together, to the issue of the institution, specifically to the necessity, on the part of the institution, to conjugate form and force without losing either one of them. It is a question of simultaneously giving solidity and endurance to force without blocking its creative potential. Under what conditions can this occur? How can the institution guarantee innovation without imprisoning it in the rigidified bulwarks of repetition? This is possible only on the condition that one keep the central void open, as is also recalled by Lacan in Seminar VII, *The Ethics of Psychoanalysis*:[99] it is a void that structures the institutional field.

This effect is obtained by making the four discourses rotate in such a manner that the institution is never identified with only one of them. Since each discourse acts as an institutional brake on enjoyment, none of the four can push beyond a certain threshold, in order not to produce a repressive effect. Let us take, for example, the master's discourse, which in Lefort's theoretical *dispositif* corresponds to the instituting – and therefore necessary – role of power with respect to social dispersion. In order for it not to crystallize into a *dispositif* for domination, as occurs in premodern societies, it needs to be removed from any belonging and emptied of substance, until it is configured like an empty pigeonhole that can be temporarily used by whoever prevails in the democratic competition, before it passes into other hands. It is only this continuous transition, which is allowed by the rotation of the positions, that is able to preserve the institution's being in harmony with the desire of the social partners, without provoking an institutional collapse as a result. This is the only way of literally keeping the institutions alive, containing the death drive that traverses them, in other words the process of bureaucratization that always threatens their functioning. This means that, just as institutions put a brake on the self-dissolving tendency of individual desire, so individual desire also contributes to putting a brake on the self-destructive tendency of institutions, freeing up the generative charge that ensures their life.

*

13. If democracy is defined by the contrast with the regime that precedes it, its relation with totalitarianism is more complex.[100] For Lefort, it constitutes, rather than its opposite, its reverse or phantasmatic extension, in the sense that it installs itself precisely into that void of substance that the democratic revolution opened up. That in Russia the totalitarian system was not born within a democracy, as occurred instead with Nazism in Germany, is not a sufficient reason to weaken the contrastive connection between the two regimes. Neither authoritarian despotism nor absolutism exhibit such characteristics as to produce a totalitarian involution – which can instead be linked to the suicidal degeneration of the democratic regime. This explains the need for the continuous critical revisiting of the concept of totalitarianism undertaken by Lefort without interruption, even if in different modalities, from the 1956 essay on *Totalitarianism without Stalin*[101] to his last writings. If in the texts from the 1950s the author's attention, which was then still located in a Marxist context, was concentrated on the bureaucratic involution of the Communist Party, in subsequent decades totalitarianism is dealt with in its absolute specificity, as a postdemocratic regime. Nevertheless, even in his last contributions, Lefort exhibits a certain caution when using the category "totalitarianism"; this was due to a dual circumstance, which he himself mentions. On the one hand, there was the superficial and deviant use of the term by the *nouveaux philosophes* [New Philosophers] in the 1970s that ended up provoking a sort of inflation of the term. On the other, there was the suspicion, if not hostility, manifested against this concept in left culture, which has always seen it as a diversion, unfounded and instrumental, with respect to the looming danger of American imperialism: unfounded from a historical point of view, because it homologizes phenomena that differ too much, such as Nazi fascism and communism – the first being based on the biopolitical mystique of race, while the second is based on the destinal mandate of a class; and instrumental because, by means of an ideological equation of dubious consistency, it ends up losing sight of the primary task of the critique of capitalism. This explains why the category of totalitarianism was for a long time left to conservatives and liberals, at least up to the point where the belated success of Hannah Arendt's book projected it at the center of

the international politico-philosophical debate. Even though he does not repropose the conceptual framework that she had elaborated, which is oriented prevalently toward an analysis of Nazism, Lefort, who was instead especially interested in communism, relaunches the issue of totalitarian society, making it a strong point of his political ontology. From this point of view, the failed elaboration of the paradigm in post-Marxist culture appears to him as the proof of its inability to think in political terms:

> Why, I asked, was the Left reluctant to employ the concept of totalitarianism? At first I replied: because it had been invented by the Right. That is true. But, I went on to ask, why did it allow itself to be outstripped by its adversaries? I would now dare to say: because this concept is *political*, and the Left does not think in political terms.[102]

But why does this happen? Why does the left not manage to think politically? We know Lefort's answer: because of its inability to recognize the symbolic dimension of power. At the same time, this is precisely the level at which, in the first decades of the twentieth century, democracy lost the match against an adversary that was not only conscious of the importance of political myths but capable of inserting itself in the contradictions of the democratic front and of providing an answer, certainly a regressive, but also a seductive one, to the issues that the latter had left open. This occurred when the indeterminacy to which the democratic regime is structurally exposed – the power vacuum, the irreducibility of conflict, the uncertainty of its outcomes – proved to be unsustainable in societies deprived of the symbolic resources of transcendence. This is the space into which totalitarianism inserted itself, filling the fractures of meaning excavated by secularization in the fragile body of democracy in a phantasmatic fashion. This, more than other reasons, explains the compromise that some of the major philosophers of the period entertained, on the one hand with Nazi fascism and on the other with communism. At the center of this collapse, both ethical and philosophical, is the illusion that the divisions within the social body could be healed by means of a reunification between state, society, and party, which democratic regimes had functionally separated. What totalitarianisms allowed one to catch a glimpse of, in a universe by now deprived of symbolic legitimation, was the reconstruction of the ancient form of the One, broken up by the separation of powers operated by the democratic form, which is constitutively multipolar. What was contested and reversed into its imaginary opposite was democracy's negative semantics – its *not* being undivided, identical, homogeneous. What was attractive in the totalitarian project was the promise to fill with affirmative substance a cavity opened up by the democratic revolution within the *ancien régime*'s organic society. Obviously, this was not to be done by restoring its symbolic configuration, centered on the king's "dual body," which had been definitively shattered by the revolution. By comparison to that theologico-political *dispositif*, which was still founded on the divine derivation of power, totalitarianism expresses a radically earthly model that excludes all transcendence. In it, society proclaims itself perfectly self-sufficient, completely relieved of theological presuppositions, simultaneously form and matter to its own immanent production. In this sense, the paradox of totalitarianism lies in the idea of creating maximum organicism – the organic community united around the prevalence of a race or a class – with maximum artificialism, in a monstruous mixture of machine and body.

Obviously the abolition of division, which is preached by totalitarian ideology, is only apparent. It is realized in a phantasmatic manner by a series of concatenated incorporations that identify society with class or race, the class or the race with the party that expresses them, the party with its leaders, and finally the leaders with the supreme leader on whom everyone depends. Actually each of these identifications hides an alterity that reaches its apex precisely in the figure of the egocrat (to adopt Solzhenitsyn's term), whose decisions are completely autonomous from the rest of the body he says he belongs to. To this first division, internal to the regime, there corresponds another one, even more decisive for its survival, which consists of the presence, or rather construction, of the public enemy. Alterity, exorcised within the social body, is projected onto the adversary that threatens it from the outside. So, far from being vanquished, political conflict is radicalized into a war against enemies real or apparent, natural or artificial, external or internal. In this fashion, the more it proclaims its unity, the more the totalitarian body, filled with itself, finds itself divided inside the separation between the One people and the Other, where the Other is the external enemy but can also be the representatives of the old society – the bourgeoisie, the kulaks in communism, and the Jews in Nazism. As has emerged from more in-depth studies, no regime more than Nazism was prey to fratricidal clashes between different and contrasting powers united only by being loyal to or terrified of the leader, who in his turn was placed in a position of immanence and at the same time transcendence vis-à-vis the social body. It can maintain itself, at least apparently, as a whole only at the cost of continuous exclusions or liquidations of those who are classified as "too many."[103] At this point what presents itself as the politics of life can transform itself seamlessly into a death machine.

Naturally this continuous exchange of opposites cannot last for a long time without colliding with the regime, as was proven by the end – albeit both the timings and the modalities were different – of the two most important twentieth-century totalitarianisms. Organicism and artificialism, unity and division, nature and history were combined in them, without any possible mediation. On the one hand the promise of an unlimited future, the production of the new human, the certainty of a radiant future; on the other, the refusal of the unexpected, the appeal to one's roots, the cult of the past. On the one hand the exaltation of the sovereign people, the spasmodic search for consensus, the horizontality of militancy; on the other, the absolute preeminence of the leader, the repression of dissent, the verticality of command. But, even prior to these issues, the failure of the totalitarian project is due to the impossibility of erasing social division by decree, of rendering the symbolic real, of superposing power, knowledge, and the law. Subjected to such discordant pressures, the totalitarian regime cannot resist the antinomies on which it rests. Although strong, it cannot stand up to the final clash with the external, as experienced by Nazism, or prevent an implosion from the inside, as occurred in communism. It is especially to the latter, even before the wall that supported it collapsed, that Lefort's attention is dedicated. Already from the 1970s, the totalitarian communist system lost ground continuously, its propaganda *dispositif* jammed, the image it had constructed became deformed and torn. Behind the veil of the imaginary, the thorny profile of the real appeared.

14. Lefort's questioning of totalitarianism does not limit itself to profiling the paradigmatic contours of democracy in the negative, but reopens the question, which is closely connected to it, of the relationship between politics and the law. It is precisely on the basis of a debate on this topic organized by the journal *Esprit* that Lefort published a programmatic essay, "Politics and Human Rights," in 1980.[104] These were the years in which, after a long period of suppression, if not of discredit, the problem of human rights reacquired importance following the increasingly detailed news, coming from Eastern European dissidents, about the Soviet camp system. Although they declared that they were not interested

in engaging in politics, with their very existence they indicted the political nature of the regime that repressed their rights ferociously. The western left's response to their revelations could not have been more impervious. Although it took sides with the dissidents as a matter of principle, the French Communist Party did not grasp the implications that existed between their condition and the totalitarian regime that determined them – leaving the relationship between politics and the law in the shadows. The presupposition that, in spite of the distance between them, the communists ended up sharing with reformists and conservatives was that, while the political confrontation was defined by power relationships, human rights concerned the private sphere of morality. Hence a certain indifference to the question posed by dissidence: deemed unavoidable in totalitarian regimes even by their adversaries, it could provoke responses of an ethical or religious character, but not of a political character. The assumption behind this attitude was that ultimately the violation of human rights did not concern politics.

Lefort identifies its genesis in the critique of the law formulated by the young Marx in *On the Jewish Question*. According to him, the Declaration of the Fundamental Rights of Man, formulated at the end of the eighteenth century first in America and then in France, expresses ideologically the dissociation of individuals within the nascent bourgeois society – in other words the separation between the latter and the political sphere of the state. Hence Marx's negative evaluation of human rights – rights to opinion, freedom, and safety. For him, these are an emanation of the only law sacralized by the bourgeoisie, that of property. This critical interpretation of human rights follows from the inadequate manner in which Marx represents the transition from feudalism to capitalism. If, in the former, all relations, both material and spiritual, seem to him to preserve a political character because they are inscribed in estates, corporations, and professions, after the bourgeois revolution they are dissociated from the political sphere, which is concentrated in the state *dispositif*. This dual process of differentiation, to which Marx does attribute an overall progressive meaning, takes on an ideological value when it is represented as the completed realization of human emancipation. The state's autonomy from the relations of production and the individuals' acquisition of inalienable rights constitute, for Marx, the two sides of one and the same political illusion, installed at the heart of bourgeois society.

According to Lefort, the Marxian analysis is caught in the same ideology that it intends to unmask. While it does contain a nucleus of truth regarding the primacy of proprietary law over all others, it reveals a series of blind spots of both a historical and conceptual nature. From the genealogical point of view, by focusing his attention on the constitutional state, Marx loses sight of the decisive role played by the monarchical state, to which one owes the overcoming of the feudal regime within the sovereign order. Rather than being consequent upon the capitalist mode of production, in accordance with the Marxist vulgate, the formation of the modern state constitutes its presupposition. Since Marx does not give the absolute monarchy its due, he also undervalues the turning point from it determined by the revolutionary transition and by the consequent formation, first of the constitutional state and then of the democratic one. It is at this stage, via the Declaration of Human Rights, that law and politics intertwine their trajectories, in a knot that has not been solved since. At its center is the dearticulation of society from the king's body, which runs parallel to the functional division between power, knowledge, and the law. For the first time the law acquires a dimension that is autonomous from sovereign power, on which it previously depended. Certainly, the power of the monarch in the *ancien régime* was also limited by the traditional rights of the estates – the clergy and the nobility in particular. But those rights remained incorporated in his person, in its turn an incarnation of the divine person. It is only after the bourgeois revolution that the law, separated from power, is ascribed to each single human being, exclusively on the basis of her or his humanity. Undoubtedly Lefort is far from attributing a substantial character to that nature, abstracted from the historical context from which it gathers its determinacy. From his point of view, it is not only Marx's critique of bourgeois universalism that remains valid, but also Burke's and De Maistre's reactionary critiques of the idea of human beings as beings without historical or national determinations. But this does not detract from the symbolic importance – which Marx confuses with the ideological level – of the dearticulation of law and power. Certainly, dearticulation does not mean absolute independence, but in democracy their role is inverted by comparison to the *ancien régime*. It is no longer power that provides the foundation for the law, but rather the latter legitimizes the former. This inversion presupposes the separation of the two spheres: in order to legitimize it, the law must enjoy an extraterritoriality in relation to power.

Naturally this complex *dispositif* of unity and separation on which the democratic regime rests is not devoid of paradoxes. First of all democratic society, articulated into its different levels, can never recognize itself as a whole – it is always put to the test of its own exteriority. Second, there is an irreducible chiasmus between the enunciation of rights and their effective validity, since they are simultaneously subject and object of the same performative declaration. Finally, those rights, which seem to belong to individual monads, each one sovereign over itself, are in reality the result of a social interrelation without which they would not be able to operate. And this is precisely where Lefort identifies Marx's error, namely assimilating these rights to private property for those who could enjoy them: because the rights of opinion, free speech, and writing cannot be expressed outside a public, supra-individual space. Similarly, the right to security, far from recalling a police state, guarantees the protection of social relationships against anyone who may want to destroy them. From whatever perspective one looks at them, therefore, fundamental rights, instead of enclosing individuals within the restricted space of their respective borders, attest to, and simultaneously produce, a new network of social relationships. This productive, performative, operative character of the law makes it impossible to separate human rights from the political, social, and civil rights that succeeded them over the course of time. None of the latter would have been possible without the former since – beyond their contents, which are relative to the historical conditions in which they were proclaimed – what counts is the symbolic threshold that their institution delineates with respect to the past. In relation to this past and the privileges it entailed, the juridical institution always has a progressively "negative" character – which is necessary in order to affirm a broadening of freedom. It negates something only to open up a space for a more emancipated condition, as when it opened up a void in the sacral body of the sovereign: "If one considers this phenomenon, the operation of 'negativity' becomes confused with the institution of political freedoms. ... Power becomes, and remains, democratic when it is revealed as the power of no one."[105]

Lefort insists on this instituting character of the law, in conformity with his political ontology. No right can be reduced solely to the claims it makes, because it always opens the door to further rights – following the unstoppable dynamic that can be traced back to the right of having rights, which is inscribed in the entry to political modernity. Certainly, this does not mean that the institution of new rights automatically arises from the historical process. They are always the object of a struggle generated by different and opposed interests. But the very possibility of this struggle for a right is in and of itself a value that is juridically assured by democracy. What is in play is an always tense confrontation with power that cannot come to an end. The law on the one hand presupposes power – since no society can exist without a *dispositif* that institutes it, dividing it into opposing parts – on the other hand is born from a resistance to it: "What we have to examine, then, is the meaning of conflicts which presuppose both the fact of power and the attempt to gain respect for different rights. These conflicts are becoming more and more characteristic of modern democratic societies."[106] They constitute its form and movement – the uninterrupted transition from the political sphere to the social, civil, and cultural spheres. Each time a right is affirmed, a threshold is crossed, a border is transgressed. The rights that are instituted on each occasion modify the power relations from which they derive, contesting the ruling powers to the point of forcing the limits of the preexisting juridical order. But the institution of new rights – their instituting power – does not only clash with constituted power, but also with positive law, incorporated in the body of established legislation. From this point of view, the dimension of the law enters into a pressing dialectic with justice, in addition to power; and it is a dialectic situated at the other extreme of juridical semantics. Since it can never be entirely objectivized in legislation, it constitutes a point of reference that, beyond the legality it has acquired, always puts the border between legitimate and illegitimate into question, following a dialectic that no judge can block via a formulation of positive law. But it is precisely this "negativity" that gives the law an affirmative power, capable of invigorating the entire instituting process:

> The legitimacy of the debate about what is legitimate and what is illegitimate presupposes, we repeat, that no one is occupying the position of supreme judge. And we emphasize: no one; neither a human invested with a superior authority nor a group, even if it is the majority. Now this negation is operative: it suppresses the judge, but it refers justice back to the existence of a public space – a space in which all are invited to speak, to listen, without being subjected to the authority of others.[107]

*

The instituting character of the juridical order – more precisely, its coinciding with the institution – was researched and elaborated upon by one of the greatest European jurists of the twentieth century. Considered even by Schmitt to be one of the indispensable authorities in the field,[108] Santi

Romano is the most rigorous theorist of that tradition of juridical thought that has taken the name of "institutionalism." Without even attempting to outline his complex perspective, let us limit ourselves to the issue, raised by Lefort, of the relationship between law and politics. Aware of the crisis of the modern state – to which he had devoted an extraordinarily prescient book in 1909[109] – Romano states without any hesitation, in his masterpiece *The Legal Order*, that the state is no more than "a species of the 'genus' law" since, "[while] the concept of law can be perfectly determined without the concept of the state, it is not possible, on the contrary, to determine the concept of the state without resorting to the concept of law."[110] Here Romano appears to be simultaneously close to and distant from Lefort. Looking at each being – people, things, actions – from the point of view of the law, like Lefort, he elaborates an ontology that encompasses all of reality. But it is an ontology of a juridical nature, not of a political kind. No discipline – not economics, not sociology, nor politics – possesses the power, both heuristic and performative, of the law, of which, in all his works, he preserves an "exalted, solemn, severe"[111] conception.

However, far from giving Romano's discourse an abstractly formalist character, the centrality of the law gives it, on the contrary, an extraordinary vitality, precisely because of the identification of the juridical order with the institution. As he had argued in the essay on the crisis of the state, "existing, and, as a consequence, legitimate is only that order that is not lacking, not only in actual life but also in vitality. It is barely necessary to demonstrate on what logical basis such a concept is founded. The transformation of a fact into a juridical status is based on its necessity, on its correspondence to social needs and exigencies."[112] What else had the crisis of the modern state arisen from, if not its inability to open up to the instances and requests of new collective subjects – groups, associations, organizations – expressed by a society that could no longer be contained within the state's perimeter? The reference to necessity as an involuntary source of the law constitutes that original point of indistinction between realism and formalism that pushes Romano's instituting thought in a direction that both differs from and goes beyond Kelsen's normativism and Schmitt's decisionism, as well as Hauriou's institutionalism, to which Romano is closer in other respects. If he gives Hauriou credit for having freed the concept of institution from the principle of juridical personhood, he criticizes its being limited to constitutional and representative organizations, conceived of "in the image and likeness" of the modern state.[113] The category of institution is instead both more ample and more general, the figure of the state being but one of its many expressions. The institution extends to all organized social forces – internal, external, or even antagonistic to the state, as are for instance criminal associations, or even revolutionary movements whose goal is to overthrow the state. That the state against which they rise up may consider them anti-juridical powers and fight them as such does not mean that, in and of themselves, they are instead perfectly juridical on account of the simple fact of being internally organized. To deny this – Romano continues, approaching the extreme limits of his ontology – derives only from an ethical estimation, which, as such, is external to the horizon of the law. To this he then adds – employing a form of argument that is, to say the least, surprising in someone who worked as a jurist under the fascist regime – "that an association, for instance a political one, whose goal is the revolutionary overthrow of a state that does not conform to fundamental needs and the dictates of justice should be judged more favorably at the ethical level than the state that declares it illegal."[114]

Notes

Notes to Introduction

1 Oliver Marchart, *Post-Foundational Political Thought: Political Difference in Nancy, Lefort, Badiou and Laclau* (Edinburgh: Edinburgh University Press, 2007), p. 2.
2 Cf. also Stephen K. White, *Sustaining Affirmation: The Strengths of a Weak Ontology in Political Theory* (Princeton, NJ: Princeton University Press, 2000).
3 Carsten Strathausen, "A Critique of Neo-Left Ontology," *Postmodern Culture* 16.3 (2006): 1–38.
4 Lars Tønder and Lasse Thomassen, *Radical Democracy: Politics between Abundance and Lack* (Manchester: Manchester University Press, 2005). For the bipolarity between theories of emptiness and theories of fullness, see also Laura Bazzicalupo, "Radicalizzare la democrazia: Produttività politica del vuoto o pienezza ontologica," in *Almanacco di Filosofia e Politica*, ed. Roberto Esposito, vol. 1: *Crisi dell'immanenza: Potere, conflitto, istituzione*, ed. Mattia Di Pierro and Francesco Marchesi (Macerata: Quodlibet, 2019), pp. 75–92, here p. 7.

Notes to Chapter 1

1 On the topic of the widespread influence of Heidegger's teaching, see Günther Anders, Hannah Arendt, Hans Jonas, Karl Löwith, and Leo Strauss, *Su Heidegger: Cinque voci ebraiche*, ed. by Franco Volpi (Rome: Donzelli, 1988). One should also consult the testimony of some of the principal protagonists of twentieth-century philosophy in Günther

Neske and Emil Kettering, eds., *Antwort: Martin Heidegger im Gespräch* (Pfüllingen: Neske, 1988).

2 Dominique Janicaud, *Heidegger en France* (Paris: Albin Michel, 2001), pp. 135ff.

3 For more on this complex issue, which is both philosophical and political, see D. Di Cesare, *Heidegger & Sons: Eredità e futuro di un filosofo* (Turin: Bollati Boringhieri, 2015).

4 As regards the antinomies of Heidegger's political ontology, one should also consult Pierre Bourdieu, *The Political Ontology of Martin Heidegger* (Stanford, CA: Stanford University Press, 1991).

5 [Translator's note (henceforth TN): I have used "unworkability" to translate the Italian *dis-operazione*. The author's discussion of Heidegger uses the Italian *opera* and derivatives to translate the Heideggerian noun *Werk* and its derivatives (which, at least partly, correspond to the English "work" and its family). In some contexts I have used "inoperativeness" for similar terms and circumlocutions. It is not always easy to assess the level of "non-action" in each specific context.]

6 See the intelligent book by Inna Viriasova, *At the Limits of the Political: Affect, Life, Things* (London: Rowman & Littlefield, 2018), esp. pp. 1–5.

7 Concerning this antinomical structure, see Manfred Riedel, *Metaphysik und Metapolitik: Studien zu Aristoteles und zur politischen Sprache der neuzeitlichen Philosophie* (Frankfurt am Main: Suhrkamp, 1975).

8 Martin Heidegger, "The Self-Assertion of the German University," in idem, *Philosophical and Political Writings*, ed. by Manfred Stassen (New York: Continuum, 2003), p. 3.

9 Selecting from the endless literature on the topic, let me refer to Francesco Fistetti, *Heidegger e l'utopia della polis* (Genoa: Marietti, 1999), to which I am indebted in some of the pages that follow.

10 Heidegger, "Self-Assertion," p. 4.

11 Ibid., p. 8.

12 Ibid., p. 6.

13 Martin Heidegger, "Der deutsche Student als Arbeiter" [1933], in idem, *Gesamtausgabe* (Frankfurt am Main: Klostermann, 1975–), vol. 16. [TN: All the quotations that do not come from published English versions specified in the notes have been translated by me from the Italian.]

14 Heidegger, "Self-Assertion," p. 5.

15 Ibid.

16 Regarding the change in semantic register in the writings on Hölderlin, one should again consult Fistetti, *Heidegger e l'utopia della polis*, pp. 137ff., as well as Alberto Altamura, "Heidegger e gli Hölderlins Hymnen *Germanien* und *Der Rhein* (Wintersemester 1934/35)," in Francesco Fistetti, ed., *La Germania segreta di Heidegger* (Bari: Dedalo, 2001), pp. 105–170.

17 Martin Heidegger, *Hölderlin's Hymns "Germania" and "The Rhine,"* transl. by William McNeill and Julia Ireland (Bloomington: Indiana University Press: 2014), p. 27.

18 Ibid., p. 31.

19 Ibid., p. 51.

20 Ibid., p. 57.

21 See Friedrich Hölderlin, *Essays and Letters on Theory*, trans. by Thomas Pfau (Albany: State University of New York Press, 1988), p. 150.
22 Philippe Lacoue-Labarthe, *Heidegger, Art and Politics: The Fiction of the Political*, trans. by Chris Turner (Oxford: Basil Blackwell, 1990).
23 Martin Heidegger, "The Origin of the Work of Art" [1935], in idem, *Poetry, Language, Thought*, trans. with introduction by Albert Hofstadter (New York: HarperCollins, 2001 [1971]), p. 38.
24 Ibid., p. 41.
25 Ibid., p. 42.
26 Ibid., p. 43.
27 Ibid., p. 58.
28 See Roberto Esposito, *Categories of the Impolitical* [1988], trans. by Connal Parsley (New York: Fordham University Press, 2015).
29 Elias Canetti, *The Human Province* (New York: Seabury, 1978), here translated from the Italian.
30 Simone Weil, *The Need for Roots* (London: Routledge, 2002), p. 215.
31 Weil, unpublished text, quoted from Simone Pétrement, *Simone Weil: A Life* [1973], trans. Raymond Rosenthal (New York: Pantheon, 1977), here translated from the Italian.
32 Ibid.
33 Simone Weil, *The Notebooks*, trans. by Arthur Wills (New York: G. B. Putnam, 1956), vol. 1, p. 415.
34 *Bhagavad Gita* II.47, quoted here from *The Bhagavad Gītā*, ed. by Christopher Key Chapple, trans. by Winthrop Smith (Albany: State University of New York Press, 2009), p. 132 = II.47. See also Lakshmi Kapani, "Simone Weil, lectrice des Upanishad Védiques et de la Bhagavad Gita: L'action sans désir et le désir sans objet," in *Cahiers Simone Weil*, 2 (1982): 95–119.
35 Martin Heidegger, *Introduction to Metaphysics* [1935], trans. by Gregory Fried and Richard Polt (New Haven, CT: Yale University Press, 2000), p. 159.
36 Ibid., p. 160.
37 On the issue of violence in Heidegger, see Giusi Strummiello, *Il logos violato: La violenza nella filosofia* (Bari: Dedalo, 2001) pp. 89ff. More generally on the concept of technology, see Eugenio Mazzarella, *Tecnica e metafisica: Saggio su Heidegger* (Naples: Guida, 1981).
38 Heidegger, *Introduction to Metaphysics*, p. 163.
39 Ibid., pp. 1, 35.
40 Ibid., p. 41.
41 Ibid., p. 40.
42 Ibid., p. 41.
43 Ibid. p. 40.
44 Ibid., p. 47.
45 Ibid., pp. 48–49.
46 Ibid., p. 45.
47 Ibid., p. 52.
48 Martin Heidegger, *Contributions to Philosophy (Of the Event)* [1936–1938], trans. by Richard Rojcewicz and Daniela Vallega-Neu (Bloomington: Indiana University Press, 1989), p. 93.

49 Ibid., p. 35.
50 For a critical examination of the complex meaning of the term, see Sandro Gorgone, *Nel deserto dell'umano: Potenza e "Machenschaft" nel pensiero di Martin Heidegger* (Milan and Udine: Mimesis, 2011).
51 Martin Heidegger, *Ponderings, II–VI: Black Notebooks, 1931–1938*, ed. by Peter Trawny, trans. by Richard Rojcewicz (Bloomington: Indiana University Press, 2014), p. 353.
52 Heidegger, *Contributions to Philosophy*, p. 100.
53 Ibid., p. 104.
54 Ibid., p. 70.
55 Ibid., p. 73.
56 Jean-Luc Nancy, "The Decision of Existence," in idem, *The Birth to Presence*, trans. by Brian Homes et al. (Stanford, CA: Stanford University Press, 1993), p. 87.
57 Ibid., p. 96.
58 Jean-Luc Nancy, "L''éthique originaire' de Heidegger: L'être-avec de l'être-là," in idem, *La pensée dérobée* (Paris: Galilée, 2001), here translated from the Italian: J.-L. Nancy, *Sull'agire: Heidegger e l'etica*, trans. into Italian by Antonella Moscati (Naples: Cronopio), 2005, p. 18.
59 Jean-Luc Nancy, *The Inoperative Community* [1986], trans. by Peter Connor, Lisa Garbus, Michael Holland, and Simona Sawhney (Minneapolis: University of Minnesota Press, 1991), p. 40.
60 On the semantics of inoperativeness, see Luca Serafini, *Inoperosità: Heidegger nel dibattito filosofico francese*, (Milan: Mimesis, 2013).
61 Nancy, *The Inoperative Community*, p. 15.
62 Jean-Luc Nancy, "Of Being-in-Common," in idem, *Community at Loose Ends*, ed. by Miami Theory Collective, trans. by James Creech (Minneapolis: University of Minnesota Press, 1991), p. 7.
63 Martin Heidegger, *The Phenomenology of Religious Life* [1995], trans. by Matthias Fritsch and Jennifer Anna Gosetti-Ferencei (Bloomington: Indiana University Press, 2004), p. 86.
64 Ibid., p. 85.
65 Ibid.
66 Ibid., p. 84.
67 Ibid., p. 77.
68 See the entry "Opera," in Roberto Esposito, *Dieci pensieri sulla politica* [1993] (Bologna: Il Mulino, 2011), pp. 155–176.
69 Karl Barth, *The Epistle to the Romans* [1922], trans. by Edwyn C. Hoskyns (London: Oxford University Press, 1933), p. 110.
70 Ibid., p. 481.
71 Ibid., p. 484.
72 Ibid., p. 488.
73 Ibid., p. 489.
74 Ibid., p. 491.
75 Martin Heidegger, *Hölderlin's Hymn "The Ister"* [1942], trans. by William McNeill and Julia Davis (Bloomington: Indiana University Press, 1996), p. 80.
76 Ibid., p. 54.

77 Ibid., p. 80.
78 Martin Heidegger, *Ponderings XII–XV: Black Notebooks, 1939–1941* [2014], trans. by Richard Rojcewicz (Bloomington: Indiana University Press, 2017), p. 34; translation slightly modified.
79 Ibid., p. 83.
80 Martin Heidegger, *Parmenides* [1942–1943], *Parmenides*, trans. by André Schuwer and Richard Rojcewicz (Bloomington: Indiana University Press, 1992), p. 90. [TN: this English translation deviates to a certain extent from what would seem more literally correct versions of the German original: *Un-wesen* would more literally be "un-essence" or "non-essence," and *Unseiende* should be "un-being" or "non-being." The Italian translation that the author relied on is closer to the literal translation in these instances.]
81 Ibid., p. 40. [TN: here again the English translation veers slightly toward the religious end of the possible spectrum of meanings. *Gebot* also includes a dimension that goes in the direction of the English "order," "command," and the author relies on an Italian translation that placed slightly more on emphasis on that element. Heidegger's ontology and interests certainly do not completely exclude an opening to the theological heritage.]
82 [TN: the author uses the verbs *aggirare* and *raggirare* to render Heidegger's noun *Hinter-gehen*: this preserves, at least in part, the play on words in German. In English I used circumlocutions, since no straightforward pun is available.]
83 Heidegger, *Parmenides*, p. 41.
84 Ibid. p. 50.
85 Ibid., p. 43.
86 Ibid., p. 44.
87 G. W. F. Hegel, *The Philosophy of History* [1970] (Kitchener: Batoche Books, 2001), p. 297.
88 On this topic, consult Luca Illetterati, "L'origine e la sua dissoluzione: La 'Romanitas' come problema in Hegel e Heidegger," in Luca Illetterati and Antonio Moretto, eds., *Hegel, Heidegger e la questione della "Romanitas"* (Rome: Edizioni di Storia e Letteratura, 2004), pp. 155–165.
89 Simone Weil, "Quelques réflexions sur les origines de l'hitlérisme" [1939], in eadem, *Oeuvres complètes* (Paris: Gallimard, 1989), vol. 2.3; here translated from the Italian: Simone Weil, "Riflessioni sull'origine dell'hitlerismo," in Giancarlo Gaeta, ed., *Sulla Germania totalitaria* (Milan: Adelphi, 1990), p. 226. On this topic, see also Rita Fulco and Tommaso Greco, eds., *L'Europa di Simone Weil: Filosofia e nuove istituzioni* (Macerata: Quodlibet, 2019).
90 Weil, *Riflessioni sull'origine*, pp. 258–259.
91 Ibid., p. 262.
92 Ibid., p. 242.
93 Martin Heidegger, *Country Path Conversations* [1944–1945], trans. by Bret W. Davis (Bloomington: Indiana University Press, 2010), p. 132. [TN: this translation uses "expanse" for what I have translated with "vastness."]
94 On "vastness/expanse" and "devastation," see Michael Marder, "Devastation," in Antonio Cerella and Louiza Odysseos, eds., *Heidegger and the Global Age* (London: Rowman & Littlefield, 2017), pp. 25–41.
95 Heidegger, *Country Path Conversations*, p. 137.

96 Ibid., p. 150.
97 Heidegger, "Science and Reflection" [1953], in idem, *The Question of Technology and Other Essays*, trans. by William Lovitt (New York: Garland Publishing, 1977), pp. 155–182.
98 Ibid., p. 159.
99 Ibid., p. 160.
100 Ibid., p. 161.
101 In Italian there is a proverbial expression *traduttore traditore*, which refers to the great difficulty of exactly conveying in one language the meaning expressed in another: all translators could be considered "traitors" or "betrayers" in this sense. The phonetic pun on which this equivalence is based is of course lost in English.
102 Ibid., p. 167.
103 Giorgio Agamben, "Epilogue: Toward a Theory of Destituent Potential," in *The Use of Bodies* [2014], trans. by Adam Kotsko (Stanford, CA: Stanford University Press, 2015), p. 266.
104 Giorgio Agamben, *Homo sacer: Sovereign Power and Bare Life* [1995], trans. by Daniel Heller-Roazen (Stanford, CA: Stanford University Press, 1998), p. 41.
105 Antonio Negri, *Il potere costituente: Saggio sulle alternative del moderno* (Rome: manifestolibri, 2002).
106 Giorgio Agamben, "Epilogue," p. 274.
107 Raffaele Laudani, *Il movimento della politica: Teorie critiche e potere destituente* (Bologna: Il Mulino, 2016), p. 13. From another point of view, which argues for destituent power, but from an insurrectional perspective, one should also consult the collective volumes *Pouvoir destituant: Les révoltes métropolitaines / Potere destituente: Le rivolte metropolitane* (Milan and Udine: Mimesis, 2008) and Marcello Tarrì and Comitato Invisibile, *L'insurrezione che viene: Ai nostri amici: Adesso* (Rome: Nero, 2019). A critique of the antinomies inherent in the concept of destituent power is formulated with his usual lucidity by Georges Didi-Huberman in "'Ne pas … encore': Destituzione, gesto, desiderio," which appears as Postface in the new edition of the declaredly destituent essay by Pierandrea Amato, *La rivolta* (Naples: Cronopio, 2019), pp. 119–138.
108 Jean Bodin, *Six Books of the Commonwealth* [1576], trans. by M. J. Tooley (Oxford: Basil Blackwell, 1955), p. 44.
109 See pp. 11–24 in Carlo Angelino's introduction to the Italian translation of Heidegger's *Gelassenheit*: Martin Heidegger, *L'abbandono* [1959], ed. and trans. by Adriano Fabris (Genoa: il melangolo, 1983).
110 Martin Heidegger, "Conversation on a Country Path about Thinking" [1944–1945], in idem, *Discourse on Thinking*, trans. by John M. Anderson and E. Hans Freund (New York: Harper & Row, 1966), p. 59. See Heidegger, *L'abbandono*, p. 47. [TN: the full Italian title in *L'abbandono*, "Per indicare il luogo dell'abbandono: Da un colloquio sul pensare lungo un sentiero tra i campi," would be in English something like this: "So as to point to the place of releasement: From a conversation about thinking, along a path among the fields."]
111 Ibid.

112 On the antinomic dialectics internal to the concept of will, see Bret Davis, *Heidegger and the Will: On the Way to Gelassenheit* (Evanston, IL: Northwestern University Press, 2007).

113 Heidegger, "Conversation on a Country Path about Thinking," p. 77.

114 Reiner Schürmann, *Heidegger on Being and Acting: From Principles to Anarchy* (Bloomington: Indiana University Press, 1986), p. 4. As regards Schürmann, a particularly useful text is the monograph by Alberto Martinengo, *Introduzione a R. Schürmann* (Milan: Meltemi, 2008).

115 See Reiner Schürmann, "Questioning the Foundation of Practical Philosophy," *Human Studies*, 4 (1978): 357–368. Bernard P. Dauenhauer, "Does Anarchy Make Political Sense? A response to Schürmann," *Human Studies*, 4 (1978): 369–375 responds to this essay, disputing its thesis.

116 Donatella di Cesare has begun some significant reflections on the philosophical category of "anarchy" in her recent book *Sulla vocazione politica della filosofia* (Turin: Bollati Boringhieri, 2018). One should especially consult "Poscritto anarchico," pp. 145–153.

117 Martin Heidegger, "Only God Can Save Us: *Der Spiegel*'s Interview," in idem, *Philosophical and Political Writings* (New York: Continuum, 2003), p. 26.

118 Ibid., p. 35.

119 Ibid., p. 33.

120 Ibid., p. 36.

121 Ibid., p. 38.

Notes to Chapter 2

1 Gilles Deleuze, *Negotiations 1972–1990* (New York: Columbia University Press, 1995), p. 170.

2 This expression can be found at the beginning of François Dosse's article "Les engagements politiques de Gilles Deleuze," *Cités*, 40 (2009): 21, a special issue titled "Deleuze politique." The biography in question is François Dosse, *Gilles Deleuze and Félix Guattari: Intersecting Lives* [2007], trans. by Deborah Glassman (New York: Columbia University Press, 2010). That "everything is politics" in Deleuze (and Guattari) is also Paolo Godani's thesis in his monograph *Deleuze* (Rome: Carocci, 2009), p. 9.

3 The editorial is from the special issue quoted in n. 2: Yves Charles Zarka, "Deleuze et la philosophie," *Cités*, 40 (2009): 4.

4 Alain Badiou, "Existe-t-il quelque chose comme une politique deleuzienne?," in *Cités*, 40 (2009), p. 17. Philippe Mengue also gives voice to some significant perplexities concerning the status and outcome of Deleuze's politics; see Philippe Mengue, *Deleuze et la question de la démocratie* (Paris: L'Harmattan, 2003).

5 Michel Foucault, preface to the American edition of *Anti-Oedipus* in Gilles Deleuze and Félix Guattari, *Anti-Oedipus: Capitalism and Schizophrenia* (Minneapolis: University of Minnesota Press, 1983), pp. xi–xiv, here xiii.

6 Slavoj Žižek, *Organs without Bodies: On Deleuze and Consequences* (London and New York: Routledge, 2004), p. 18.
7 Ibid.
8 Ibid., p. 31.
9 Deleuze, *Negotiations*, p. 88.
10 Peter Hallward, *Out of This World: Deleuze and the Philosophy of Creation* (London and New York: Verso, 2006).
11 See Benjamin Noys, *The Persistence of the Negative: A Critique of Contemporary Continental Philosophy* (Edinburgh: Edinburgh University Press, 2010). On the relation between politics and negation, see Diana Coole, *Negativity and Politics: Dionysus and Dialectics from Kant to Poststructuralism* (London and New York: Routledge, 2000) and Roberto Esposito, *Politics and Negation: For an Affirmative Philosophy* (Cambridge: Polity, 2019).
12 Noys, *Persistence of the Negative*, p. ix.
13 Gilles Deleuze and Félix Guattari, *What Is Philosophy?* (New York: Columbia University Press, 1994), pp. 108–109.
14 See Gavin Rae, *Ontology in Heidegger and Deleuze: A Comparative Analysis* (Basingstoke and New York: Palgrave Macmillan, 2014).
15 On the ambivalent relationship between Deleuze and Heidegger, see Janae Scholtz, *The Invention of a People: Heidegger and Deleuze on Art and the Political* (Edinburgh: Edinburgh University Press, 2015). In addition, also consult Alain Badiou, *Deleuze: The Clamor of Being* (Minneapolis: University of Minnesota Press, 2000).
16 See Constantin V. Boundas, "Martin Heidegger," in Graham Jones and Jon Roffe, eds., *Deleuze's Philosophical Lineage* (Edinburgh: Edinburgh University Press, 2009), pp. 326–327.
17 See Rae, *Ontology in Heidegger and Deleuze*, p. 4.
18 For a radically immanentist reading of Deleuze, see Rocco Ronchi, *Gilles Deleuze* (Milan: Feltrinelli, 2015) and *Il canone minore: Verso una filosofia della natura* (Milan: Feltrinelli, 2017).
19 Jean-Noël Vuarnet, "On Nietzsche and the Image of Thought," in Gilles Deleuze, *Desert Islands and Other Texts, 1953–1974* [2002], trans. by Michael Taormina (Los Angeles, CA: Semiotext(e), 2004), p. 136.
20 Gilles Deleuze, "Hume" [1952], in Gilles Deleuze, *Desert Islands and Other Texts, 1953–1974* [2002], trans. by Michael Taormina (Los Angeles, CA: Semiotext(e), 2004), p. 163.
21 Gilles Deleuze, *Difference and Repetition* [1968], trans. by Paul Patton (New York: Columbia University Press), p. 36.
22 Jean-Luc Nancy, "Les différences parallèles: Deleuze et Derrida," in André Bernold and Richard Pinhas, eds., *Deleuze épars* (Paris: Hermann, 2005), pp. 7–30, here 11–12.
23 On the different meaning of death in Deleuze, Hegel, and Heidegger, see Brent Adkins, *Death and Desire in Hegel, Heidegger, Deleuze* (Edinburgh: Edinburgh University Press, 2007).
24 Deleuze, *Difference and Repetition*, pp. 64, 66.
25 Ibid., p. 53.
26 Ibid., p. 202.

27 Ibid., p. 51.
28 Laurent de Sutter, *Deleuze and Law* (Edinburgh: Edinburgh University Press, 2012).
29 On the inevitable return of transcendence within the ontology of immanence, see Miguel de Beistegui, *Immanence: Deleuze and Philosophy* (Edinburgh: Edinburgh University Press, 2012). Federico Luisetti, *Una vita: Pensiero selvaggio e filosofia dell'intensità* (Milan: Mimesis, 2011) argues that Deleuze never entirely manages to free himself of the negative – that there remains a residue of Kantian transcendentalism in him. For a thorough critical revisitation of the category of immanence, see Roberto Ciccarelli, *Immanenza: Filosofia, diritto e politica della vita dal XIX al XX secolo* (Bologna: Il Mulino, 2008).
30 Noys, *Persistence of the Negative*, p. 73.
31 Gilles Deleuze, "Instincts and Institutions," in idem, *Desert Islands and Other Texts, 1953–1974* [2002], trans. by Michael Taormina (Los Angeles, CA: Semiotext(e), 2004), p. 19. One should also consult Ubaldo Fadini, *Il tempo delle istituzioni: Percorsi della contemporaneità: Politica e pratiche sociali* (Rome: Ombre Corte, 2016). Useful observations on the same topic can be gleaned from the discussion between Adalgiso Amendola, Dario Gentili, Paolo Napoli and Elettra Stimilli, "Filosofia e diritto fra 'French Theory' e 'Italian Thought,'" in Enrica Lisciani-Petrini and Giuseppina Strummiello, eds., *Effetto Italian Thought* (Macerata: Quodlibet, 2017), pp. 175–206.
32 Deleuze, "Instincts and Institutions," pp. 19–20.
33 Gilles Deleuze, *Empiricism and Subjectivity: An Essay on Hume's Theory of Human Nature* [1973], trans. by Constantin V. Boundas (New York: Columbia University Press, 2001), p. 45.
34 Ibid., p. 46.
35 Ibid., p. 47. [TN: Boundas in his translation of this passage uses the term "drive(s)" where other translators in other texts have used "tendency/-ies." Esposito has used the Italian equivalent of the second term, and I have followed his usage.]
36 Deleuze, "Instincts and Institutions," p. 20.
37 Ibid., p. 21.
38 Ibid.
39 On Nietzsche "at the heart of the debate between Deleuze and Heidegger," see Véronique Bergen, *L'ontologie de Deleuze* (Paris: L'Harmattan, 2001), pp. 208ff.
40 Gilles Deleuze, *Nietzsche and Philosophy*, trans. by Hugh Tomlinson (London and New York: Continuum, 1983), p. 3.
41 Ibid., p. 8.
42 Ibid., p. 9.
43 Ibid., p. 40.
44 Ibid., pp. 176–177.
45 Friedrich Nietzsche, "Ecce homo," in idem, *Opere*, vol. 6.3: *Nascita della tragedia*, ed. by Giorgio Colli and Mazzino Montinari (Milan: Adelphi, 1969), p. 321.
46 Friedrich Nietzsche, *Nachgelassene Fragmente 1885–1887*, in idem,

Sämtliche Werke: Kritische Studienausgabe in 15 Bänden, ed. by Giorgio Colli and Mazzino Montinari (Berlin: de Gruyter, 1999), vol 12, p. 215.
47 Deleuze, *Nietzsche and Philosophy*, p. 176.
48 Ibid.
49 Ibid., p. 186.
50 Ibid., p. xi.
51 Ibid., pp. xi–xii.
52 Deleuze, "Conclusions on the Will to Power and the Eternal Return," in idem, *Desert Islands and Other Texts, 1953–1974* [2002], trans. by Michael Taormina (Los Angeles, CA: Semiotext(e), 2004), p. 122.
53 Ibid.
54 Deleuze, *Nietzsche and Philosophy*, p. 174.
55 Gilles Deleuze, *Proust and Signs* [1964], trans. by Richard Howard (Minneapolis: University of Minnesota Press, 2000), p. 49.
56 Ibid., p. 15.
57 Ibid., p. 16.
58 Ibid., pp. 17–18.
59 Ibid., p. 5.
60 Ibid., p. 8.
61 Ibid., p. 11.
62 Ibid., p. 50.
63 Ibid., p. 95.
64 Ibid.
65 Ibid.
66 Michael Hardt, *Gilles Deleuze: An Apprenticeship in Philosophy* (Minneapolis: University of Minnesota Press, 1993), p. 13.
67 Ibid., p. 22.
68 I am referring to Frédéric Worms. See one of his most recent statements, an interview with Caterina Zanfi, "A partire da Bergson," *Lo sguardo*, 26 (2008): 185–192, as well as his exhaustive monograph: Frédéric Worms, *Bergson ou les deux sens de la vie* (Paris: Presses Universitaires de France [PUF], 2004).
69 Henri Bergson, *Creative Evolution* [1907], trans. by Arthur Michell (New York: Random House, 1944), p. 313.
70 Gilles Deleuze, *Bergsonism*, trans. by Hugh Tomlinson and Barbara Habberjam (New York: Zone Books, 1991), p. 18.
71 Gilles Deleuze, "Bergson's Conception of Difference" [1956], in idem, *Desert Islands and Other Texts, 1953–1974* [2002], trans. by Michael Taormina (Los Angeles, CA: Semiotext(e), 2004), p. 42.
72 For these theoretical transitions in Bergson adopted by Deleuze, one can now consult Enrica Lisciani-Petrini, "Quartetto per un'ontologia del virtuale: Bergson, Jankélévitch, Merleau-Ponty, Deleuze," *Il Pensiero*, 1 (2008).
73 Gilles Deleuze, "Intuition as Method," in *Bergsonism*, trans. by Hugh Tomlinson and Barbara Habberjam (New York: Zone Books, 1991), p. 20.
74 Hardt, *Gilles Deleuze*, p. 13.
75 Gilles Deleuze, "Conversation avec Toni Negri," *Futur antérieur*, 1 (1990); for the English translation used here, visit https://thefunambulist.net/law/

philosophy-control-and-becoming-a-conversation-between-toni-negri-and-gilles-deleuze (from Deleuze's response to Negri's first question).
76 Ibid.
77 Ibid. (from Deleuze's response to Negri's second question).
78 Ibid. (from Deleuze's response to Negri's third question).
79 Ibid., (from Deleuze's response to Negri's question about *Foucault* and *The Fold*).
80 Gilles Deleuze, *Expressionism in Philosophy: Spinoza* [1968], trans. by Martin Joughin (New York: Zone Books, 1990), p. 80.
81 Baruch Spinoza, "Letter to Jarig Jelles, March 25, 1667," in idem, *Complete Works*, trans. by Samuel Shirley (Indianapolis, IN: Hackett, 2002), p. 865.
82 Baruch Spinoza, *Ethics*, in idem, *Complete Works*, trans. by Samuel Shirley (Indianapolis, IN: Hackett, 2002), p. 279 (III, Proposition 1).
83 Deleuze, *Expressionism*, p. 253.
84 Gilles Deleuze, "Préface à *L'anomalie sauvage*," in idem, *Deux régimes de fous: Textes et entretiens 1975–1995* (Paris: Minuit, 2003), pp. 175–178, here 175.
85 Ibid., p. 176.
86 Antonio Negri, *Time for Revolution* [2006], trans. by Matteo Mandarini (New York: Continuum, 2003), p. 234 (paragraph 13.4).
87 Ernesto Laclau, "Can Immanence Explain Social Struggles?," *Diacritics*, 31.4 (2001): 3–10, here 7.
88 Ibid., p. 5.
89 Émile Bréhier, *La théorie des incorporels dans l'ancien stoïcisme* (Paris: Vrin, 1928), p. 13.
90 On the fracture that traverses *The Logic of Sense*, one should consult the detailed analysis by José Gil, *O imperceptível devir da imanência* (Lisbon: Relógio d'Água, 2008).
91 Gilles Deleuze, *The Logic of Sense* [1969], trans. by Mark Lester (London: Athlone Press, 1990), p. 84.
92 Ibid., p. 90.
93 Ibid., p. 93.
94 Gilles Deleuze and Félix Guattari, "Deleuze and Guattari Fight Back" [1971], in Gilles Deleuze, *Desert Islands and Other Texts, 1953–1974* [2002], trans. by Michael Taormina (Los Angeles, CA: Semiotext(e), 2004), pp. 216–229, here 216.
95 I am quoting from Arnaud Bouaniche, *Gilles Deleuze: Une introduction* (Paris: La Découverte, 2007), p. 148. (Originally from a piece by Gilles Deleuze and Félix Guattari published in *L'arc* (1980); quotation at p. 102.)
96 Gilles Deleuze and Claire Parnet, *Dialogues*, trans. by Hugh Tomlinson and Barbara Habberjam (New York: Columbia University Press, 1987), p. 96.
97 Gilles Deleuze, "Nomadic Thought," in idem, *Desert Islands and Other Texts, 1953–1974* [2002], trans. by Michael Taormina (Los Angeles, CA: Semiotext(e), 2004), pp. 252–261, here 261.
98 Gilles Deleuze and Félix Guattari, *Anti-Oedipus: Capitalism and Schizophrenia* [1972], trans. by Robert Hurley, Mark Seem, and Helen R. Lane (Minneapolis: University of Minnesota Press, 1983), p. 311.
99 Ibid., p. 8.

100 On the destructive and self-destructive dialectics of desire, see Igor Krtolica, *Gilles Deleuze* (Paris: PUF, 2015), pp. 62 ff.
101 Deleuze and Parnet, *Dialogues*, p. 133.
102 Deleuze and Guattari, *Anti-Oedipus*, p. 277.
103 Ibid., p. 140.
104 Ibid., p. 254.
105 Friedrich Nietzsche, *On the Genealogy of Morality* [1997], trans. by Carol Diethe (Cambridge: Cambridge University Press, 2006), p. 38.
106 Ibid., p. 58.
107 Franz Kafka, "The Great Wall of China," in idem, *The Complete Stories* (New York: Schocken, 1971), p. 158.
108 Deleuze and Guattari, *Anti-Oedipus*, p. 250.
109 Ibid., pp. 239–240.
110 Deleuze and Parnet, *Dialogues*, p. 59.
111 Gilles Deleuze, *Essays Critical and Clinical* [1993], trans. by Daniel W. Smith and Michael A. Grieco (London and New York: Verso, 1998), p. 85.
112 Ibid., pp. 85–86. The quotation is from Herman Melville, "Redburn," in idem, *Redburn, White-Jacket, Moby-Dick* (New York: Library of America, 1983), p. 185 (ch. 33).
113 Gilles Deleuze and Félix Guattari, *Kafka: Toward a Minor Literature* [1975], trans. Dana Polan (Minneapolis: University of Minnesota Press, 1986), p. 16.
114 Ibid., pp. 17–18.
115 Deleuze, *Essays Critical*, p. 4.
116 Ibid.
117 Deleuze and Guattari, *Kafka*, p. 41.
118 Ibid.
119 Ibid., p. 57.
120 Ibid.
121 Gilles Deleuze and Félix Guattari, *A Thousand Plateaus: Capitalism and Schizophrenia* [1980], trans. by Brian Massumi (Minneapolis: University of Minnesota Press, 1987), p. 357.
122 Ibid., p. 416.
123 Ibid., p. 421.
124 Ibid., p. 422.
125 See David Lapoujade, *Deleuze: Les mouvements aberrants* (Paris: Minuit, 2014).
126 Ibid., pp. 83–84.
127 Gilles Deleuze, *Foucault*, trans. by Seàn Hand (Minneapolis: University of Minnesota Press, 1988).
128 Deleuze, *Negotiations*, p. 88.
129 Ibid., p. 95.
130 Ibid., p. 106.
131 Deleuze, *Foucault*, p. 113.
132 Ibid., p. 111.
133 Ibid., p. 113.
134 Ibid., p. 112.
135 Ibid. p. 86.

136 Ibid., pp. 89–90.
137 Michel Foucault, *The History of Sexuality*, vol. 1: *An Introduction*, trans. by Robert Hurley (New York: Pantheon, 1978), p. 145.
138 Deleuze, *Foucault*, pp. 92–93.
139 Ibid., p. 94.
140 Deleuze, *Negotiations*, p. 109.
141 Deleuze, *Foucault*, p. 94.
142 Ibid., p. 97.
143 Ibid., pp. 97–98.
144 See Michel Foucault, "The Life of Infamous Men," in *Power, Truth, Strategy*, trans. by Paul Foss and Meaghan Morris (Sydney: Feral Publications, 1979), pp. 76–91.
145 Deleuze, *Foucault*, p. 109.
146 Ibid., p. 95.
147 Ibid., p. 96.
148 Ibid., p. 114.
149 Gilles Deleuze, "Desire and Pleasure," in *Two Regimes of Madness: Texts and Interviews 1975–1995* [2003], trans. by Ames Hodges and Mike Taormina (Los Angeles: Semiotext(e), 2006), p. 124.
150 Ibid., p. 129.
151 Ibid., p. 130.

Notes to Chapter 3

1 On Lefort's as yet inadequate recognition, see Alain Caillé, *Claude Lefort, les sciences sociales et la philosophie politique*, in Claude Habib and Claude Mouchard, eds., *La démocratie à l'oeuvre: Autour de Claude Lefort* (Paris: Esprit, 1993), pp. 51–76.
2 See the interview Claude Lefort gave in 1988 to the journal *Autrement*, 102, now published as "La pensée du politique," in idem, *Le temps présent: Écrits 1945–2005* (Paris: Belin, 2007), pp. 599–609.
3 Claude Lefort, *Machiavelli in the Making* [1972], trans. by Michael B. Smith (Evanston, IL: Northwestern University Press, 2012), p. 198.
4 Bernard Flynn insists on Lefort's ties to Heidegger's ontology in an important monograph; see Bernard Flynn, *The Philosophy of Claude Lefort: Interpreting the Political* (Evanston, IL: Northwestern University Press, 2005), especially pp. 205ff.
5 Claude Lefort, "La dissolution des repères et l'enjeu démocratique," in idem, *Le temps present: Écrits 1945–2005* (Paris: Belin, 2007), pp. 551–568.
6 Ibid., p. 558.
7 See Oliver Marchart, *Post-Foundational Political Thought: Political Difference in Nancy, Lefort, Badiou and Laclau* (Edinburgh: Edinburgh University Press, 2007), pp. 85–108.
8 On the concept of institution in the phenomenological school, see Roberto Terzi, "Événement, champ, trace: Le concept phénoménologique

d'insitution," *Philosophie*, 131 (2016): 52–68 and idem, "Institution, événement, histoire chez Merleau-Ponty," *Bulletin d'analyse phénoménologique*, 3 (2017): 1–29. On the topic of the institution, one should also consult Petar Bojanič, "La violenza come origine dell'istituzione (Deleuze con Hume e Saint-Just)," *Iride*, 65 (2012): 79–90 and idem, "Biopolitica: Il 'fuori' dell'istituzione," in Dario Gentili and Elettra Stimilli, eds., *Differenze italiane* (Rome: DeriveApprodi, 2015), pp. 113–120.

9 On the intrinsically political character of Merleau-Ponty's philosophy, which appeared in all its depth in the radical confrontation with Sartre in the 1950s, one can now consult the exhaustive and convincing essay by Enrica Lisciani-Petrini, "Merleau-Ponty/Sartre: Una insanabile divergenza filosofico-politica," *aut-aut*, 381 (2019): 61–90 (a special issue edited by Lisciani-Petrini herself and by Raoul Kirchmayr). More generally on Merleau-Ponty, one can examine another work by Lisciani-Petrini, *La passione del mondo: Saggio su Merleau-Ponty* (Naples: Esi, 2002). One should also consult the substantial essay by Judith Revel, *Foucault avec Merleau-Ponty: Ontologie politique, présentisme et histoire* (Paris: Vrin, 2015).

10 Claude Lefort, "Foreword," in Maurice Merleau-Ponty, *Institution and Passivity: Course Notes from the Collège de France (1954–1955)*, trans. by Leonard Lawlor and Heath Massey (Evanston, IL: Northwestern University Press, 2010).

11 Maurice Merleau-Ponty, "Cézanne's Doubt," in idem, *Sense and Non-Sense* [1945], trans. by Hubert L. Dreyfus and Patricia Allen Dreyfus (Evanston, IL: Northwestern University Press, 1964), pp. 9–25.

12 Maurice Merleau-Ponty, *Signs*, trans. by Richard C. McCleary (Evanston, IL: Northwestern University Press, 1964), p. 59.

13 Ibid.

14 Ibid.

15 Maurice Merleau-Ponty, "The Algorithm and the Mystery of Language," in idem, *The Prose of the World* [1969], trans. by John O'Neill (Evanston, IL: Northwestern University Press, 1973), pp. 115–129.

16 Maurice Merleau-Ponty, "Institution in Personal and Public History," in idem, *In Praise of Philosophy and Other Essays*, trans. by John Wild and James Edie John (Evanston, IL: Northwestern University Press, 1963), pp. 107–113, here 108.

17 Ibid., p. 112.

18 Pierre Dardot and Christian Laval, *Common: On Revolution in the 21st Century* [2014], trans. by Matthew MacLellan (London: Bloomsbury Academic, 2019). The chapter in question is "Instituting Praxis," pp. 277–309.

19 Michael Hardt and Antonio Negri, *Comune: Oltre il privato e il pubblico* (Milan: Rizzoli, 2010), p. 373.

20 Cornelius Castoriadis, *The Imaginary Institution of Society* [1975], trans. by Kathleen Blamey (Cambridge: Polity, 1987). Fabio Ciaramelli, one of the first researchers to study Castoriadis in Italy, in addition to editing Castoriadis, has written on institutions; see Fabio Ciaramelli, *Istituzioni e norme: Lezioni di filosofia del diritto* (Turin: Giappichelli, 2006), especially pp. 135ff.

21 Cornelius Castoriadis, "Power, Politics, Autonomy," in idem, *Philosophy, Politics, Autonomy*, trans. by David Ames Curtis (Oxford: Oxford University Press, 1991), p. 168.
22 Cornelius Castoriadis, *Le monde morcelé: Les carrefours du labyrinthe 3* (Paris: Seuil, 1990), p. 246.
23 Claude Lefort, "Le pouvoir," in idem, *Le temps present: Écrits 1945–2005* (Paris: Belin, 2007), translated here from the Italian: Claude Lefort, "Il potere," in Dario Malinconico, ed., *Almanacco di Filosofia e Politica*, vol. 1, p. 292.
24 Claude Lefort, "Sur la démocratie: Le politique et l'institution du social," ed. by Marcel Gauchet, *Textures*, 2–3 (1971): 7–78.
25 Lefort, "La pensée du politique," p. 601.
26 On the complex relationship of differential and mutual implication between the social and the political, see Jean-Yves Pranchère, "Un monde habitable par tous: Claude Lefort et la question du social," *Esprit*, 451 (2019): 111–122.
27 Lefort, "Sur la démocratie," p. 13.
28 Ibid., p. 17.
29 Ibid.
30 Carl Schmitt, "Un giurista davanti a se stesso" [1982], an interview with Fulco Lanchester, in Carl Schmitt, *Un giurista davanti a se stesso: Saggi e interviste*, ed. by Giorgio Agamben (Milan: Neri Pozza, 2005), pp. 166–167; also Carl Schmitt, *The* Nomos *of the Earth in the International Law of the* Jus Publicum Europaeum, trans. by Gary L. Ulmen (New York: Telos Press Publishing, 2006), p. 210.
31 I am referring especially to Neil MacCormick and Ota Weinberger, *An Institutional Theory of Law* (Dordrecht: Reidel, 1985).
32 Maurice Hauriou, *La théorie de l'institution et de la fondation* [1925], translated here from the Italian version: Maurice Hauriou, *Teoria dell'istituzione e della fondazione*, trans. into Italian by Widar Cesarini Sforza (Milan: Giuffrè, 1967), pp. 12–13.
33 Ibid., p. 18.
34 Paolo Napoli, "Ritorno a 'instituere': Per una concezione materialistica dell'istituzione," in Francesco Brancaccio and Chiara Giorgi, eds., *Ai confini del diritto: Poteri, istituzioni e soggettività* (Rome: DeriveApprodi, 2017), pp. 77–88.
35 Paul Ricoeur, "Le problème du fondement de la morale," *Sapienza: Rivista internazionale di filosofia e teologia*, 3 (1975): 313–337. For the topic of the institution as it relates to conflict, one should also consult another essay by Paul Ricoeur, "Le conflit: Signe de contradiction ou d'unité?" in *Contradictions et conflits: Naissance d'une société* (Lyon: Chronique sociale de France, 1971), pp. 189–204.
36 For more on this formulation, I refer readers to the fundamental works by Yan Thomas, most particularly *Les opérations du droit* (Paris: Gallimard, 2010). For a better understanding of the importance of Thomas's work to a theory of the institution, one should consult the keen reflections by Gabriella Bonacchi, "Fictio legis e disforie del femminile," in Francesco Brancaccio and Chiara Giorgi, eds., *Ai confini del diritto: Poteri, istituzioni*

e soggettività (Rome: DeriveApprodi, 2017), pp. 141–151. For Roman law more generally, I refer readers to the masterful synthesis by Aldo Schiavone, *The Invention of Law in the West*, trans. by Jeremy Carden and Antony Shugaar (Cambridge, MA and London: Belknap Press of Harvard University Press, 2012).

37 Claude Lefort, *Éléments d'une critique de la bureaucratie* (Paris: Gallimard, 1979), p. 9.

38 Ibid., p. 12.

39 Claude Lefort, "Préface," in idem, *Les formes de l'histoire: Essais d'anthropologie politique* (Paris: Gallimard, 1978), translated here from the Italian version: Claude Lefort, *Le forme della storia: Saggi di antropologia politica*, trans. into Italian by Benedetta Aledda and Pietro Montanari (Bologna: Il Ponte, 2012), p. 11.

40 Claude Lefort, "Lo scambio e la lotta tra gli uomini," in idem, *Le forme della storia: Saggi di antropologia politica*, trans. into Italian by E. Aledda and P. Montanari (Bologna: Il Ponte, 2012), p. 17.

41 Of Georges Bataille's many works one should consult *The Accursed Share* [1949], trans. by Robert Hurley (New York: Zone Books, 1988).

42 Bronislaw Malinowski, *Argonauts of the Western Pacific* (London: Routledge & Kegan Paul, 1922), here translated from the Italian version in the original.

43 Lefort, "Lo scambio e la lotta," p. 25.

44 Ibid., p. 26.

45 Ibid.

46 Ibid., p. 27.

47 Ibid.

48 Ibid., p. 29.

49 See Abram Kardiner, *The Individual and His Society* (New York: Columbia University Press, 1939). Lefort's preface to the French translation of Kardiner's work is republished in Italian as Claude Lefort, "Le ambiguità dell'antropologia culturale: Introduzione all'opera di Abram Kardiner," in idem, *Le forme della storia: Saggi di antropologia politica*, trans. into Italian by E. Aledda and P. Montanari (Bologna: Il Ponte, 2012), pp. 85–118.

50 Lefort, "Le ambiguità," p. 108.

51 Pauline Colonna d'Istria, "La division originaire du social: Lefort lecteur de Lacan?," *Politique et sociétés*, 341 (2015): 131–147. As regards the relationship between Merleau-Ponty and Lacan more broadly, see Guy-Félix Duportail, *Les institutions du monde de la vie: Merleau-Ponty et Lacan* (Paris: Millon, 2008).

52 Lefort, "Le ambiguità dell'antropologia culturale," pp. 107–108.

53 This is what Bruno Moroncini argues in *Lacan politico* (Naples: Cronopio, 2015). On this topic more generally, see Yannis Stavrakakis, *Lacan and the Political* (London: Routledge, 1990) and idem, *The Lacanian Left: Psychoanalysis: Theory: Politics* (Edinburgh: Edinburgh University Press, 2007). For an encompassing examination of Lacan's views, one should consult the exhaustive two-volume monograph by Massimo Recalcati, *Desiderio, godimento e soggettivazione* (Milan: Cortina, 2012) and idem, *La clinica psicoanalitica: Struttura e soggetto* (Milan: Cortina, 2016).

54 In addition to the introduction we quoted previously, one should also consult Claude Lefort, "L'idea di 'personalità di base'" [1951], in idem, *Le forme della storia: Saggi di antropologia politica*, trans. into Italian by E. Aledda and P. Montanari (Bologna: Il Ponte, 2012), pp. 74–84.
55 The text discussed by Lefort is Gregory Bateson, "Culture Contact and Schismogenesis," in *Man*, 199 (1935): 178–183.
56 Claude Lefort, "Società 'senza storia' e storicità" [1952], in idem, *Le forme della storia: Saggi di antropologia politica*, trans. into Italian by E. Aledda and P. Montanari (Bologna: Il Ponte, 2012), p. 4.
57 Pierre Clastres, *Society against the State: Essays in Political Anthropology* [1974], trans. by Robert Hurley (New York: Zone Books, 1987).
58 Claude Lefort, "Dialogue with Pierre Clastres," in idem, *Writing: The Political Test*, trans. by David Ames Curtis (Durham, NC and London: Duke University Press, 2000), pp. 207–235, here 214.
59 Ibid.
60 Claude Lefort, "Le nom d'Un," in Étienne de la Boétie, *Discours de la servitude volontaire* (Paris: Payot, 1993).
61 Lefort, "Dialogue with Pierre Clastres," p. 224.
62 There are diverging interpretations about the effects of Lefort's encounter with Machiavelli. If some, such as Bernard Flynn, recognize a clear paradigm shift occurring as a consequence, others tend to see a greater continuity. As an example of the latter, see Mattia Di Pierro's noteworthy doctoral thesis, *L' "esperienza del mondo": Claude Lefort e la fenomenologia del politico*, defended at the Scuola Normale Superiore di Pisa in the course of the 2018–2019 academic year.
63 Claude Lefort, "Riflessioni sociologiche su Machiavelli e Marx," in idem, *Le forme della storia: Saggi di antropologia politica*, trans. into Italian by E. Aledda and P. Montanari (Bologna: Il Ponte, 2012), p. 184.
64 Lefort, *Machiavelli in the Making*, p. 21.
65 Maurice Merleau-Ponty, "A Note on Machiavelli," in idem, *Signs*, trans. by Richard C. McCleary (Evanston, IL: Northwestern University Press, 1964), p. 216.
66 [Translator's note: All the quotations from *The Prince* are taken from Niccolò Machiavelli, *The Prince*, trans. by Harvey C. Mansfield (Chicago, IL: University of Chicago Press, 1998).]
67 For an examination of Merleau-Ponty's phenomenological reading of Machiavelli, one should consult the stimulating doctoral thesis by Caterina Di Fazio, *Phénomenologie de l'espace politique*, defended in 2018 at the Université Paris I Panthéon-Sorbonne.
68 Merleau-Ponty, "A Note on Machiavelli," p. 217.
69 Ibid., p. 218.
70 Ibid., p. 215.
71 "Machiavel et nous" is the title of Louis Althusser's essay on Machiavelli; see Louis Althusser, *Machiavelli and Us*, trans. by Gregory Elliot (London and New York: Verso, 1999).
72 Eric Weil, "Machiavel aujourd'hui," in idem, *Essais et conferences* (Paris: Vrin, 1991), vol. 2, p. 190.
73 J. G. A. Pocock, *The Machiavellian Moment* (Princeton, NJ: Princeton

University Press, 1974). At this point in time, in this "Machiavellian moment," I would like to point to some current scholarship that is worthy of note: Alberto Asor Rosa, *Machiavelli e l'Italia: Resoconto di una disfatta* (Turin: Einaudi, 2019); Michele Ciliberto, *Niccolò Machiavelli: Ragione e pazzia* (Rome and Bari: Laterza, 2019); Carlo Ginzburg, *Nondimanco: Machiavelli, Pascal* (Milan: Adelphi, 2018); Gabriele Pedullà, *Machiavelli in Tumult: The Discourses on Livy and the Origins of Political Conflictualism* (Cambridge: Cambridge University Press, 2018).

74 Miguel Abensour, *Democracy against the State: Marx and the Machiavellian Moment* [2004], trans. Max Blechman and Martin Breaugh (Cambridge: Polity, 2011), p. xliv.

75 On the topic of the post-Marxist interpretation of Machiavelli, see the keen observations by Miguel Vatter, "Machiavelli after Marx: The Self-Overcoming of Marxism in the Late Althusser," *Theory and Event*, 4 (2005) (no page numbers).

76 Abensour, *Democracy against the State*, p. xxv.

77 Ibid., p. xxvi.

78 Gilles Deleuze, *Instincts and Institutions*, in idem, *Desert Islands and Other Texts, 1953–1974* [2002], trans. by Michael Taormina (Los Angeles, CA: Semiotext(e), 2004).

79 On the problematic nature of the concept of "savage democracy," one should consult Antoine Chollet, "L'énigme de la démocratie sauvage," *Esprit*, 451 (2019): 136–146.

80 For a valuable examination of the mutual (co)implication(s) of order and conflict, one can now consult the excellent study by Francesco Marchesi, *Cartografia politica: Spazi e soggetti del conflitto in Niccolò Machiavelli* (Florence: Olschki, 2018).

81 Lefort, *Machiavelli in the Making*, p. 228

82 Lefort, *Éléments d'une critique de la bureaucratie*, p. 77.

83 Lefort, *Machiavelli in the Making*, p. 468; translation slightly modified

84 For a discussion of Lefort's complex interpretation of modernity, see Hugues Poltier, *Passion du politique: La pensée de Claude Lefort* (Geneva: Labor et fides, 1998), pp. 175ff.

85 Claude Lefort, "The Permanence of the Theologico-Political?" [1986], in idem, *Democracy and Political Theory*, trans. by David Macey (London: Polity, 1988), pp. 213–255.

86 Claude Lefort, "La modernité de Dante," introduction to the French edition of Dante's *De monarchia / La monarchie* (Paris: Belin, 1993), p. 11, translated here from the Italian.

87 For this interpretation of political theology, see Roberto Esposito, *Two: The Machine of Political Theology and the Place of Thought* [2013], trans. by Zakiya Hanafi (New York: Fordham University Press, 2015).

88 I am obviously referring to Ernst Kantorowicz, *The King's Two Bodies: A Study in Medieval Political Theology* (Princeton, NJ: Princeton University Press, 1957).

89 Lefort, "Permanence of the Theologico-Political?," pp. 242–243.

90 Ibid., p. 255.

91 Claude Lefort, "La question de la démocratie," in idem, *Essais sur le*

politique, XIX–XX siècles (Paris: Seuil, 1986), translated here from the Italian.

92 Lefort, "Permanence of the Theologico-Political?," p. 226.

93 Ibid.

94 Ibid.

95 See Nicholas Poirier, *L'ontologie politique de Castoriadis: Création et institution* (Paris: Payot & Rivages, 2011). On the antinomies of Castoriadis's political ontology, one can also consult Stavrakakis, *The Lacanian Left*, pp. 37–65.

96 For a series of reasons why the social cannot be transparent to itself, see Esteban Molina, *Le défi du politique: Totalitarisme et démocratie chez Claude Lefort* (Paris: L'Harmattan, 2005), pp. 173ff.

97 Massimo Recalcati, *Il vuoto centrale: Quattro brevi discorsi per una teoria psicanalitica dell'istituzione* (Alberobello: Poiesis, 2016).

98 Jacques Lacan, *The Other Side of Psychoanalysis* [1991], trans. by Russell Grigg (New York: Norton, 2007).

99 Jacques Lacan, *The Ethics of Psychoanalysis. 1959–1960* [1986], trans. by Dennis Porter (New York: Norton, 1992).

100 Another work by Claude Lefort that one should consult is Claude Lefort, "The Image of the Body and Totalitarianism," in idem, *The Political Forms of Modern Society: Bureaucracy, Democracy, Totalitarianism* (Boston, MA: MIT Press, 1986), pp. 292–306. This piece has been translated into Italian and is now part of a collection edited by Simona Forti under the title *La filosofia di fronte all'estremo: Totalitarismo e riflessione filosofica* (Turin: Einaudi, 2004). The collection places Lefort's perspective within the context of a wide-ranging selection of essays on totalitarianism. Forti herself has contributed works on the subject, including the weighty study *Il totalitarismo* (Rome-Bari: Laterza, 2001), as well as *The New Demons: Rethinking Power and Evil Today* [2012], trans. by Zakiya Hanafi (Stanford, CA: Stanford University Press, 2015).

101 Claude Lefort, "Totalitarianism without Stalin," in idem, *Political Forms of Modern Society: Bureaucracy, Democracy, Totalitarianism* (Boston, MA: MIT Press, 1986), pp. 52–88.

102 Claude Lefort, "The Logic of Totalitarianism," in idem, *Political Forms of Modern Society: Bureaucracy, Democracy, Totalitarianism* (Boston, MA: MIT Press, 1986), p. 277.

103 Claude Lefort, *Un homme en trop* (Paris: Belin, 2015).

104 Claude Lefort, "Politics and Human Rights," in idem, *Political Forms of Modern Society: Bureaucracy, Democracy, Totalitarianism* (Boston, MA: MIT Press, 1986), pp. 239–272.

105 Claude Lefort, "Les droits de l'homme et l'État-providence," in idem, *Essais sur le politique, XIX–XX siècles* (Paris: Seuil, 1986), p. 39.

106 Lefort, "Politics and Human Rights," p. 265; translation modified.

107 Lefort, "Les droits de l'homme," p. 66.

108 Carl Schmitt, *On the Three Types of Juristic Thought* [1935], trans. by Joseph W. Bendersky (Westport, CT: Praeger, 2004). On the topic of the complex relationship between Schmitt and Romano, one should consult the important observations by Alfonso Catania, "L'ordinamento giuridico

concreto e la teoria dell'istituzione: Santi Romano e Carl Schmitt," in idem, *Lo stato moderno: Sovranità e giuridicità* (Turin: Giappichelli, 1996), pp. 85–114.

109 Santi Romano, *Lo stato moderno e la sua crisi: Saggi di diritto costituzionale* [1909] (Milan: Giuffrè, 1969).

110 Santi Romano, *L'ordinamento giuridico* [1917–1918], ed. with an essay by Mariano Croce (Macerata: Quodlibet, 2018), p. 101.

111 See Paolo Grossi, "'Lo stato moderno e la sua crisi': A cento anni dalla prolusione pisana di Santi Romano," in Paolo Grossi and Alberto Romano, *Ricordando Santi Romano*, ed. by Eugenio Ripepe (Pisa: Pisa University Press, 2013), p. 23. One should also consult Biagio de Giovanni, *Alle origini della democrazia di massa: I filosofi e i giuristi* (Naples: Editoriale Scientifica, 2013) and idem, *Elogio della sovranità politica* (Naples: Editoriale Scientifica, 2015).

112 Romano, "'Lo stato moderno e la sua crisi': A cento anni," p. 97.

113 Romano, *L'ordinamento giuridico*, p. 43.

114 Ibid., p. 110.

Index